JULIA ROBERTS CONFIDENTIAL

JULIA ROBERTS
CONFIDENTIAL
The Unauthorised Biography

Paul Donnelley

For Tracy and Brendan
May your life together be filled
with much laughter and happiness.
I love you both very much.
Mr D.

This is an unauthorised biography and was researched and
written without the direct involvement of the subject,
Julia Roberts

First published in Great Britain in 2003 by
Virgin Books Ltd
Thames Wharf Studios
Rainville Road
London
W6 9HA

A catalogue record for this book is available from the British
Library.

ISBN 1 85227 023 3

Plate section designed by Anita Ruddell
Typeset by TW Typesetting, Plymouth, Devon
Printed and bound in Great Britain by
Mackays of Chatham PLC

Stuart Graham (Tom Cullen), Sean McGinley (Smith), Gerard McSorley (Cathal Brugha), Jonathan Rhys-Myers (Collins's assassin), Charles Dance (Soames), John Kenny (Patrick Pearse), Ronan McCairbre (Thomas McDonagh), Ger O'Leary (Thomas Clarke), Michael Dwyer (James Connolly), Martin Murphy (Captain Lee-Wilson), Gary Whelan (Hoey), Frank O'Sullivan (Kavanagh), Frank Laverty (Sean McKeoin), Owen O'Neill (Rory O'Connor), Liam d'Staic (Austin Stack), Owen Roe (Arthur Griffith), Paul Bennett (Cosgrave), Tom Murphy (Vinny Byrne).

EVERYONE SAYS I LOVE YOU (1996)
(US opening 6 December 1996; UK opening 18 April 1997; 97 minutes; Rated R (USA), 12 (UK))
Director/Writer: Woody Allen.
CAST: Edward Norton (Holden Spence), Drew Barrymore (Schuyler Dandridge), Diva Gray (Nanny), Ami Almendral (Nanny), Madeline Balmaceda (Nanny), Vivian Cherry (Nurse), Tommie Baxter (Old woman), Jeff Derocker (Homeless man), Cherylyn Jones, Tina Paul, Vikki Schnurr (Mannequins), Natasha Lyonne (D.J. Dandridge), Kevin Hagan (Doorman), Alan Alda (Bob Dandridge), Gaby Hoffmann (Lane Dandridge), Natalie Portman (Laura Dandridge), Lukas Haas (Scott Dandridge), Trude Klein (Frieda), Goldie Hawn (Steffi Dandridge), Itzhak Perlman (Himself), Navah Perlman (Pianist), Barbara Hollander (Claire), John Griffin (Jeffrey Vandermost), JULIA ROBERTS (Von), Waltrudis Buck (Psychiatrist), Patrick Cranshaw (Grandpa), Isiah Whitlock Jr (Policeman), Woody Allen (Joe Berlin), Edward Hibbert (Harry Winston salesman).

MY BEST FRIEND'S WEDDING (1997)
(US opening 20 June 1997; UK opening 19 September 1997; 101 minutes; Rated PG-13 (USA), 12 (UK))
Director: P.J. Hogan; Writer: Ronald Bass.
CAST: JULIA ROBERTS (Julianne Potter), Dermot Mulroney (Michael O'Neal), Cameron Diaz (Kimmy Wallace), Rupert Everett (George Downes), Philip Bosco (Walter Wallace), M. Emmet Walsh (Joe O'Neal), Rachel Griffiths (Samantha Newhouse), Carrie Preston (Mandy Newhouse), Susan Sullivan (Isabelle Wallace),

Christopher Masterson (Scotty O'Neal), Raci Alexander, Jennifer Garrett, Kelly Sheerin, Bree Turner (Title sequence performers), Cassie Creasy (Flower girl), Lucina Paquet (Kimmy's grand-mother), Rose Abdoo (Seamstress), Phillip Ingram (Wedding singer).

NOTES: Ron Bass who wrote this film also wrote *Sleeping with the Enemy*.

The 'I Say a Little Prayer' scene took seven days to film.

CONSPIRACY THEORY (1997)

(US opening 8 August 1997; UK opening 29 August 1997; 130 minutes; Rated R (USA), 15 (UK))

Director: Richard Donner; Writer: Brian Helgeland.

CAST: Mel Gibson (Jerry Fletcher/Dr Fine), JULIA ROBERTS (Alice Sutton), Patrick Stewart (Dr Jonas/Henry Finch), Cylk Cozart (Agent Lowry/Hatcher), Steve Kahan (Mr Wilson), Terry Alexander (Flip/Undercover agent), Alex McArthur (Cynic), Rod McLachlan/Michael Potts/Jim Sterling (Department of Justice guards), Rich Hebert (Public works man), Brian J. Williams (Clarke), George Aguilar (Piper), Cece Neber Labao (Henry Finch's secretary), Saxon Trainor (Alice's secretary).

STEPMOM (1998)

(US opening 25 December 1998; UK opening 29 January 1999; 120 mins; Rated PG-13 (USA), 12 (UK))

Director: Chris Columbus; Writer: Gigi Levangie.

CAST: JULIA ROBERTS (Isabel Kelly), Susan Sarandon (Jackie Harrison), Ed Harris (Luke Harrison), Jena Malone (Anna Harrison), Liam Aiken (Ben Harrison), Lynn Whitfield (Dr P. Sweikert), Darrell Larson (Duncan Samuels), Mary Louise Wilson (Mrs Franklin), Andre Blake (Cooper), Russel Harper (Photo assistant), Jack Eagle (Craft service man), Lu Celania Sierra, Lauma Zemzare, Holly Schenck, Michelle Stone, Annett Esser, Monique Rodrique (Photo shoot models), Sal Mistretta, Rex Hays, Alice Liu, Chuck Montgomery (Advertising executives), Mak Gilcrist (Rapunzel), Mrozek Michael (Dylan the prince).

NOTES: Ron Bass who wrote *Sleeping with the Enemy* and *My Best Friend's Wedding* was an uncredited contributor to the film.

NOTTING HILL (1999)

(UK première 26 April 1999; US opening May 1999; 119 mins; Rated PG-13 (USA), 15 (UK))

Director: Roger Michell; Writer: Richard Curtis.

CAST: JULIA ROBERTS (Anna Scott), Hugh Grant (William Thacker), Richard McCabe (Tony), Rhys Ifans (Spike), James Dreyfus (Martin), Dylan Moran (Rufus the thief), Roger Frost (Annoying customer), Henry Goodman (Ritz concierge), Julian Rhind-Tutt (*Time Out* journalist), Lorelei King (Karen), John Shrapnel (PR chief), Clarke Peters (*Helix* lead actor), Arturo Venegas (Foreign actor), Yolanda Vazquez (Interpreter), Mischa Barton (Twelve-year-old actress).

RUNAWAY BRIDE (1999)

(US opening 30 July 1999; 116 mins; Rated PG (USA), PG (UK))

Director: Garry Marshall; Writers: Josann McGibbon, Sara Parriott.

CAST: JULIA ROBERTS (Maggie Carpenter), Richard Gere (Ike Graham), Joan Cusack (Peggy Flemming), Hector Elizondo (Fisher), Rita Wilson (Ellie Graham), Paul Dooley (Walter Carpenter), Christopher Meloni (Coach Bob Kelly), Donal Logue (Priest Brian), Reg Rogers (George Bug Guy), Yul Vazquez (Dead Head Gill), Jane Morris (Mrs Pressman), Lisa Roberts (Elaine from Manhattan), Kathleen Marshall (Cousin Cindy), Jean Schertler (Grandma), Tom Hines (Cory Flemming).

ERIN BROCKOVICH (2000)

(US opening 2000; UK opening 7 April 2000; 125 mins; Rated R (USA), 15 (UK))

Director: Steven Soderbergh; Writer: Susannah Grant.

CAST: JULIA ROBERTS (Erin Brockovich), Albert Finney (Ed Masry), David Brisbin (Dr Jaffe), Dawn Didawick (Rosalind), Aaron Eckhart (George), Valente Rodriguez (Donald), Conchata Ferrell (Brenda), George Rocky Sullivan (Los Angeles judge), Pat Skipper (Defence lawyer), Jack Gill (Defendant), Irene Olga López (Mrs Morales), Emily and Julie Marks (Eight-month-old Beth Brockovich), Ashley and Brittany Pimental (Eighteen-month-old Beth Brockovich), Scotty Leavenworth (Matthew Brown), Gemmenne de la Peña (Katie Brown), Erin Brockovich-Ellis (Julia),

Adilah Barnes (Anna), Randy Lowell (Dr Brian Frankel), Jamie Harrold (Scott), Sarah Ashley (Ashley Jensen), Scarlett Pomers (Shanna Jensen), T.J. Thyne (David Foil), Joe Chrest (Tom Robinson), Meredith Zimmer (Mandy Robinson), Michael Harney (Pete Jensen), William Lucking (Bob Linwood), Mimi Kennedy (Laura Ambrosiano), Scott Sowers (Mike Ambrosiano), Judge Leroy A. Simmons (Himself), Gina Gallego (Miss Sanchez), Peter Coyote (Kurt Potter). NOTES: Albert Finney was nominated for a Best Supporting Actor Oscar and Steven Soderbergh for Best Director. He was also nominated for *Traffic* and won for that film.

THE MEXICAN (2001)
(US opening 2001; UK opening 27 April 2001; 123 mins; Rated R (USA), 15 (UK))
Director: Gore Verbinski; Writer: J.H. Wyman.
CAST: Brad Pitt (Jerry Welbach), JULIA ROBERTS (Samantha Barzel), James Gandolfini (Winston Baldry), J.K. Simmons (Ted Slocum), Bob Balaban (Bernie Nayman), Sherman Augustus (Leroy the hitman), Michael Cerveris (Frank), Gene Hackman (Arnold Margolese), Richard Coca (Car thief), David Krumholtz (Beck), Castulo Guerra (Joe the pawnshop owner), Mayra Serbulo (Emanuelle), Salvador Sánchez (Gunsmith), Alan Ciangherotti (Gunsmith's assistant), Melisa Romero (Gunsmith's daughter).

AMERICA'S SWEETHEARTS (2001)
(US opening July 2001; UK opening 19 October 2001; 99 mins; Rated PG-13 (USA), 12 (UK))
Director: Joe Roth; Writers: Billy Crystal and Peter Tolan.
CAST: JULIA ROBERTS (Kathleen 'Kiki' Harrison), Billy Crystal (Lee Phillips), Catherine Zeta-Jones (Gwen Harrison), John Cusack (Eddie Thomas), Hank Azaria (Hector Gorgonzolas), Christopher Walken (Hal Weidmann), Stanley Tucci (Dave Kingman), Seth Green (Danny Wax), Alan Arkin (Wellness guide), Scot Zeller (Davis), Larry King (Himself), Steve Pink (Limousine driver), Rainn Wilson (Dave O'Hanlon), Eric Balfour (Security guard), Marty Belafsky (Security guard), Keri Lynn Pratt (Leaf Weidmann), Maria Canals (Adinah), Charlie Steiner (Nevada television host), Shaun Robinson (Nevada television presenter),

Jeff Michael (Network TV presenter), Sibila Vargas (Reporter), Jane Yamamoto (Reporter on patio), Byron Allen (Himself), Wendy Schenker (Maura Klein), Jim Ferguson (Mort Josephson), Lisa Joyner (Laura Messinger), Patrick Stoner (Bob), Sam Rubin (Ken), Susan Katz (Interviewer), Maree Cheatham (Matronly interviewer), Alex Enberg (*Larry King Live* producer), Sarah Loew (*Larry King Live* producer), Joseph Feingold (Judge), Sherry Jennings (Bar hostess), Julie Sorrels (Mother), Austin L. Sorrels (Little boy), Julie Wagner (Caller #1), Leilani Muenter (Caller #2), Dimitri Moraitis (Agent), Shawn Driscoll (Sean), Misti See (Misti), Gail Laskowski (Gail), Amber Barretto (Alison), Heather Charles (Reporter #7), Ann Cusack (Assistant to Lee Phillips), Michelle Gold (Gwen's greeter), Michael A. Tessiero (Film Critic #6).

OCEAN'S ELEVEN (2001)

(US opening 2001; UK opening February 2002; 181 mins; Rated PG-13 (USA), 12 (UK))

Director: Steven Soderbergh; Writers: Ted Griffin based on a 1960 screenplay by George Clayton Johnson and Jack Golden Russell.

CAST: George Clooney (Danny Ocean), Matt Damon (Linus Caldwell), Andy Garcia (Terry Benedict), Brad Pitt (Rusty Ryan), Casey Affleck (Virgil Malloy), Scott Caan (Turk Malloy), Elliott Gould (Reuben Tishkoff), Edward Jemison (Livingston Dell), Bernie Mac (Frank Catton), Shaobo Qin (Yen), Carl Reiner (Saul Bloom), JULIA ROBERTS (Tess Ocean), Joe La Due (Billy Tim Denham), Cecelia Ann Birt (Parole board member #1), Paul L. Nolan (Parole board member #2).

FULL FRONTAL (2002)

(US opening 2 August 2002; Rated R (USA), 18 (UK))

Director: Steven Soderbergh; Writer: Coleman Hough.

CAST: David Duchovny (Bill/Gus) Nicky Katt (Hitler), Catherine Keener (Lee), Mary McCormack (Linda), David Hyde Pierce (Carl), JULIA ROBERTS (Catherine/Francesca), Blair Underwood (Nicholas/Calvin), Enrico Colantoni (Arty/Ed), Erika Alexander (Lucy), Tracy Vilar (Heather), Brandon Keener (Francesca's assistant), Jeff Garlin (Harvey), David Alan Basche (Nicholas's agent), Nancy Lenehan (Woman on plane), Brad Rowe (Sam Osbourne).

CONFESSIONS OF A DANGEROUS MIND (2002)
(US opening December 2002; Rated R (USA), 15 (UK))
Director: George Clooney; Writer: Charlie Kaufman based on the book by Chuck Barris.
CAST: Sam Rockwell (Chuck Barris), Drew Barrymore (Penny), George Clooney (CIA Agent Jim Byrd), JULIA ROBERTS (Patricia Watson), Rutger Hauer (Keeler), Jennifer Hall (Georgia), Linda Tomassone (Monica), Steve Adams, Krista Allen (Pretty woman), Tanya Anthony (Prostitute), Barbara Bacci (Veiled woman), Shaun Balbar (Beanpole bachelor), Samantha Banton (Black spinster), Chuck Barris (Himself), Richard Beaudet, Ron Di Lauro, Andre Minicozzi, Bruce Pepper, Francois St-Pierre, Peter N. Wilson (*Gong Show* Band), Carlo Berardinucci (Waiter), Maria Bertrand (Stud spinster), Claudia Besso (Chuck's Mother), Isabelle Blais (Chuck's second date), Sara Brookshire, Robert John Burke (Instructor Jenks), Carlos Carrasco (Brazioni), Melissa Carter (Chuck's third date). Chelsea Ceci (Eight-year-old Tuvia), Michael Cera (Young Chuck Barris), Dick Clark (Himself), Joe Cobden (The Unknown Comic), Bill Corday (Justice of the Peace), Leslie Cottle (LA bar woman), Matt Damon (Gameshow contestant), Pascale Devigne (Critic), Joey Elias (Drunk), Ilona Elkin (Mary-Ann/Georgia's girlfriend), Michael Ensign (Simon Oliver), Marlida Ferreira (Woman in pub), Marlene Fisher (Casting executive woman), Frank Fontaine (ABC executive), Kelli Garner, Gene Gene Patton (Real Gene Gene), Benoit Guerin (Jim Byrd looka-like), Maggie Gyllenhaal (Debbie), Tommy Hinkley (Hambone Man), David Julian Hirsh (Freddy 'Boom Boom' Cannon), Mariah Inger (Principal), Isabelle Juneau (Amana Girl), Eric Jungmann, Martin Kevan (Chuck's father), Suyun Kim (Game Show Contestant, Asian Folk Singer), Richard Kind (Casting Executive), Janet Lane (Blonde spinster), Artie Lange (Bellboy), Jim Lange (Himself), Murray Langston (Real Unknown Comic), Jeff Lefebvre (Frizzy-haired bachelor), Rachelle Lefevre (25-year-old Tuvia), Molly Rose Livingstone, Jaye P. Morgan (Herself), Nathalie Morin (Spinster winner), Cheryl Murphy (Midget), Shu Lan Noma (Asian Folk singer #2). Keshav Patel (Elvis singer), Mike Paterson (Employee #3), Christian Paul (Black bachelor), Brad Pitt (Gameshow contestant), Conrad Pla (Fat man), Sergei Priselkov

(Shaving man), Andrée-Anne Quesnel (*Gong Show* model), George Randolph (Gene Gene the dancing machine), Emilio Rivera (Manny Benitez), Aimee Rose Ambroziak (Chuck's first date), Norman Roy (Colbert), Anna Silk (Headset woman), Michelle Sweeney (Housekeeper), Ethan Thomas C. Dempster (Three-year-old Chuck), Jérôme Tiberghien (Englishman), John Todd Anderson (Stud bachelor), Dino Tosques (LA barman), Sean Tucker (Barfly), James Urbaniak (Rod Flexner), Jerry Weintraub (Larry Goldberg), Alicia Westelman (Employee), Kristen Wilson (Loretta), Brian D. Wright, Daniel Zacapa (Renda), Tony Zanca (Bachelor winner).

MONA LISA SMILE (2003)

(In production)

Director: Mike Newell; Writers: Lawrence Konner, Mark Rosenthal.

CAST: JULIA ROBERTS (Katherine Watson), Kirsten Dunst (Betty Warren), Julia Stiles (Joan Brandwyn), Maggie Gyllenhaal (Giselle Levy), Ginnifer Goodwin (Constance Baker), Dominic West (Bill Dunbar), Juliet Stevenson (Amanda Armstrong), Marcia Gay Harden (Nancy Abbey), John Slattery (Paul Moore), Marian Seldes (President Jocelyn Carr), James Callahan (John Brandwyn), Terence Rigby (Dr Edward Staunton), Laura Allen (Susan Delacorte), Topher Grace (Tommy Donegal), Jordan Bridges (Spencer Jones).

CONTENTS

ACKNOWLEDGEMENTS

Julia Roberts is not known to be a vindictive person. Many speak of her kindness, but such is the power that someone who is paid $20 million per film can wield in Hollywood that very few people were willing to talk on the record to me. This is only natural, and I am very grateful to those that did and they will find their names in the appropriate place in the book.

Like Julia at the Oscars in 2001, I would like to thank a number of people for their help and kindness; it would probably take more than 45 seconds to mention them all. I would like to thank my editor at Virgin Books, Mark Wallace, whose judicious eye has ensured this is *the* book for fans of Julia or J Ro as she became known in my household. My agent Chelsey Fox arranged the contract. This is the fourth book that we have worked on together and I hope there are many more to come.

Thanks go to my friends: Peter Blackbrow, Jeremy Beadle, Steve Dyer, Jim Haspiel, Lis Williams, Shannon Whirry, Sarah Bastow, Natalie Partridge, Nicola Wilson, Mark Bego (who is also writing a book about Julia), Mitchell Symons, Jo Knowsley and David Hensley, Karen and Barry Kemelhor, Robin and Larry Goetz, Suzanne Kerins, Sinéad Heffernan, Laura Jones, Jacqui Fuller, John Gibbens, James Steen and, of course, the dedicatees Tracy Calway and Brendan O'Mahony.

If you would like to contact the author, you can do so c/o Virgin Books or direct via email – filmbiographer@hotmail.com

JULIA ROBERTS

THE BARE FACTS
Full name: Julia Fiona Roberts
Nickname: Jules
Date of birth: 28 October 1967
Starsign: Scorpio
Place of birth: Crawford Hospital, Atlanta, Georgia
Father: Walter Grady Roberts (1933–3 December 1977)
Mother: Betty Lou Bredemus (b. 13 August 1934)
Religion: Roman Catholic
Stepfather: Michael Motes
Stepmother: Eileen Sellars (1945–18 September 1977)
Brother: Eric (b. 18 April 1956)
Sister: Lisa (b. May 1965)
Half-sister: Nancy Dabbs Birmingham Motes (b. 19 May 1976)
Education: Fitzhugh Lee Elementary School
    Griffin Middle School
    Campbell High School
Height: 5 ft 9 in
Weight: 121 lb
Hobbies: Knitting. She likes to knit sweaters.
Tattoos: Julia has a butterfly tattoo in the small of her back.
Hair: 'My real hair colour is kind of a dark blonde. Now I just
    have mood hair.'
Eyes: Brown
Marriages: (1) 27 June 1993 to Lyle Lovett
           (2) 4 July 2002 to Danny Moder
First film: *Blood Red* (1986, released 1990)
Academy Awards: Best Actress – *Erin Brockovich* (2000)
Academy Award nominations: Best Supporting Actress – *Steel
    Magnolias* (1989)
    Best Actress – *Pretty Woman* (1990)

CAST OF CHARACTERS

Bratt, Benjamin	Actor
Clooney, George	Actor
Day-Lewis, Daniel	Actor
Devine, Mick	Chauffeur
Gere, Richard	Actor
Goldsmith, Elaine	Agent
Lovett, Lyle	Singer
Manocchia, Pat	Fitness trainer
Marshall, Garry	Film-maker
McDermott, Dylan	Actor
McGowan, Bob	Manager
Moder, Danny	Cameraman
Motes, Michael	Stepfather
Motes, Nancy	Half-sister
Neeson, Liam	Actor
Partridge, Ross	Barman
Patric, Jason	Actor
Perry, Matthew	Actor
Roberts, Betty	Mother
Roberts, Eileen	Stepmother
Roberts, Eric	Brother
Roberts, Lisa	Sister
Roberts, Walter	Father
Schumacher, Joel	Film-maker
Shapiro, Risa	Agent
Soderbergh, Steven	Film-maker
Sutherland, Kiefer	Actor

PROLOGUE: STAY AT HOME BRIDE

'I was born to love and to be the wife of this man . . .'

Julia Roberts

1329 PASEO PBLO SUR, TAOS, NEW MEXICO, 87571,
4 JULY 2002

The tall, slim redhead looked up and down the crowded shelves of the grocery store in Taos, her adopted home, a village in northern New Mexico that lies at the foot of the Sangre de Cristo mountains, 69 miles northeast of Santa Fe. Taos, pronounced Tous, was established in 1615 as Don Fernando de Taos and is one of the oldest white settlements in the United States.

Since the late nineteenth century Taos has been known for attracting writers and artists although the main income is from ranching, farming, lumber and the ski industries.

Despite the attraction of literary and artistic types, a grocery store in Taos was perhaps not the most obvious place to be if you wanted to go star-spotting. Nor did the grocer's seem to be a place where a bride-to-be might be found just a few short hours before her wedding. But the unlikely setting was where you would have found Julia Roberts, one of Hollywood's most successful, if occasionally unorthodox, stars, wandering the aisles and examining the produce. She had invited several friends to what she claimed was a Fourth of July party at her 51-acre ranch, which is reputed to be worth $2 million.

The invitation read:

*Come celebrate our **Independence Day** on the green*
grass under the stars
With the dogs and the horses.

Theme: *Midsummer Night's DreamISH*
meets Great Gatsby like combined with Wild West Bohemian

***Attire** – Think Linen, try Seersucker, Dawn Sweet Summer Hats.*

Free yourself from black.
Look fabulous staying cool.

Admittance: Bring along a lively/lovely addition to our garden.

RSVP

The press had been on high alert expecting Julia to marry her boyfriend cameraman Daniel Moder not least because they had been watching the construction of a redbrick chapel on her ranch in May 2002. A neighbour who wishes to remain anonymous remarked, 'Straight away we thought there might be wedding bells. How many people have a chapel in their back garden?' A large white marquee also appeared in the grounds of Julia's house but still she kept to the story of holding an Independence Day party. A source close to Julia Roberts revealed, 'Danny told his family that they must be at the party. [Julia and Danny] always wanted to get married as soon as [his] divorce was sorted. Independence Day seemed like a good idea.'

Danny Moder received his divorce on 16 May 2002. Reportedly, his ex-wife received a six-figure divorce settlement, almost certainly paid by Julia. The lovers celebrated his freedom with a romantic break in Cabo San Lucas, Mexico.

Yet when the wedding finally occurred Julia managed to wrong-foot the fourth estate's finest. A simple announcement was later made by Julia's publicist: 'Julia Roberts and Daniel Moder married during a midnight ceremony before close family and friends at their home in New Mexico.'

The wedding was the culmination of a love match that had been played out in secret and then later quite publicly and at times in an unpleasant way. Julia did herself and her public image no good whatsoever by being photographed in October 2001 in a home-made T-shirt bearing the legend 'A Low Vera'. It was a very unsubtle dig at make-up artist Vera Steinberg, Moder's estranged wife.

Julia Roberts met Danny Moder in February 2000 on the set of *The Mexican*, the film in which she co-starred with Brad Pitt. There was a major problem in their romance. Moder was already married and Julia was supposedly 'sickeningly, ecstatically happy' with Benjamin Bratt, her long-term boyfriend, who had accompanied her to the Oscars for her *Erin Brockovich* triumph. Julia and Moder managed to keep their romance under wraps until August of the following year (2001) when it became very public.

Vera Steinberg discovered the affair when she examined his itemised mobile phone bill and noticed lots of long-distance calls made by her husband to Julia.

In June 2001 Julia announced that she and Bratt had parted. In fact, the split had occurred the previous month after Julia had worked with Moder on the low-budget film *Grand Champion* (2001) which starred her 11-year-old niece, Emma. Julia helped to finance the film and Moder was chief cameraman.

On location Julia and Moder maintained propriety by having separate rooms at the hotel, although they were next door to each other.

Julia's people went to great lengths to portray her friendship with Moder as 'innocent' but that charade ended when Moder left his wife of five years. On 7 September 2001 Danny Moder separated from his wife and filed for divorce the following month. Vera Steinberg was bitterly hurt by her husband's betrayal and pleaded with him to give their marriage another try. Rather unkindly, she pointed to Julia's admittedly shaky romantic track record. However, Julia may have had her fair share of boyfriends but a story doing the rounds in Hollywood has Moder as something of a Lothario who has slept with more than a thousand women.

Julia, however, was determined to stand by her man even if, legally, he was actually still someone else's. 'I'm in love again,' she said, 'and I don't care if my man is married.'

Julia rang the Moder home and when Vera picked up the telephone asked, 'I think your husband is yummy – may I borrow him?'

Vera, believing that Julia was joking, replied, 'As long as you return him like you found him.'

'I'll give him a wash and brush up first,' quipped Julia.

Vera later recalled, 'When she first met Danny on the set of *The Mexican*, it was like she was all friendly. She rang me and asked in this giggly voice, "Is it OK if your husband takes me to dinner?" '

The merry banter hid the real truth. The lovers set up home in a £5 million house in Malibu Colony. The couple spent nights having romantic dinners in Wolfgang Puck's Granita restaurant. By the time Julia's 34th birthday came around on 28 October 2001 the couple were living in a suite at the L'Ermitage Hotel in Beverly Hills.

Meanwhile, Julia offered Vera $100,000 to quickly divorce her husband. It was claimed that the Moder family – mother Patty, film producer father Mike, brother John and sisters Jyl, Jane and Debbie – were heartbroken by the split. They all adored Vera. Mike Moder commented, 'Vera is a wonderful girl. We all love her. She was one of us – part of the family. When Danny first told me he was dating Julia Roberts I asked him, "Son, what are you smoking?"[1] I made it clear to Danny and Julia that we weren't pleased. Vera stuck with him when he was down on his luck. She washed his shirts and underwear. We are all wondering if Julia will do that.'

Tragedy hit the Moder family as the affair was revealed. Danny's mother, Patty, died aged 63 on 21 August 2001 from a heart attack, just days after learning of the romance. A family friend said, 'Dan is distraught. He cannot help thinking that the publicity over his affair may have contributed to [Patty's death].'

A month after Patty's death Julia travelled to Big Bear Resort, Mike Moder's home a hundred miles from Los Angeles, in Toluca Lake. There she convinced the grieving widower that the romance was not just another fling but that she truly loved his son and wanted to make him happy. At first Mike Moder was naturally hesitant. As a film producer in Hollywood[2] he was well aware of Julia's apparent commitment phobia. Julia was older than his son and an international film star, and fabulously wealthy to boot.

Julia managed to bring him round, resulting in the gathering of the Moders and the Robertses at her home in Taos on that warm summer's day in July 2002 to witness the midnight marriage.

---

[1] Coincidentally, in December 2001 newspapers and magazines published pictures, taken during a break in the filming of *Full Frontal*, of Julia and Moder sharing a joint. While he ate a lunch of artichoke salad she rolled the joint and, after taking a few puffs, she passed it to her boyfriend.
[2] His films include *Crimson Tide* and *Beverly Hills Cop*.

Aside from the unusual time of ceremony there were other odd elements about the wedding. The cake was a red and white carrot cake confection decorated with the elephant head of the Hindu god Ganesh, the deity of good luck.

Julia's wedding ring cost Moder $2,500, a small fortune for the cameraman who earns about $42,000 a year but small change to Julia whose most recent pay packet topped $20,000,000.[3] Rather than having some fancy Beverly Hills jeweller design the ring, Moder bought it in a shopping centre.

The bride wore a pink off-the-shoulder dress with a trailing white veil. Unlike her first wedding, she was not barefoot but wore flat Manolo Blahnik shoes so as not to tower over her new husband. Her hair was done by Serge Normand. Manhattan florist Cornucopia, owned by Julia's friend Dorothy Pfeiffer, supplied the flowers. The groom wore a red ruffled shirt and trousers.

The ceremony was performed by Barry Hirsch who is also Julia's lawyer. The white tent in which the reception was held was decorated with scented jasmine candles, lilacs and red roses.

The guests, aside from the members of the Roberts and Moder families, included very close friends and a very small sprinkling of celebrities such as George Clooney, Brad Pitt and Bruce Willis. All of the female guests were presented with custom-made necklaces featuring Buddhist elephant charms on ribbons.

One guest said, 'It was such a magical, intimate gathering, it felt like we were eavesdropping into someone's secret. There was great relief, complete and utter joy that these two people found each other.'

Julia's father had died when she was ten and she was not about to ask her stepfather to give her away, of which more later. The man she turned to was a bespectacled, bearded, grey-haired Irishman called Mick Devine, nineteen years her senior. Julia met Devine, a married father-of-three, when she was dating the Irish actor Liam Neeson. He was then running a successful chauffeuring company, Michael Devine Chauffeur Services, and he regularly drove Julia around.[4] However, she and Devine established a close

---

[3] When Michael Douglas married Catherine Zeta Jones in 2000 he spent £250,000 on her wedding ring.

[4] Other celebrities driven by Mick Devine include pop knights Mick Jagger and Paul McCartney.

friendship in 1991 after she dumped Kiefer Sutherland, three days before they were due to marry. She travelled to Ireland to find consolation in the arms of Jason Patric, who happened to be a friend of Sutherland.

When she landed at Dublin Airport Julia was met by Devine and he drove her to her hotel but found the paparazzi were camping outside. Devine suggested they visit a favourite café until the photographers got bored. But when they returned to the hotel, the paparazzi were still much in evidence. He offered Julia the chance to stay at his house. Relieved to be with someone she sensed she could trust, Julia agreed. When she arrived at the house Devine shares with his wife Breda and their family she was surprised. Mick Devine's three-bedroomed semi-detached house in Palmerstown, West Dublin, had only one bathroom.

Mick Devine is almost trappist on the subject of Julia Roberts. He has turned down vast sums to talk to journalists in detail about the star. He has said of that encounter in 1991, 'The only place I could bring her was to my home in the Dublin suburbs, so I took her home to the wife. Since then we have become great friends.'

Julia admits that at the time the pain of the split from Kiefer Sutherland had sent her to the edge of a nervous breakdown. It was Mick Devine's down-to-earth friendly behaviour towards her that saved her sanity. She refers to him as her 'surrogate dad'. Oddly, he calls her Alice rather than Julia or her nickname Jules but won't explain the reason to anyone.[5] At the end of her stay he drove her to the airport. As he carried her bags to check-in she said, 'I'll either pay you the agreed fee or you can take a gamble and have whatever's in my purse.'

Devine chose the purse and was delighted to find it chock-full of traveller's cheques. He cashed them all apart from one which to this day he keeps in his wallet. When Julia's relationship with Jason Patric went sour, it was to Mick Devine's home that she flew for comfort. The journey took fourteen hours but it was in the bosom of the Devine family that she wished to be.

A close friend of Julia who wishes to remain anonymous says,

---

[5] A number of celebrities have been called names other than the one by which they are known to the public. Doris Day, perhaps tellingly, called Rock Hudson 'Ernie' because 'he's certainly no Rock'. Lauren Bacall is known to intimates as Betty Bacall. Her real name is Betty Perske.

'Julia has always looked to Mick for guidance. She's taken most of her boyfriends to meet him over the years. It's like a ritual.

'Mick doesn't talk about their relationship. When it comes to Julia he is extremely protective. But if Danny hadn't got the thumbs up from Mick, I doubt Julia would have married him. She values Mick's opinion more than anything.'

Such is the romance of the story of the chauffeur and the film star that it became the subject of a film. An Irish writer called Barry Devlin penned a script entitled *Limo Man* based loosely around the story. The plan reached the casting stage and Melanie Griffith, ten years older than Julia, was selected to play the lead role. But for some reason, probably to Mick Devine's pleasure and relief, the project never went ahead.

Julia Roberts trusts very few people. Her agent is one, her sister Lisa is another. A third is Mick Devine. Julia has on several occasions asked Mick to leave Ireland and come to work for her on a full-time basis. Each time his answer has been firm but polite. He loves Ireland too much to ever leave it for good and, besides, he does not want to uproot his family. Julia makes do with regular trips to Ireland and invites for the Devine family to her home.

Less than a fortnight after the wedding Julia went on television to sing the praises of her new husband. Appearing on ABC's *Good Morning America*, she gushed, 'Danny is astounding. He is formidable. He is a man among men, unselfish and all-encompassing and he stands by the choices that he's made. He will never blame it on somebody else. And I've never seen anybody else ever do that. We will have a family in due course. I hope there are some people who agree that I have done some good, some kind things in my life, but to really, ultimately stand fully in a moment of realising that I was born to love and to be the wife of this man.'

Speaking of her marriage, Julia claimed that the midnight wedding was not secret: 'People just weren't paying enough attention. Ultimately, more than anything it wasn't about keeping secret and being clever and pulling something off than it was about what will make us most happy and most fulfilled at the moment. And if that's what we pulled off, then I would say, absolutely, we pulled it off because we were levitating with happiness.' She refused to reveal the specially written vows that the couple made to each other but did say that they had had their initials tattooed on each other.[6] However, she denied that the engravings were done for the wedding. 'It was a long time ago, actually. People kind of missed it for a long period of time and somebody gave us up.'

Speaking of her relationship with Benjamin Bratt, who had said that the constant media intrusion during the affair was like a mosquito constantly buzzing in his ear, she commented, 'It sounds to me like Benjamin came up with more bad than good, but that he's participating in that. I figure he's kind of making his choices, so, all the better because he was unhappy and he left and moved along and found happiness where there aren't any mosquitoes.'

The marriage to Danny Moder has hopefully given Julia Roberts the stability that she has been looking for since her parents' divorce and her father's untimely death in December 1977 when Julia was just six weeks past her tenth birthday. It has been a long, hard struggle, one that saw her on the front pages of the world's newspapers for the wrong reasons but one that saw her rise to become, in terms of financial reward, the most successful actress the world has ever known.

It is a struggle that began in Georgia, thousands of miles from Hollywood, in the 1960s . . .

---

[6] *Baywatch* star Pamela Anderson and Tommy Lee eschewed wedding rings having their names tattooed on the other's ring finger. Anderson now has a permanently scarred ring finger where she had the tattoo removed.

1. A STAR IS BORN

'Walter had a tremendously intense feeling toward theatre, and a zest for what he was doing, so ultimately it hurt him deeply that he did not get the attention he wanted. But, truthfully, although his ideas and ambitions were good, his productions didn't live up to them. He never had enough time, enough talent. He was a tough man, very short-tempered. I liked him and respected him, but I also thought he was unreasonable at times.'

Journalist Terry Kay on Walter Roberts

ATLANTA, GEORGIA, 28 OCTOBER 1967

Despite what you will see and read in innumerable sources such as supposedly reliable reference books, magazines and websites, Julia Fiona Roberts was not born in Smyrna, Georgia. In fact, she came into the world in Atlanta, the state capital and largest city of Georgia, the third child of Walter and Betty Roberts.

In 1960 when her elder brother Eric was four, the city of Atlanta had a population of 487,455 (the metropolitan area numbered 1,017,188) but by 1970 it had grown to 496,973 (metropolitan area 1,390,164). The state saw a population rise of 16.4 per cent in that decade. Georgia[1] is the largest state east of the Mississippi River. It was founded in 1733 as a British colony by General James Edward Oglethorpe and named for King George II. General Oglethorpe was governor of the colony for ten years until 1743. Georgia was the youngest of the thirteen colonies when the American Revolution began and on 2 January 1788 it became the fourth state to ratify the constitution. It is a predominantly white state and more than 95 per cent of the population are protestants. Three per cent are Roman Catholics and one per cent Jewish. Julia was among the three per cent of Catholics.

Atlanta, a city of 131 square miles, is the financial, distribution and communications capital of southeastern America. The city was founded in 1845 three years after it was chosen as the final

---

[1] Jimmy Carter, the 39th US president, was governor of Georgia from 1971 until 1975. Franklin D. Roosevelt, the 32nd president, convalesced in Georgia in 1921 after he was struck down by poliomyelitis. He died from a cerebral hæmorrhage in the Little White House, Warm Springs in Georgia on 12 April 1945. He was the seventh president to die in office.

location for the terminus of the Western and Atlantic Railroad. It was originally called The Terminus then Marthasville. On 15 November 1864, during the American Civil War, it was burned on the orders of Union General William Tecumseh Sherman.

Julia was born in the maternity ward of Crawford Long Hospital in downtown Atlanta on Saturday 28 October 1967.[2] The Robertses had already a son, Eric, and a daughter, Lisa, when Julia completed the family.

In the week of Julia's birth anti-Vietnam War protests began in Arlington, Virginia, and demonstrators attempted to march on the Pentagon. The Americans lost three jets but had also raided Hanoi. If you switched on the television that Saturday night you would be entertained by *The Dating Game*, *The Newlywed Game*, *The Lawrence Welk Show*, *Iron Horse*, *The Jackie Gleason Show*, *My Three Sons*, *Hogan's Heroes*, *Petticoat Junction*, *Mannix*, *Maya*, *Get Smart* and a film on NBC. Lulu was spending her second week on top of the Billboard pop charts with 'To Sir, With Love'.

BILOXI, MISSISSIPPI, 1955

Julia's parents had been married for a dozen relatively unhappy years by the time of her arrival. Her mother, short and blonde, was born in Minneapolis, Minnesota on 13 August 1934 as Betty Lou Bredemus, the second child and only daughter of Elizabeth and Wendell Bredemus, an American football-coach-turned-salesman. She has an elder brother, John. Unusually for someone of her family background and generation, on 27 August 1953 Betty Lou Bredemus enlisted in the US Army Air Force. She was a fortnight past her nineteenth birthday. In fact, it was her family background that virtually forced Betty to sign up. Her father squandered money. Her intention had been to study drama but

---

[2] Other 28 October celebrants include: French chef Georges-Auguste Escoffier (1846), surgeon Robert Liston (1794), lesbian Oscar-winning designer Edith Head (1897), novelist Evelyn Waugh (1903), bisexual actor Elsa Lanchester (1902), painter Francis Bacon (1909), scientist Jonas Salk (1914), singer Dame Cleo Laine (1927), actor Tony Franciosa (1928), actor Joan Plowright (1929), composer Carl Davis (1936), TV presenter David Dimbleby (1938), actor Jane Alexander (1939), Shadows guitarist Hank Marvin (1941), *NYPD Blue* star Dennis Frantz (1944), actor Telma Hopkins (1948), actor-athlete Bruce Jenner (1949), actor Annie Potts (1952), golfer Mark James (1953), computer genius Bill Gates (1955), actor Daphne Zuniga (1962), actor Jami Gertz (1965) and actor Leaf Phoenix (1974).

her parents could not afford the tuition fees and so she joined up hoping to use the GI Bill of Rights when she was demobbed to pay for her studies.[3]

History was to deal Betty a different hand. After basic training at San Antonio, Texas, she was posted to Chanute Air Force Base before being stationed at the Keesler Air Force Base in Biloxi, Mississippi. At Keesler Betty worked in Special Services spending her time in the library and appearing in various amdram shows. One day she met Airman First Class Walter Grady Roberts, a Korean War veteran and a medic, and a year older than Betty. Walter Roberts was one of two children of Walter Thomas and Beatrice Roberts and had been born in Atlanta. He wanted to be a short-story writer. Physically he was the opposite of his future wife – he was tall with dark, wavy hair. By all accounts he was a very striking man. Oddly, Betty always referred to him as 'Rob', never by his Christian name.

The pair found that they had a shared interest in the theatre and this drew them closer together. They befriended another couple, Rance and Jean Howard. The Howards had a young son, Ronald, born on 1 March 1953, who would grow up to play Richie Cunningham on the popular television sitcom *Happy Days* and later to become a highly successful film director.[4]

In 1955 Rance and Jean Howard moved to Los Angeles (where he became a successful television director) and tried to persuade Walter and Betty to accompany them. Sadly for Betty, Walter still had a year to serve and reluctantly she stayed with him. It seemed to her that showing that kind of commitment necessitated Walter showing another kind of declaration.

---

[3] The GI Bill of Rights was a government grant designed to help ex-servicemen back into civvy street. Among those actors who benefited were Jeff Corey who took a degree in speech therapy at the University of California at Los Angeles, and Walter Matthau, who took advantage of the GI Bill and returned to New York to study at the New School for Social Research Dramatic Workshop under the renowned German director Erwin Piscator, from whom he acquired 'the real feeling for acting'. Using the same government grant Vic Morrow went to Florida State University to study law. Many lawyers need to be good actors and while at university Morrow discovered he preferred acting on stage to acting in a court of law. Using the grant, Rod Steiger moved to New York where he began to study acting at the New School for Social Research Dramatic Workshop and the Actors' Studio.

[4] In fact, when Richie Cunningham was the lead actor in *Happy Days*, the show suffered poor ratings. When the emphasis switched to Henry Winkler – Arthur 'The Fonz' Fonzarelli – the show took off. As a director Howard's films include *Splash* (1984), *Cocoon* (1985), *Apollo 13* (1995) and *EDtv* (1999).

On 1 July 1955 Walter Roberts and Betty Lou Bredemus were married at a friend's home on the base by Reverend Victor Augsberger of the First Presbyterian Church in Biloxi. On 26 July 1955 Betty was demobbed but stayed on the base because of Walter's extra year of service. On 18 April 1956 their first child, a son they named Eric Anthony, arrived.[5] 'My mother was about to have me and the aeroplane landed in Biloxi, Mississippi, so I was born there,' he was to say.

Not long after Eric was born, Walter was finally demobbed and went up to Tulane University in New Orleans where he studied English literature and psychology. Betty worked for an insurance company to support the family and also went to night school at Tulane where she, too, studied English lit. With fewer than three months to go before graduation Walter mysteriously dropped out of university. Betty was to later say that 'He had a great deal of animosity towards the professors and was convinced there was nothing more they could teach him.'

ATLANTA, GEORGIA, 1960–71

The family moved back to Atlanta and settled on Scott Boulevard in Decatur, a small town on the outskirts of Atlanta. '[Walter] came from nothing and was going to be something, make something of himself,' says journalist Terry Kay. 'He didn't want to leave Georgia so he stayed and beat his brains out. He was a brilliant man who was in the wrong town to be doing what he was doing. That was his downfall. Also, he expected everyone to work as hard as he did, to be as committed as he was.' Walter worked for Atlanta Dairies Co-op as a wholesale milk salesman while Betty worked in the public relations department of Emory University as a secretary. In May 1965 Lisa Billingsley Roberts was born.

The same year that Lisa arrived Walter launched his first actors' workshop in the living room of their home. From the time that they had returned to Atlanta Walter had worked his way through several jobs, one of which was as a publicist for Academy Theatre. His boss, Frank Wittow, remembered, 'Walter Roberts was one of

---

[5] On the day that Eric was born Hollywood ice maiden Grace Kelly married Prince Rainier III of Monaco.

the most charming people I have ever met. He was extremely good-looking, sort of like Armand Assante, and had very dark, piercing eyes. He was very dynamic, very verbally adept and, since he had some background in theatre, he seemed well suited for the position.' Less than a year after he had started, Walter left. 'I became aware that he clearly had other interests, which were distracting him from doing the job. Walter decided to have an art exhibit in the lobby of the theatre, which was a converted Baptist church then. The lobby was less than 60 feet in diameter and not conducive to an art exhibit. But Walter wanted to have an exhibit and then pretend one of the paintings had been stolen, which he believed would get a lot of publicity. He left shortly afterward. He was very bright and he was king where his family was involved. But he was somewhat manipulative and I felt that he had some emotional problems.'

Walter went to work at the Harrington Scenic and Lighting Studio. Never one to doubt his own abilities, he simply walked in and introduced himself to the owner and was quickly taken on. He stayed there a year and formed a friendship with Edith Russell Harrington who had an interest in the theatre. Some years before, she had founded the Civic Children's Theatre. Walter took the mailing list of the theatre and almost certainly used it to begin his own. Charles Walker who now owns the studio recalled, 'I remember [Edith] being quite upset about it saying, "That renegade so-and-so tried to take our kids." [Walter] was kind of like a butterfly. He seemed to want to dig in, but then he'd fly away. [He was a] moody fellow. He was all right unless you crossed him. He was a bit pompous and I remember he got on Mr Harrington's nerves. He had very definite political views, especially about the Vietnam War, and he enunciated everything perfectly. When he talked, it was better than listening to the radio.'

In a large, two-storey house at 849 Juniper Street in midtown Atlanta Walter opened his Actors' and Writers' Workshop. The venue was just two blocks from his former employ with the Harringtons. The workshop took up the ground floor of the house and the Robertses lived on the first.

Philip De Poy was one of the pupils at The Actors' and Writers' Workshop during its five-year existence. He said, 'The house stood high above the street so you had to climb up ten or fifteen steps and then five more steps up to the front porch. Once you were inside, immediately to your left was a library. There was a staircase going upstairs, where the family lived, and on the right were a large dining room and a sun room, as well as a kitchen and oversized pantry, which is where they stored the costumes. I remember that each of the rooms had sliding wooden doors and lots of woodwork. The house seemed enormous to me at the time.'[6]

In November 1967 Julia came home from Crawford Long Hospital to a vibrant, buzzing house full of young aspirant actors. One of them was Eric, then eleven. Eric claimed not to have spoken for the first five years of his life and when he did he had a stutter but later found that acting partially cured the disability. 'My dad always found ways of making acting magical to me. He would wake me up in the middle of the night to see something special on television. And I learned in grade school, if I memorised something, I wouldn't stutter, which made acting a cure.' He also memorised large passages of text in case he was called upon to read aloud in class. 'If I didn't get it memorised first, I thought I would stutter and the class would laugh. But what really bothered me more than that was that I was always so much shorter than the other kids. I was short until I was fifteen and then I grew six inches in ten months.' Eric's plan usually worked except on the days when the teacher called the students in a different order and Eric realised he had not memorised the text he was about to be called upon to read. He developed the ability to learn very quickly.

It was while at the pictures one Saturday afternoon that Eric's life was changed. He watched the film *Red River* (1948) which starred John Wayne and Montgomery Clift. He was inspired by the cowboys because they lived their own lives beholden to no one. The only difference was that the cowpokes had no fathers and Eric idolised the ground that Walter walked upon.

Yolanda King, one of the older students and the daughter of Martin Luther King, recalls Eric as being 'very, very skinny. He was not quiet but he was very introspective, very thoughtful.' By

---

[6] The house was demolished apart from one wall, now covered in graffiti, in the mid-1970s.

the time he was offered a place at RADA when he was fifteen Eric had appeared in more than eighty plays including *Charley's Aunt*, *A Member of the Wedding* and *The Taming of the Shrew*. That year, 1971, he also became America's cross-country running champion. Ed Danos, an Atlanta actor, saw fifteen-year-old Eric in a production of *Othello*. 'He had a strong man's voice and, truthfully, was better than some Shakespearean actors I'd seen. He was head and shoulders above everyone else in the play. Nobody had that kind of voice at his age, with that kind of resonance and stage presence.' When Eric graduated from RADA he enrolled at the American Academy of Dramatic Art in New York.

Walter's plan was to create a southern version of Lee Strasberg's Actors Studio[7] but he found that most adults were uninterested in the theatre for themselves but did have an interest in the possible future stardom of their children.

One patron was Coretta Scott King, the wife of Reverend Dr Martin Luther King. Their children – Yolanda, Martin Luther Jr, and Dexter – attended Walter's school. Yolanda went to Walter's from the age of nine until she was fifteen and studied movement, drama and speech. She said, 'My mother was immediately attracted to the workshop because it was an integrated group. It was a constant struggle to get funds to keep going. My mother was very much committed to them. But it was always a case of just barely getting by, paying the rent, getting the costumes.' In fact, once the rent had been paid the Robertses had just $50 a week to live on, well below the poverty line for the first six years of Julia's life.

Walter managed to wangle a grant worth $2,500 from the Guggenheim Foundation after The Actors' and Writers' Workshop staged a production of *Othello*. Walter played the Moor and Betty was Desdemona. The money enabled their next shows to be staged. *The Nightingale*, a traditional Chinese fable, was followed

---

[7] From 1948 Strasberg ran the infamous Actors Studio in New York and numbered some of Hollywood's greats under his patronage: Marlon Brando, Montgomery Clift, Robert De Niro, James Dean, Sally Field, Jane Fonda, Julie Harris, Steve McQueen, Paul Newman, Al Pacino, Geraldine Page, Maureen Stapleton and Rod Steiger. The Method required actors to dredge up personal feelings in order to play a rôle. Some believed in it wholeheartedly, others like Laurence Olivier dismissed it. Strasberg once opined that he had taught two great acting talents: Marilyn Monroe and Brando.

by a version of Joel Chandler Harris's Uncle Remus stories. Eric played Brer Rabbit, Philip De Poy was Brer Fox and Yolanda King covered herself completely in green food colourant to play Ma Alligator.

In the summer of 1970 with a grant courtesy of the Economic Opportunity Act the Robertses toured the ghettos of Atlanta in a 'showmobile'. This was simply a flatbed truck in which the back doubled as a stage. Betty remembers, 'When we toured that summer I would put Julia in a stroller while I set up the sound system. In the ghetto areas the kids would come up and ask, "Can I take her for a walk?" and I'd say, "Sure." Then one time someone said, "Are you sure she's coming back?" But the black children were fascinated with her because a lot of them had never seen any white children. She was about two years old and she had all this soft blonde hair. It was a wonderful summer.'

Once again Walter's inability to get on with people created problems. The Actors' and Writers' Workshop relied on volunteers and Walter believed that they should work as hard as he did. He was adored by his students but many others found him difficult to be around. Some believed that he was able to get on with the students because they were young and impressionable and did not threaten to undermine him or question his beliefs and opinions.

Yolanda King, who often babysat Lisa and Julia, remembers, '[He] was a larger than life person. He was a cauldron of energy. He seemed to be bubbling over with it. I remember feeling very comfortable with him, never intimidated, even though he had a temper. He would scream and rant, but I think he was very paternal, very protective. I think he represented a father figure to me.'

Philip De Poy has similar views: 'Rob didn't act like any ordinary adult we'd ever seen. He was outside mainstream adult behaviour. To us, he was an artiste, something most of us had never met before. He didn't put on a suit or go to an office. He wore sweatshirts, jeans and loafers. He was absolutely the coolest man I'd ever met.'

Stuart Culpepper, an actor in Atlanta, said, 'Walter Roberts had more dreams than talent. He was one of those men I didn't want to pursue a friendship with because I never quite trusted him. He was quite pompous, something of a con man, I think. Anyway, he just didn't fit in with anything. It was a workshop for kids. I don't think there was any substance there at all. My impression was that it was a very shoestring operation, run by family members and close friends.'

Atlanta actor Ed Danos concurs with Culpepper's opinion: 'Whenever I talked to Walter I had an idea in the back of my head that he didn't really know much. Walter was somebody on the fringes of society and, frankly, I didn't have a good impression of him. There was something about him that was not quite on the up-an-up. He was a little sleazy, a little oily. He seemed like somebody living hand-to-mouth. And I remember his clothes never seemed pressed. He always seemed to be wearing the same baggy, nondescript suit. But his assurance had to come from somewhere, not just his family.'

Journalist Terry Kay, the drama critic of the *Atlanta Constitution*, partly disagrees with the sentiments of both actors. His view of Walter Roberts was very different. 'The workshop was a real serious attempt to create the first repertory company in Atlanta. Walter had a tremendously intense feeling toward theatre, and a zest for what he was doing, so ultimately it hurt him deeply that he did not get the attention he wanted. But, truthfully, although his ideas and ambitions were good, his productions didn't live up to them. He never had enough time, enough talent. He was a tough man, very short-tempered. I liked him and respected him, but I also thought he was unreasonable at times. He felt he knew more about theatre than anyone in Atlanta. He was passionate and temperamental, and he didn't like criticism. Walter was the kind of guy who argued with you because *his* interpretation was the *only* interpretation. He had a drive to teach because he was ambitious. He was trying to establish a school that would have his name stamped on it. But he was headstrong, the kind of guy who would fight the system too, head first.'

Walter's theatre was a fine experiment but although it was loved by the children it was, with one or two notable exceptions, merely tolerated by their parents. It was somewhere for the kids to go to keep out of mischief. It did not get the recognition Walter thought it deserved. In 1966 he had produced a thirteen-week television show on Atlanta's Channel 11, which starred Betty as a character with the unlikely name of Bum Bum. It, too, sank without trace.

ATLANTA, GEORGIA, 1971–72

Both Walter and Betty put a lot of work into the workshop. Perhaps they put so much of themselves into the project that they had nothing left to put into their relationship. In February 1971 Walter bought a three-bedroomed bungalow for $17,800 at 432 Eighth Street. The building was across the road from Grady High School where Eric had just entered the third year. But it was too little, too late to save their marriage. On 13 June 1971 Betty filed for divorce. Four weeks later, they agreed visitation rights plus child support which was set at $195 per month. The decree become absolute on 28 January 1972. To outsiders it seemed a very amicable split.

The last production of The Actors' and Writers' Workshop was a version of the farce *The Owl and the Pussycat*, which starred Yolanda King as a black prostitute opposite a white boy. In the bigoted South of the 1970s such racial desegregation did not go down well with either whites or blacks.

'People were saying my father was turning over in his grave. People even threatened to leave my father's church. My grandfather, the Reverend Martin Luther King Sr, decided he was not coming. But, at the last minute, he did come to the première. I think Walter saw *Owl* as a way to rejuvenate the company but it was too daring. It was artistically successful but financially it was not.'

The Owl and the Pussycat ran for a fortnight and when it closed so did The Actors' and Writers' Workshop. Walter landed a job selling vacuum cleaners in a department store. Betty became a secretary.

2. STEPMOM AND DYING YOUNG

'My childhood was real weird to me. I feel like I grew up twice. Once till I was about ten. After that it was completely different. My father died . . . then, which probably changed me a lot more than I realised. I don't think I'd be what I am today if that hadn't happened.'

Julia on the loss of her father Walter

'I just didn't have the energy to work with her. I was very stressed out, the office was in total chaos, and I realised instantly that this demure, shy, waiflike girl sitting across from me needed somebody special and kind-hearted to take care of her, that she was going to need 24-hour-a-day nurturing. And frankly, I just didn't have it in me at the time.'

Agent Mary Sames on why she turned Julia down

ATLANTA AND SMYRNA, GEORGIA, 1971–85

On leaving the family home in June 1971 Walter moved into a bachelor flat in Ansley Forest, still near to his children and estranged wife. Betty took up with a man by the name of Michael Motes a month after the divorce was finalised. As a consequence Betty often left the children with Walter at weekends, a situation he loved. Betty moved out of the family home in Atlanta, unable to pay the mortgage, and in with Motes in Smyrna, a town of approximately 20,000 people in northwestern Georgia, twelve miles from Atlanta. Apart from the connection to Julia, Smyrna was the scene of an American Civil War battle on 4 July 1864. It was on a nearby hill that William T. Sherman[1] watched Atlanta burn, an incident immortalised in Margaret Mitchell's epic novel *Gone With the Wind*.

Michael Motes was born in Smyrna in 1945 and was educated at Campbell High School, just like Julia and Lisa. He collected *Gone With the Wind* memorabilia. He was working for the *Atlanta Constitution* when he met Betty. She was appearing in an amdram production of *Arsenic and Old Lace* and he was on the drama desk. A tall and hefty man, Motes wore horn-rimmed glasses, had a pale complexion and, unlike Walter, was not sure of everything he

---

[1] General William T. Sherman (1820–91) has several claims to fame. The tank is named after him and he popularised the expression 'War is hell' in 1880.

knew. Motes also suffered from alopecia from an early age and attempted to compensate by wearing a wig. A friend of his commented, 'They weren't very attractive and they were obviously hairpieces, sort of reddish coloured. I remember he came into the office one day with a different hairpiece. Same colour but obviously a different hairpiece. But he didn't seem to care. He was a funny guy with a sort of comedian's look, sort of your typical second banana. He was the comic relief. He wore those wigs until Betty convinced him not to because after they were married he stopped and just went around bald.'

With his three children at his side, Walter would go to the cinema or 'the flicks' as he called the entertainment. One day in the summer of 1971 Walter was on the pavement in front his flat with his two daughters when they bumped into one of his neighbours, Eileen Sellars. Julia, then three years old, decided to do the introductions. 'This is my daddy. His name is Walter, but you can call him daddy.' Not long after, Walter plucked up the courage to ask Eileen Sellars out for a drink. For Walter, 1972 began well: he had an attractive new girlfriend, a steady job and saw his children whenever he wanted. Then it all began to go horribly wrong.

On a Thursday in May 1972 Eric and Michael Motes had a fight. Two days later, with the rain pouring down, Eric left the house. Eric, a month past his sixteenth birthday, rang his father but Walter was out with Eileen Sellars and not contactable. So instead he rang Eileen Sellars's mother, Virginia, who picked him up in Atlanta where he had hitchhiked from Smyrna. She recalls, 'I felt so sorry for him. He couldn't get in touch with his father and he didn't have any money. He was just soaking wet and he was so upset he was stuttering something awful.' In later years, Eric would become estranged from Julia but that rain-soaked night began his virtual estrangement from his mother. The two have rarely spoken since. Once he left school he flew to London where he joined RADA.

On 13 September 1972 Betty married Michael Motes in Atlanta. The following month Walter applied for sole custody of his children. He told the court that Motes 'has and continues to mistreat our minor children' and that 'during the winter months our daughters had colds, appeared extremely tired and listless, and had fevers'. He accused Betty of 'neglect[ing] the minor children by staying out late at night without providing any adult care and supervision'. Betty countersued accusing him of theft from their former home, not paying his maintenance and 'telling malicious lies to the minor children concerning her behaviour in order to prejudice them and induce them to leave her custody'. The court's decision, published on 30 October, was to award Betty temporary custody of Lisa and Julia and to award custody of Eric to Walter. On 31 January 1973 Betty was awarded permanent custody and Walter's access decreased to a fortnight during the summer holidays and either Christmas Eve or Christmas Day. He was heartbroken by the decision. That month also saw the old family home in Atlanta sold at auction at Fulton County courthouse. What might have tipped the scales of justice in Walter's favour was the knowledge that Michael Motes was in dire financial straits. In November 1972 he was sued for non-payment of rent on a flat in Smyrna. It was the first of several lawsuits that he and Betty would face over the next ten years.

In December 1973 Motes went into Rich's department store and bought some items for $23.33. He paid by cheque. It bounced. In America writing a rubber cheque is a far more serious offence than it is in England and on 21 March 1974 the store sued Motes for the return of its money. Neither Motes nor Betty made any attempt to repay the debt and eventually the money was recovered from Betty's wages on 18 June. At the time she was working for the *Georgia Bulletin*, a Catholic newspaper. The couple managed to survive the embarrassment.

On 4 April 1974 40-year-old Walter Roberts married 28-year-old Eileen Sellars in a register office. The newlyweds moved into a three-bedroomed apartment in Stone Mountain, Georgia. With his new wife by his side Walter felt empowered to again seek custody of his children and filed suit on 20 June.

It was shortly after the suit was filed that the Motes house at 154 Privette Road in Smyrna was raided by drugs officers acting on a tip-off. The authorities had been told that there was a hoard of drugs hidden inside a hollowed-out Bible on the coffee table in the lounge. When the book was searched there were indeed drugs inside. Neither Motes nor Betty were arrested. Drugs officer Troy Ballinger remembers, 'The husband started crying. He got really upset and began wringing his hands, saying he had young children in the house and how he would never have drugs around them. And then the wife said that the stuff had probably been planted by her ex-husband. They were involved in some court problems at the time. Things just didn't fit . . . we never charged them and the whole thing was dropped.'

Was Walter so determined to gain custody of Lisa and Julia that he attempted to frame his ex-wife? Or did Eric take revenge on his hated stepfather and mother by planting the narcotics? Despite Betty's suspicions, there was no evidence to suggest that either male Roberts had the opportunity or inclination to behave in that way, although there was certainly a motive. The suspicions must also have arisen in the mind of the judge at the custody hearing which occurred in the middle of July. Walter was banned from going to the house or even setting foot in any part of Privette Road. The court's decision on 8 August 1974 was not what Walter wanted to hear. His visitation rights were still limited to a fortnight in the summer holidays and either 24 or 25 December. However, he was allowed a fifteen-minute telephone call every Wednesday to each girl between 7 p.m. and 7.30 p.m.

In 1976 Walter and Eileen bought a house in Riverdale, a suburb of Atlanta. That was the year that Eric landed a rôle on a daytime soap opera. It was also the first time he told a journalist that his mother was dead. Since he was only able to see them occasionally and Betty did her best to block his telephone calls, Walter took to writing letters to Julia and Lisa. Julia kept one written by Walter on 6 July 1977, the only one of his missives she managed to hang on to and the one that today still 'moves me in a different way every time [I read it]'.

The letter from Walter was composed when he took his daughters to visit their brother in New York and when he left them at Betty's he was naturally upset. He would not get to see the girls again for five months.

Eileen tried to cheer her husband up by reminding him that they had a weekend away planned for September at Six Mile Creek on Lake Lanier, where Walter leased a houseboat.

The couple set out in high spirits on the afternoon of Friday 16 September 1977. Eileen had just begun to pursue a career as a court stenographer and Eric decided to visit them at the lake. On the Sunday morning Eric and his stepmother went for a paddle in their own canoe. It was around 9.30 a.m. and the sun was shining brightly as the pair began to paddle away from the houseboat where Walter stayed. Then without warning a speedboat shot by the canoe creating a violent backwash. Eileen stood up and the boat tipped over throwing her and Eric into the water. Eileen was a non-swimmer but had decided not to wear a life jacket because of the warm weather. Walter heard Eric's screams for help but it was all to no avail. Eileen never again broke the surface. The search and rescue teams arrived less than fifteen minutes after the alarm was sounded but it took them several hours to find Eileen's corpse.

On 21 September Eileen Sellars Roberts was buried. She was just 31 years old. In her coffin she held a small nosegay that had been placed in her hands by Eric.

Like many grieving people Walter found it difficult to cope with his wife gone. He would often break down weeping without warning. His health began to suffer although some believed it was in reaction to Eileen's death rather than anything more serious. He was sent for tests at Emory University Hospital and shortly before he went he rang Eileen's aunt, Vivien McKinley, and then Walter's mother rang her to say that he would be in touch. Vivien McKinley never heard from Walter or his mother again. On 3 December 1977 Walter Roberts died of throat cancer. He was 43 and had never smoked a cigarette in his life. (Julia would later become a smoker.) Walter's funeral was arranged by Eric, and Betty brought Lisa and Julia to the ceremony.

'My childhood was real weird to me. I feel like I grew up twice,' said Julia. 'Once till I was about ten. After that it was completely different. My father died . . . then, which probably changed me a lot more than I realised. I don't think I'd be what I am today if that hadn't happened. It was just a rough time. I miss my dad. I don't feel that boundless injustice over his death any more, which is good, because that's not a fun bag to carry. It was just something that happened to me.'

In September 1977, the month that Eileen died, the Motes moved to a new three-bedroomed house on Maner Road on the outlying area of Smyrna. The house was comparatively expensive and it is a mystery as to how the couple managed to afford it especially as they now had an extra mouth to feed. On 19 May 1976 Nancy Dabbs Birmingham Motes had been born. Eileen Roberts had died intestate so her worldly goods immediately reverted to Walter. On 1 December 1977 he had signed a will leaving everything to his children. The document, witnessed by nurses at the hospital, appointed Eric as executor and trustee and guardian of Lisa and Julia. The estate amounted to around $20,000. In late December 1977 Eric appealed to the court to be made Lisa and Julia's legal guardian and also for the will to be probated. A hearing was scheduled for February 1978 but on 17 January Betty issued proceedings that sought to have herself appointed trustee and for the will to be overturned. 'Eric Anthony Roberts is not a fit and proper person to serve as guardian and trustee. He is a New York City actor with no regular income and caveators (i.e. Lisa and Julia) fear the waste of their inheritance.' She also harked back to the property allegedly taken without permission by Walter and used this as leverage to persuade the court that Walter couldn't bequeath items that he had no right to. On 26 January Eric asked the court to name him as executor of Eileen's estate. Legal delays ensured that the hearing due to be heard in February 1978 was delayed until 4 April 1979. To complicate matters, on 22 February 1978 Barbara Louise Floyd Wood filed suit asking the court to alter the status of the Roberts children as recipients of Eileen's largesse. It was learned that Eileen had a 25 per cent share in an office building and thus her estate was worth five times as much as it was originally thought. Wood was another shareholder and she wanted what she regarded as her money. The Cobb County Superior Court ruled in favour of Eric, Lisa and Julia so Wood appealed. Fortunately for the Roberts children, the Georgia Supreme Court upheld the ruling of the Cobb County Superior Court and awarded Eileen's estate – worth around $90,000 – to them. Further good news was received when Betty and Eric ended their squabble and agreed to C.R. Vaughn, a lawyer in Cobb County, being appointed guardian for Lisa and Julia.

Julia – or Julie or Jules as she was called by her family and friends – enjoyed school and had several friends, although a not especially subtle colour bar still operated in the South. When Julia was eleven she entered a dancing competition with a black boy as her partner. Some people did not approve of her decision because, not long after, her school locker was vandalised and she was insulted by some other pupils who called her 'a nigger lover'.

At Griffin Middle School on King Spring Road she wanted to be a vet. Betty remembers, 'That's all Julie ever talked about for a long time because she just adored animals – still adores them ... especially dogs.' Julia would go on to 'adopt' a dog on the set of *Pretty Woman*.

Julia said, 'I thought I was Dr Doolittle. I was convinced I could talk to the animals. But then I went to school and discovered science, which I hated, so that went out of the window.'

When she was thirteen Julia thought about entering the fine profession of journalism and competed in a speech-writing contest. Julia's speech was a feminist tract although later in interviews she was to claim that she was not a feminist: 'I'm Julia.'

Feminist or not, there was one man for whom she held little regard – her stepfather, Michael Motes. Despite the fact that they lived under the same roof for eleven years Julia has never mentioned him in interviews. With their big brother away in New York and their stepsister too young to understand, Lisa and Julia turned to each other to establish a strong bond. Until the move to Maner Road and their own bedroom, they slept in the same bed. 'Lisa has this celestial thing,' said Julia. 'I would wait until she was asleep and touch her, to tap into this safe place so I wouldn't be scared at night.' Although the sisters are devoted, physically they are dissimilar. Julia is dark blonde and 5 ft 9 in while Lisa is a lighter blonde and a much more petite 5 ft 3 in.

After leaving Griffin Middle School, Julia enrolled at Campbell High School on Ward Street in 1981. Campbell was designated a 5A school which made it among the larger of scholastic establishments in the area. The daily attendance was around a thousand children but only around ten of them were black. Classmate John Briglevich, now a successful music producer in Atlanta, remembers Julia as an average student. 'She was developed. I wouldn't say more developed than other girls.' Julia gave no clue that she would go on to become the world's leading female at the box office. Briglevich says, 'One of the things I tell young aspiring music stars that I deal with today is that I went to high school with Julia Roberts and it goes to show that if she can be famous anyone can. I don't mean that as a knock to her. She was just an everyday girl. She was a very normal girl, which is part of her success. One thing that has stuck with her is that she has a very infectious smile. She could light up a room. I am not saying that because now she is a star. I remember her being like that at school. She could walk into a class and her infectious smile would light up that room. But star quality? No. I never thought of her like that.'

Kelly Jones recalls Julia as 'very nice, very outgoing at school and at parties. She always had a lot of girlfriends. She always wanted to have fun. Julia was very easy-going and I have really fond memories of her. She always said my hair was perfect and she'd run her hands through it, saying "Oh, I feel so much better now." She was always joking.'

In March 1991 the *National Enquirer* ran an article which described Julia as boy crazy. It claimed her nickname was 'Hot Pants Roberts'. This is not the Julia that Briglevich recalls. 'She was not running around with boys. There were some girls in high school who were aggressive. She was wholesome and beautiful and sexy in her own way but she was not a floozy. She was not a prissy girl either. There is a Southern belle type, very preppy – she was definitely not that.'

Another classmate, Jeff Hardigree, says, 'I tried to seduce her a number of times and failed, so did all my friends. Nearly all the girls were having sex with the football team. But not Julia. She'd go so far but never all the way.'

Again John Briglevich: 'In American high schools there are numerous cliques – jocks, geeks, freaks, London leather boys, headbangers, etc. Julia was the type of girl who got on with many cliques. She could move between the circles readily and get along with those people. I think she was well-respected by many people.'

Romance did figure in Julia's life when she met Keith Leeper, two years her senior, during a junior disco in a club in downtown

Atlanta. 'I was standing at the bar and she came over to me and said I looked like Sting. I asked her to dance and we exchanged phone numbers. She was a good kisser.' Julia lost her virginity when she was sixteen to Leeper in his bedroom in Smyrna on 25 December 1983. He recalls, 'We were alone and kissing [during a Christmas party]. It wasn't anything we planned. The timing was right. I took her by the hand and led her upstairs to my bedroom. We stayed there for about an hour before rejoining the party.'

During the next four months he and Julia would drive off in his pick-up truck and park on a remote road where they would make love. 'We were always naked,' he says.

'I saw her differently after we had sex. I started to fall in love with her. I was physically attracted to her at first but then we also became best friends. It was puppy love at first.' The last time he saw Julia was just before she left for New York.

John Briglevich says, 'Some preppy girls think that work is beneath them and are more concerned with breaking a nail. Julia was not like that. I remember for one year she was a statistician/trainer for the soccer team. She was not afraid to get her hands dirty. She had a good work ethic.'

Julia's work ethic resulted in a job as a waitress at the Pizza Inn on South Cobb Drive in Smyrna. The Pizza Inn was a popular place for Campbell pupils to spend their spare time so Julia managed to work and socialise at the same time. She also worked as a shop assistant at the Cumberland Mall and on the tills at the Piggly Wiggly supermarket. In 1984 she spent the summer selling popcorn and sweets at the Galleria Mall Cineplex. Julia had to wear a white blouse with red vest and bow tie and black trousers. She was paid $3.35 an hour and was allowed all the junk food she could eat.

The Cineplex's assistant manager at the time was Jeff Feasal. He remembers, 'She wasn't shy, but I don't recall her being loud or boisterous. She seemed to fit in with the rest of the kids, but she was not someone who would stand out. I was surprised when I saw her in *Mystic Pizza*. She's slimmed down and lost her girlish look.'

There was a man who could and did withstand Julia's 'girlish look'. He was Joe Thompson, a 6 ft 5 in West Point dropout who now lives a reclusive life. Julia fell for Thompson in a heavy way but he was simply not interested. Julia wrote him love letters and attempted to find him in Vermont where she believed he lived. High school friend Tom Acres says, 'I don't really believe she was interested in anyone apart from Joe Thompson.'

More domestic problems arose both with the relationship or lack of one with Eric – John Briglevich says that her friends knew that Julia was not close to her brother – and when Betty was sued by a loan company. On 26 August 1980 Motes was sued by a debt collector and in October by a photographer. It all became too much for Betty. On 28 February 1983 she filed for divorce. The papers stated that the couple had separated in October 1982. On 16 March 1983 Betty filed another suit in a bid to have C.R. Vaughn replaced as the girls' guardian and Betty herself put in his stead. Betty did not mention that she had filed for divorce a month earlier and named Motes on the suit albeit mentioning that he was without a job. In May 1983 Vaughn resigned his position and Betty took over. She gave Lisa a cheque for $37,210.27 in May 1984. Betty stepped down in November 1985, a short period after Julia turned eighteen and had received her inheritance of $28,857.07. On 6 July 1983 Motes sued his estranged wife claiming that she had committed a fraud by moving back in with him but not rescinding the divorce papers. Motes claimed that the separation, far from occurring in October 1982, was actually on 15 June 1983. This led to a bitter and long court case that only ended as Julia was preparing to leave for New York.

Betty wanted sole custody of Nancy and the deeds to the home on Maner Road. She also wanted their property to be divided equally. Her lawyer was James J. Macie. Motes was furious at this hiring and his lawyer, James C. Strayhorn, sought to have Macie replaced. The reasoning was as bizarre as it was unusual. Macie had once been a Catholic priest. More pertinently, he had once been Michael Motes's parish priest and had taken his confessions. Macie refused to stand aside.

Motes asked the court to give him a divorce but also order that the Maner Road house be sold and any moneys divided equally. Betty refused to countenance this demand and in revenge asked him to supply all his income tax records, bank statements and credit card bills from 1979 until 1983. As the court deliberated Motes was ordered to pay $200 a week maintenance for Nancy. A temporary decision was reached on 18 October 1983. The terms of the agreement stated that Motes would pay $75 a week maintenance, Betty got the family car and the house but had to take responsibility for all the bills. When the decree absolute was issued on 8 March 1984 the child support was reduced to a weekly amount of $25.

In July 1985 when she graduated from Campbell High School Julia moved to New York to begin her biggest adventure. Eric had a luxury apartment at 45 West 73rd Street near Central Park but Julia moved in with Lisa at her tiny flat at 306 West 18th Street in Chelsea, near Greenwich Village.

In the Big Apple Julia did not have a glamorous start to her new life. She landed a job selling pizza and then began to sell training shoes in a shop called Athlete's Foot on 72nd Street and Broadway.

If Julia had been maligned as the school bike by the *National Enquirer* when she was at Campbell High School, then her sexuality blossomed when she moved to New York. One friend of the time says, 'I don't know how she is now, but in those days Julia was very outgoing, very much a party girl, and had a lot of friends, especially boyfriends. She had a lot of flings, at least four I personally know of in New York. From what I've heard, she didn't change her lifestyle on movie sets either.'

Julia also began to enjoy a tipple or two. A friend says that her drink was tequila or beer. 'She drank straight out of the bottle. She was wild, very free-spirited, always up for a good time, a real party girl.'

In school Julia dressed smartly and often in designer labels. In New York she adopted the style that she still has today – bag lady chic – which has led to her being named on several worst-dressed lists.

Julia was also a networker. Although she lived in Chelsea, she spent much of her time in her brother's manor. This was where people like Tom Cruise, Robert De Niro, Mick Jagger, Oliver Stone and other movers and shakers either owned or rented property.

It was on Columbus Avenue in that area that Julia was spotted by Mary Sames, an agent, and Glenn Daniels, a casting director.

Sames was knocked out by Julia but Daniels who had met her a month earlier thanks to Eric was unimpressed then and at the subsequent meeting. Sames gave Julia her card and invited the scruffy teenager to her office. 'She seemed so innocent,' said Sames, 'so completely without guile, and yet at the same time so guarded, so wary, that I was fascinated by what I perceived to be a unique personality. I mean, here was this free spirit, this breathtakingly beautiful young girl who was nevertheless shy and awkward and gave off the vibes of a wounded fragile bird.'

Despite the attraction, Sames did not agree to represent Julia and she passed her on to Bob McGowan who was just beginning his career as a personal manager. Says Sames, 'I just didn't have the energy to work with her. I was very stressed out, the office was in total chaos, and I realised instantly that this demure, shy, waiflike girl sitting across from me needed somebody special and kind-hearted to take care of her, that she was going to need 24-hour-a-day nurturing. And frankly, I just didn't have it in me at the time.'

McGowan found himself not only her manager but her personal guardian at times. He loaned her money on several occasions and also paid rent more than once even though he didn't actually know where she lived. Julia also tried to get McGowan to represent Lisa but he found it impossible to get her work and so he passed her, without notable success, to other agents.

McGowan tried to get Julia to take acting classes and also speech therapy in a bid to lose her thick Southern accent. Julia went to the classes on just three occasions before dropping out. She later recalled, 'I went to acting classes a few times but it never seemed very conducive to what I wanted to do . . . Things just sort of happened. Basically, I've learned on the job. It's an instinctive thing with me. I don't quite know what I'll be doing until it's done.'

3. SOMETHING TO TALK ABOUT

'I gave her her first break. My sister got her first movie because I was right in the middle of it. There's more competition as an actor and she's pretty so her career skyrocketed. You notice she hasn't asked me to be in any of her movies. Not that I'd necessarily accept, but she could ask.'

Eric Roberts

NEW YORK, 1986

Usually it is the case in families that children squabble with their siblings and then, as they become adults, they become close and rely on each other. Brothers stand for each other as best man at their respective weddings and sisters are bridesmaids. Not everyone has this close tie. In Hollywood everything is magnified – the people are richer, sexier, vainer, the arguments are fiercer, the feuds longer lasting.[1]

Eric Roberts moved to New York in the mid-1970s and in December 1976 got his big break playing Ted Bancroft in the soap opera *Another World*. Six weeks later, he was sacked. 'I kept falling over furniture. I would walk across the set and break a chair. I was the world's worst soap opera actor,' he confessed. Three years later in 1979 he made his film debut in *King of the Gypsies* playing the son of Susan Sarandon, who would later befriend Julia. The movie made him a star. Four years later, he played Paul Snider, the husband of tragic *Playboy* Playmate of the Year Dorothy Stratten, in *Star 80*.[2] He appeared in *Raggedy Man* (1981), *The Pope of Greenwich Village* (1984), *The Coca-Cola Kid* (1985) and *Runaway Train* (1986), in which he played Buck, an escaped convict, and was nominated for an Oscar as Best Supporting Actor. Eric also refused work. After *King of the Gypsies*, for which he was nominated for a Golden Globe,[3] he was offered a three-year contract but turned it down to work in the theatre. He was offered

---

[1] Sisters Olivia de Havilland and Joan Fontaine have been feuding for more than sixty years for many reasons including de Havilland not inviting Fontaine to their mother's funeral.

[2] Snider was a small-time pimp and hustler who saw an opportunity to make money in the young and beautiful Stratten. When she left him for the film director Peter Bogdanovich, Snider enticed her to see him one more time. At that meeting in August 1980 he raped and murdered her and then sodomised her corpse before committing suicide by blowing his own head off.

[3] Eric won a second Golden Globe nomination for *Star 80*.

a part in *Breaking Away* but rejected it lest he be cast as a juvenile lead. He also turned down the lead in *An Officer and a Gentleman*, a rôle that ironically was played by Richard Gere. By the mid-1980s Eric Roberts's career was if not over then in serious trouble. Julia's was going in the opposite direction to her brother's.

Off screen Eric began to develop a reputation as something of a loose cannon. He was traumatised by the early death of his father and was estranged from his mother. He told *Playboy* in 1985, 'There has never been a relationship between us. I just don't like the woman. It's as simple as that.' He also said, 'I haven't talked to my mother since I was fourteen, except once. I went through all those years without a mother. But when I met Lee Grant . . . we really bonded. And now she's what I call my surrogate mother. What's wonderful about it is that I got to choose her, which doesn't happen often with mothers.'

On 3 June 1981 Eric was involved in a serious car crash that nearly killed him. He was driving home from the apartment of his then girlfriend, the actress Sandy Dennis, in Wilton, Connecticut. He later told crash investigators that he had Dennis's alsatian in his Jeep and when he looked over at the dog, the animal seemed to be trying to get out of the vehicle or possibly falling out. Eric reached over and pulled its collar. When he looked back at the road, he was heading for a tree. Unable to avoid a collision he smashed into it. The dog was thrown clear and landed on its feet but Eric was thrown through the windscreen. He lay comatose in a hospital for three days, his face shattered and innumerable bones broken. He had reconstructive surgery on his face but to this day he has a crooked nose and a large scar over his left eye.

The year before, Eric had been cast in a low-budget straight-to-video western called *Blood Red*.[4] Playing his sister in the film and making her movie debut was Julia. Now how Julia got the part depends on who you listen to. Her CV was bare and Eric claims that he pulled a few strings to get his baby sister a job. Betty Roberts, not her son's number one fan and as such reluctant to give him credit for anything, alleges that it was Bill Trevsch, Eric's manager, who was responsible for Julia's job. Betty says that the

---

[4] *Blood Red* wrapped in November 1986 but did not find a release until 1990.

producers could not find an actor to play Eric's sister in the film because none of those who auditioned looked sufficiently like him. Bill Trevsch just happened to be carrying a picture of Julia that he showed to the producers. They were amazed by the unknown actor's resemblance to Eric and cast her. The way Eric tells it has him asking Peter Masterton, the director, if Julia could play his screen sister. Eddie Bunker is a Hollywood scriptwriter and friend of Eric. He recalls, 'It was Eric who went to the director. It was Eric who introduced her to contacts in New York and who kicked open doors for her in Los Angeles. How else do you get into Hollywood? There's a thousand girls out there as pretty as she is, and she was not even a trained actress. The hardest thing was getting through the door.'

Another version is that Julia's then manager Bob McGowan received a telephone call from the producers and sent a picture of Julia to them. This only after Eric mentioned his sister to the executives.

The announcement of her casting appeared in the People column in the *New York Daily News* on 17 August 1986 and Julia told the journalist that her brother had no idea she was auditioning let alone had landed the job. She further claims that he was furious when he found out. That seems unlikely. The feud between Julia and Eric Roberts may have its genesis here. The truth of how Julia landed her first film role is now lost in time but it would seem likely that it was, indeed, Eric who was responsible rather than his manager. In fact, in early interviews Julia credited her brother: 'Eric has given me advice and, of course, my first movie rôle.'

Speaking in 1992 Eric said, 'I love Julia dearly. Julia's very beautiful, she's very bright, she's very everything. I see what I think I helped her to accomplish and what she accomplished on her own. I am nothing but proud of her.' Despite the glowing testimonial, there has been no rapprochement between Eric and his sisters. Nor does it seem likely that there will be any. Julia refuses to believe any ill of her mother and Lisa's closest ally is Julia, one of the few people she trusts. Eric was not invited to either of Julia's weddings.

4. SLEEPING WITH A CO-STAR

'What's nice about my dating life is that I don't have to leave my house. All I have to do is read the paper: I'm marrying Richard Gere, dating Daniel Day-Lewis, parading around with John F. Kennedy Jr, and even Robert De Niro was in there for a day.'

Julia Roberts

NEW YORK, CALIFORNIA, SOUTH CAROLINA AND MARYLAND, 1986–87

Throughout the hundred or so years of Hollywood history sex has always been a potent force both in front of and behind the cameras. As soon as the technology was available women began acting in the nude. Annette Kellerman was the first actress to appear nude on screen. Hedy Lamarr ran naked through the woods in *Ecstasy* (1933) and D.W. Griffith's early films were replete with nudity. Portrayals of sex were rife, so much so that Hollywood moguls were threatened with prosecution by the State of California. To head off the attempt at state-imposed censorship the moguls appointed their own film tsar. Postmaster General Will Hays was offered a renewable three-year contract on 14 January 1922 with a salary of $115,000 a year, a $2 million life insurance policy and unlimited expenses, taking office exactly two months later. In 1930 he created the Motion Picture Production Code whose aim was to 'govern the making of talking, synchronised and silent motion pictures'. Many in the industry were outraged by the appointment of the Republican Hays. John T. Hays, Hays's father, himself a Republican lawyer, instilled strict puritanical views into his sons including not borrowing money and abstaining from alcohol. Despite two decades in Republican politics, Hays actually only held elective office once. Hays resigned as head of the Motion Picture Producers and Distributors Of America, Inc. (MPPDA) in September 1945.

However, while the on-screen canoodling had stopped, off screen it was as rampant as ever. It was not just directors and producers who used the casting couch to entice young starlets into their beds and their films. Many actors coupled with their co-star oblivious to their spouse at home. Affairs lasted as long as the shoot and wrapped when the film wrapped.

For a time Julia did indeed meet her boyfriends on movie sets. After *Blood Red* she appeared in two television series: *Crime Story* in an episode called 'The Survivor' broadcast on 13 February 1987 and then in 'Mirror Image', the 22nd episode of the fourth series of *Miami Vice* on 6 May 1988. At home in Smyrna for Christmas 1987 Julia went shopping with a friend and both girls noticed that people were staring at Julia. At first Julia thought that they were imagining it until one or two approached her and said that they had seen her on *Crime Story*. It was a very small indication of the fame that was to come Julia's way in the future. Another bit part followed in a forgotten film called *Firehouse*. Film critics Mick Martin and Marsha Porter described it as a '*Charlie's Angels* clone set in a firehouse' and rated it as a turkey. The film did have some female nudity in it, albeit not from Julia. Gianna Rains bares her breasts twice while Jennifer Stahl[1] goes topless on just the one occasion.

Meanwhile, Julia's manager Bob McGowan continued to work hard for his client sending her picture and CV to numerous casting agents and anyone else he thought might be able to help Julia. One landed on the desk of Johanna Ray in Los Angeles. She had been hired to cast a film about an all-girl rock band. Liking what she saw, she rang McGowan and asked if Julia could play the drums. McGowan lied and said that, of course, she could. Ray decided to fly to New York for a closer look at this talented drum-playing actor. Meanwhile, McGowan paid for Julia to take drum lessons. In the end she was cast in the film but as a bass guitar player, Daryle Shane.

The film was called *Satisfaction* and was co-produced by Aaron

---

[1] Jennifer Stahl was born in Titusville, New Jersey in 1962. On 10 May 2001 she was murdered along with two other people in her New York apartment, above the Carnegie Deli. Two more guests were injured but survived. When not acting or dancing in New Jersey strip joints, Stahl produced CDs on her own label, Girl Jam Records. However, she made more money with a thriving marijuana business. At the time of her death police found six bundles of the drug each with a street value of $10,000. Her killer, Sean Salley, was captured in Miami, Florida, after an appeal on *America's Most Wanted*.

Spelling.[2] Having landed the rôle Julia faced another problem. She had to join the Screen Actors' Guild (SAG), the American version of Equity. Although she was baptised with the name Julia, she was known to family and friends as Julie or Jules. There was already an actor called Julie Roberts in SAG so Julia rang her mother for advice. The two women discussed the problem and Julia suggested either reverting to her real Christian name or using her middle name and becoming Fiona Roberts. They decided that it would be best to use her original name and so Julie Roberts once again was known as Julia Roberts. Many actors forsake their original names for stardom; Julia was unusual in that she adopted hers.

Another problem was that now she needed an agent. Although Bob McGowan was doing a fine job as her manager, by law he was prevented from negotiating contracts for his client. He put a call in to Risa Shapiro at the William Morris Agency. But Shapiro wasn't interested in handling the young actor. McGowan hustled for Julia telling the agency that Julia would be paid $50,000 and that they could have a piece of that, but it was only when he mentioned that Aaron Spelling was a producer on the project and that Julia would be hired if the film led to a television series that William Morris changed its mind and agreed to represent Julia. Her career was put in the hands of two agents, Risa Shapiro and Elaine Goldsmith. However, at the beginning neither wanted to handle Julia. She also met Sally Field and her husband, the producer Alan Greisman, around this time. Sally Field would become a close friend and mentor to the younger actor.

In the month leading to the beginning of shooting Julia learned how to play the guitar. She was to say, 'There's nothing more frustrating than having this great instrument and a great song and not being able to put the two together.' Nevertheless Julia persevered and became an adequate guitarist.

---

[2] Aaron Spelling (b. Dallas, Texas, 22 April 1923) is one of the most successful producers in television history. Beginning as an actor he turned to writing and producing. Among the shows he has been responsible for are: Beverly Hills 90210 (which co-starred his gorgeous daughter Tori), Burke's Law, Charlie's Angels, The Colbys, Dynasty, Fantasy Island, Glitter, Hart to Hart, The Love Boat, Melrose Place, The Mod Squad, Models, Inc., Savannah, Starsky & Hutch, Sunset Beach, T.J. Hooker, Vega$, and many, many more. His home, the 123-room mansion The Manor at 594 Mapleton Drive in Bel Air, is the largest single-family home in California.

Satisfaction was originally called *Sweet Little Rock'n'Rollers* and has also become known as *Girls of Summer*. Whatever the title, it was filmed between 13 May and 24 June 1987 in Charleston, South Carolina and Baltimore, Maryland. It was during filming that she had her first on-set romance. It was to be the first but not the last romance of its kind. Julia has never denied that she met many of her lovers in this way but she feels that it is perfectly normal for someone who does what she does for living. You work on a film set, you meet people on the film set, you are attracted to some of those people and you begin a relationship.

Julia's attraction was for the quietly spoken but apparently spectacularly well-endowed Irish actor Liam Neeson.[3] He played a fading and ageing rock star but realised almost from the start that the film would be a flop. All Neeson has ever said of his work is, 'Unsatisfactory. I have no intention of ever seeing it.' He refused to attend the première in February 1988. Julia, on the other hand, has seen *Satisfaction* at least twice. On one occasion she was in the company of her brother Eric.

She said, 'Eric laughed but, when it was over, we talked and he made it seem not so bad. But the film taught me a lot about what I hope to never do again in a movie. There's only one scene I was embarrassed about that I was supposedly in. But I had the day off so it was kind of funny.

'In the film there's a scene where I'm supposedly in the van with my boyfriend, and the van is rocking, and a grand amount of time passes, as if we've been going at it for a quite a long time. Well, actually, it was an empty van and there were a couple of grips[4] behind it pushing it back and forth. I was at the beach all day.'

However, the affair between Neeson and Julia made working on the film a much more enjoyable experience. The director Joan Freeman had a first-hand view of the romance. She recalls, 'Doing the film wasn't a pleasant experience for Liam. He felt it was creatively stifling – and Liam needs very much to be creative. There were people, too, who were not happy with him. The end

---

[3] Another of Neeson's lovers, Helen Mirren, confirmed that he is possessed of an extremely large penis. Neeson's other lovers have included Brooke Shields, Diane Keaton, Sinéad O'Connor, Barbra Streisand, Kate Capshaw and Natasha Richardson, whom he married.

[4] A grip is a technician or skilled labourer on a film set. He works under a key grip.

result was that he felt underappreciated. But there was one bonus. He met Julia through it.'

Within weeks of their initial meeting, the couple were living together intermittently. Reports had them living together for over a year but, in fact, it was a much briefer affair that burned itself out quickly. A friend of the couple who wishes to remain anonymous because they are still working in Hollywood and are fearful of upsetting either party says, 'They were absolutely nuts about each other. They couldn't keep their hands off each other. It was incredible to watch. Liam is so cool but he was very, very responsive to Julia. In contrast, she's a very tactile person. She seemed to spark him off and they would be crawling over one another. They didn't seem to notice who saw them – or if they did, they certainly didn't seem to care.'

OKLAHOMA, 1988

Almost as soon as the filming ended on *Satisfaction*, Julia appeared in a film for Home Box Office. HBO, a cable channel launched nationally in America in December 1975, produces television programmes and films some of which would not be suitable for mainstream American television because of content such as nudity or language.[5] Julia appeared in *Baja Oklahoma*, in which she plays Candy Hutchens, the eighteen-year-old daughter of Lesley Ann Warren's character, Juanita, a barmaid who aspires to being a country and western songwriter.

As with nearly all her films – *Hook* was an exception – Julia befriended cast and crew and spent a lot of time when not working socialising with them.

One member of the crew said, 'Julia was one of the nicest people I've ever met on a set. There was no attitude from her. She didn't have the barracuda mentality that often affects actors. She wasn't obsessed with acting. She was very natural. She had an interesting mix of being very real, very focused. She knew what she wanted and where she wanted to go in terms of her career and she felt confident it was going to happen at her pace.'

---

[5] Home Box Office fare includes: *Dream On, Fraggle Rock, Larry Sanders Show, Sex and the City* and *The Sopranos*.

It looked as if Julia had the world at her feet. Her career was progressing nicely and she had a well-endowed Irishman who was madly in love with her at home.

MYSTIC, CONNECTICUT, AUTUMN 1987–88

When filming wrapped on *Baja Oklahoma* Julia flew to New York to prepare for an audition for what she hoped would be her next film, *Mystic Pizza*. There were three leading female parts in the film, which would be filmed on location in Mystic, Connecticut. The film is a coming-of-age tale of three young women who work in a pizza parlour. Competition for each of the rôles was fierce. More than a hundred actors had sent their CVs to the producers in the hope of landing the job. Julia read the script that she was sent but was unaware of which of the three parts they wanted her to read for.

'I just assumed I was Jojo who was described as cute, earthy and unable to commit to marriage with her boyfriend, because Kat was too young and Daisy was too voluptuous or something,' she said.

Julia was surprised when Jane Jenkins, the casting director, told her that it was the part of the Portuguese Daisy Arujo that she was up for. The director Donald Petrie and the producer Mark Levinson asked Julia to read at a second audition. Julia went to see her manager Bob McGowan and borrowed one of his suits to wear at the reading. She also dyed her hair jet-black with a mixture of mousse, hair dye and shoe polish. This marked the start of Julia's propensity for wearing male attire. She would wear a man's suit with nothing underneath.

When Julia turned up for the audition she found a roomful of 'Daisys', some of whom were indeed Portuguese. Julia took a seat and began leafing through her sides. She was wearing McGowan's suit without a blouse or bra underneath, her jet-black hair cascaded over her shoulders. Clamped to her head was a Sony Walkman playing Jimi Hendrix's live version of 'Wild Thing' at Monterrey over and over again. She would often select a particular song to psyche herself up for a rôle and then listen to it on her Walkman continuously.

Julia was called into the room before the producer and director and began her second audition. It went well until the moment the actor playing opposite Julia ran his fingers through her hair and pulled away only to find his hand jet-black from the hair dye and shoe polish. The whole room broke up. 'Julia was real smart to put that rinse in her hair and make it jet-black,' said director Daniel Petrie, 'like the colour of the Portuguese character she played in the film. It worked. It made her look exotic and just right for the part. She was exactly what I needed for the rôle . . . unpredictable and willing to take chances, fiery, spirited and yet very real.'

Julia got the part and the two other girls in the film were played by Annabeth Gish (Kat) and Lili Taylor (Jojo). Julia had to put on some weight to play the curvy Daisy and suffered some good-natured stick from the crew. 'I would walk around the set and the crew would kid me. They'd say, "There's that girl that men are going to kill for today." Now how the f*** can you live up to that? Daisy was someone I might have been if I had been different, if that makes any sense. I could relate to her in a lot of ways, but at the same time she had a lot of gusto, a lot of chutzpah that I've never had. It was a little scary being Daisy, though, because she's kind of like 10 feet tall and I'm happy being 5 ft 8 in.'[6]

Of the picture, Julia opined, 'Our characters and our generation are a little more independent and open about the philosophy of friendship. If women didn't play the kind of women that they wouldn't hang out with, there would be fewer of those rôles. We shouldn't see so many surface cheese puffs.

'I like to see movies that are real. Things with heart and soul, not ones that are just about sex or silly surface feelings. *Mystic Pizza* isn't *Apocalypse Now*, but we have a little heart and soul. All our characters are honest.'

Filming continued apace with a lot of laughter around the set until 28 October 1987. It was Julia's twentieth birthday, a fact that she hadn't mentioned to the cast and crew in case they thought her swollen-headed. As the day rolled on it was like any other normal day on a film set – boring with interludes for shooting. Julia was unhappy. She loved working on the film but was missing her boyfriend, Liam Neeson, and missing home. Then there was

---

[6] Julia is actually 5 ft 9 in.

a commotion in the afternoon and when Julia looked up a crew member was wheeling a huge cake designed to look like a pizza towards her. One of the crew had discovered it was her birthday and they all planned a surprise party. Julia was overwhelmed by the gesture and fled blushing from the set. 'I'm shy and I'm an extrovert. So everyone seems to get a kick out of the fact that I blush very easily. But I do. Certain things kind of make me go, "Well, I've got to run, see you later . . ."'

Julia takes her art very seriously and spent a lot of time going over her lines making sure each nuance was how she felt it should be. Director Daniel Petrie was not convinced that this was the best way for Julia to achieve a good performance. 'She has a wonderful spontaneity on-screen that really makes her light up,' he said. 'Most actors have that in their eyes. But Julia has it in her eyes, her face, everywhere. She's the kind of actor you want to shoot without a rehearsal because she's so quirky that you never know what you'll get.'

Julia later recalled, 'I used to be curvaceous and roundish when I filmed *Pizza*. I said that I put on twenty pounds weight to play the part. But actually I used to be heavier. It was adolescence – I was nineteen. And I had a big Oreo cookie fetish. I was big, and I felt very uncomfortable with myself. I had very low self-esteem. I hated playing that part in *Pizza* because the confident character was the antithesis of me. I was not that girl.'

The film opened on 21 October 1988 and received mixed reviews. It had cost $3.5 million and earned $14 million at the box office. Considering the cast were little-known or unknown, it was a more than respectable performance.

It also made Julia more recognisable, which helped her agents when it came to negotiating her next contract. Julia recalled that, one day while visiting her mother at home in Smyrna, Georgia, the two women decided to go to the pictures. Once there Julia had to visit a comfort station. As Julia was answering the call of nature she heard a woman's voice call out, 'Excuse me, girl in stall number one. Weren't you in *Mystic Pizza*?'

'Yeah,' replied Julia.

'Can I have your autograph, please?' said the voice and a pen and piece of paper appeared under the stall door.

'I don't think now is the right time,' replied the easily embarrassed actor.

VENICE BEACH, CALIFORNIA, 1988

Around a month after *Mystic Pizza* wrapped, Julia packed her bags and moved to the West Coast. There were a number of reasons behind the move not the least being she missed her boyfriend Liam Neeson. In March 1988 they were living in a flat in a three-storey, ivy-covered, stucco house on 26th Avenue in Venice, California.

On 6 May 1988 the 22nd episode of the fourth series of *Miami Vice* aired in which Julia was a guest star playing Polly Wheeler. Julia was not in a position to enjoy the show because at the time she was suffering from spinal meningitis. Julia was feeling run-down but put her tiredness down to her working schedule. A couple of days off would do her the world of good, she thought. However, as the time went on she became more and more ill. Eventually, Liam Neeson persuaded her to call a doctor who upon examining her rushed Julia into hospital. It was a fortunate decision of Neeson to insist on the phone call because when Julia was admitted she was delirious and running a high temperature. Betty flew in from Georgia to be with her daughter and Eric also visited his sister. Julia lay very ill for several weeks but gradually pulled through. She believed that she had contracted the disease when swimming in the sea off Miami while filming the cop show, although this has never been proved. It could also be the case that she contracted the meningitis from swimming off the shores of Venice Beach.

'I thought I was going to die and so did everybody else. So I was forced to face it,' she said, 'and found that I wasn't scared to die, that it wasn't a scary thing. Not that I want to die, I want to live forever. It's just that having been there I found out it wasn't such a bad thing.'

By mid-June of 1988 Julia was still recuperating but was sufficiently well enough for her agents to put her name forward for a new film. The part was playing the diabetic daughter of Sally Field, Julia's old friend, and Meg Ryan had signed to play the exotically-named Shelby Eatenton Latcherie. Then Ryan was offered the rôle of Sally opposite Billy Crystal in *When Harry Met Sally* and pulled out of the film.

Julia's agents immediately sent her CV and picture to Herb Ross, the film's director, but he was not interested in Julia. Off-screen Julia's language can be slightly salty as indeed can Liam Neeson's – another reason they made a great couple. Julia did rather a lot of swearing in *Mystic Pizza* and Herb Ross wanted a refined lady to play the rôle of Shelby Eatenton Latcherie. It was here that Sally Field came into her own. As well as being Julia's friend, Field was also a great admirer of the younger actor and persuaded Ross to at least audition Julia, so her name was added to a list of 75 other wannabes.

Julia learned that the rest of the cast included Dolly Parton, Shirley MacLaine, Daryl Hannah, Olympia Dukakis, Tom Skerritt and Sam Shepard and knew that she had no hope of landing the part and joining this august company. Nevertheless, Julia put her heart and soul into the auditions and was called back five times to read for the part. The fourth and fifth readings were with Field. Three hours after the fifth audition she received a call telling her that she had the part. Director Herb Ross still seemed unsure of his new actor and told her to lose weight, lighten her hair and alter the shape of her eyebrows, a tall order since filming was due to start in a week. Julia was no more enamoured of him.

She was, however, ecstatic about playing the rôle and she, Bob McGowan, Elaine Goldsmith and Risa Shapiro went to the Polo Lounge in the Beverly Hills Hotel where they proceeded to get drunk on champagne.

Recovered from her hangover, Julia went home to prepare to pack for the trip to Louisiana. The trip would change her personal and professional life. The film she had just signed to make was called *Steel Magnolias* and one of her co-stars would be an actor called Dylan McDermott.

5. STEEL BACKBONES

'I am a taskmaster. I never spoke privately to anyone. If I had criticism or advice, I would say it in front of the other women. But Julia worked hard. She stayed in bed for the coma scenes eight, twelve hours a day, until she was ill and dizzy.'

Director Herb Ross

NATCHITOCHES, LOUISIANA, SUMMER 1988

Natchitoches is a small town in Louisiana with a population of around 16,000 people. The oldest town in Louisiana, Natchitoches was founded in 1714 as a French military and trading post and came under American control in 1803. Natchitoches was incorporated in 1819 and is 55 miles southeast of Shreveport. It makes money from producing plywood, cotton, bricks and tiles. It is also a centre of soybeans and pecans. Not very much happens in the sleepy town except once in a while a film crew comes to stay. It happened in 1959 when John Wayne and William Holden arrived with John Ford to film *The Horse Soldiers*. It happened again in 1988 when a film crew turned up to shoot *Steel Magnolias*. The all-star cast included Shirley Maclaine, Daryl Hannah, Dolly Parton, Olympia Dukakis and Julia's old friend and mentor Sally Field.

The townsfolk were fascinated by the celebrities in their midst and did anything but take the invasion in their stride. Many got up early to watch filming before going to work. Others staked out the town's two restaurants in the hope of spotting a star. The more enterprising had special *Steel Magnolias* T-shirts printed to sell to visitors.

The stars coped in their own way with being far from family and friends. In fact, Dolly Parton made sure she wasn't far at all. She invited her eleven siblings to visit as often as they could. The whole Parton clan would retreat to Dolly's rented home and enjoy her home-cooked food. Daryl Hannah rented a farm on the outskirts of Natchitoches and when not filming spent her time riding horses. With just seven years between them Julia became friendly with Daryl Hannah and the two actors often went riding together. Sally Field brought her two-year-old son Sam with her and, when she was not before the cameras, she would be playing with him. She also advised Julia on acting and life in general. She later said, 'People thought I wasn't old enough to play Shelby's mother.[1] There was no problem, I was so tired on set that I aged drastically. Every morning I was totally wrung out so it was a perfect time to shoot the film.'

Of looking after Julia, Field said, 'Something about her makes you care for her, watch her. And it goes beyond her looks. The part of Shelby did not call for a great beauty which was fortunate because no one, including Julia, agreed with me that she was one. She grew up as a kind of ugly duckling, not a pretty woman, and the impression we form of ourselves in early adolescence always remains. 'I think we were a good combination. I became the mother rôle for her and I think she felt she was able to lean on my steadiness and my experience while I was able to use my delight and affection for her.

'Julia is much more independent than I ever was. She's a real free spirit and that's one thing I've never been or ever will be. I've often wished I was, but I'm sort of grounded, which is why I think I get a kick out of the Julias of the world. I'm delighted by them.'

Julia was both touched and amazed by Field: 'Sally's inexhaustible support staggered me. It got so that I didn't call my real mother for three months. I would call Sally and say "Momma" and she would just answer me back.' So close did the bond grow that when Betty did visit the set and Julia called 'Mum' both women answered. Daryl Hannah also suffered from nerves at the commencement of filming 'but they rallied around me. We all bonded immediately.'

That was not strictly true. Julia, by her own admission, is insecure and this can cause conflicts when people take her shyness for rudeness. When they began filming, Shirley Maclaine and Julia did not hit it off despite living in rented homes that were next to each other, but once the two women got to know each other they became close friends. 'The first time we met I felt she was looking right though me,' remembers Julia. 'It was my most tense moment, which is very funny to me now. I went over to her house one day

---

[1] She is in fact 21 years older that Julia.

and we got into this intense conversation in which I talked nonstop for an hour and a half about feelings and families and ideas and goals. And when I finished this amazing woman dissected everything I'd said, starting from the beginning. I was absolutely blown away by her extraordinary gift of really listening to a person.'

Julia was also probably reassured by the fact that Maclaine did not become especially close to any of the other actors on the film with the exception of Dolly Parton. The actor and the 'Jolene' hit-maker became very close friends and spent a lot of their spare time laughing and telling each other dirty jokes. Olympia Dukakis threw a bizarre dinner party one night at which all the food was comprised of leftovers. Olympia explained the oddity by saying that she was busy with her cousin.[2]

Filming was due to begin on 12 July 1988 but since all the cast and crew were *in situ* by Independence Day the film bosses decided to throw a Fourth of July party. As filming progressed cast and crew could often be found in the local bar called the Bodacious Club. On more than one occasion Dolly Parton even performed there much to the pleasure of the regular patrons. The wonderfully down-to-earth and self-deprecating Dolly Parton – 'Honey, it costs a fortune to look this cheap', 'I don't get upset when people say I'm a dumb blonde because I know I'm not dumb. I'm not a blonde either' – summed up the feelings of the female cast aptly, if not quite accurately: 'I think the reason we all became such good friends is because we all had the same exact Winnebagos, we didn't have beautiful clothes to fight over, and there were no available men in the cast.' Dolly Parton had missed a young 25-year-old actor called Dylan McDermott who played Jackson Latcherie, Julia's on-screen husband. But Julia didn't. Her relationship with Liam Neeson had been going on for a year but soon the on-screen passion ignited into one off screen and Liam Neeson was soon history. Neeson has never spoken publicly about the break-up with Julia and a letter from this author to Neeson went, unsurprisingly, unanswered. Only once did Neeson albeit

---

[2] Her cousin was the Democrat Michael Dukakis who that November lost the presidency to George Bush by a landslide – 79.18 per cent of the electoral votes went to Bush.

obliquely mention Julia when an interviewer asked him about his romances and he sighed: 'Is this what it's going to say on my tombstone? "He dated Julia Roberts and Barbra Streisand."'

For the most part Julia found filming, for which she was paid $90,000, to be a pleasant experience. 'It's one thing to watch [the others] act,' she said, 'but it's another thing to work with them and see first-hand that they're not just really great actors but also really great people.' Behind the cameras was a different matter. The director Herb Ross did not always see eye to eye with his young star. 'Herbert has his ideas of action and result and I have mine,' said Julia tactfully, 'and they don't always receive each other perfectly. But you have that relationship and that's one you deal with every day and you do what you have to do to get the result you feel is most true.'

Ross was at the time courting Princess Lee Radziwill, the younger sister of Jacqueline Kennedy Onassis, the former First Lady. She accompanied him on recces and most weekends would fly down to be with him. On 23 September 1988, less than a month after the film wrapped, he became her third husband when they married in her lavish New York apartment.

Many of the cast felt that Ross was too tough on the still relatively inexperienced actor. Sally Field remembers, 'Herb was a good director but in some ways he was extremely hard on Julia. We all felt it was uncalled for, but she's a warrior.'

Ross himself later confessed, 'I am a taskmaster. I never spoke privately to anyone. If I had criticism or advice, I would say it in front of the other women. But Julia worked hard. She stayed in bed for the coma scenes eight, twelve hours a day, until she was ill and dizzy.' When the film wrapped he did suggest that Julia take acting lessons 'now you have some time on your hands'.

To relax Sally Field did needlepoint[3] and taught the rest of the female cast her particular skill. Once again Herb Ross interfered. Apparently, the needlework so relaxed the actors that he claimed it interfered with shooting. He banished all the needlework from the film.

Some of the crew, unusually for a Julia Roberts film, did not take to her. According to cast members who understandably wish

---

[3] Another aficionado of on-set needlepoint was Rock Hudson.

to remain anonymous, particularly now that Julia is one of the most powerful actors in Hollywood, she was, to put it lightly, demanding of the hair and make-up teams.

Said one, 'She was a monster. She couldn't sit still. She was always late getting to the set, which meant everyone had to hurry to get her ready so that shooting wouldn't be held up. She was never happy with her hair or make-up.'

Another explained Julia's tardiness by simply stating that she was a young girl having fun. 'Julia was a wild, fun party girl. She'd stay out all night and that's why she was always late for her call. Dolly Parton wasn't joking later when she called Julia "a sleepyhead".'

The role of Shelby was the most emotionally draining that Julia had attempted. 'It was a really difficult part. In terms of the friends I made on the set, it was tremendous. In terms of the things I've received from the outcome of it, it was tremendous. But it was not an easy road to travel. Challenge-wise it was difficult, like taking the S[tudent] A[ptitude] T[ests] every day.'

Steel Magnolias was written by the Broadway playwright Robert Harling and it was based on the story of his sister, Susan, who had died in 1985, just three years beforehand, from the effects of diabetes. Before filming began Julia became very close to the author and his family and regularly dined *chez* Harling. Julia would become involved in long, intense conversations with Harling's parents and pored over the family photograph albums but always to look at the pictures of Susan. 'I thought if I ever looked in her eyes I would lose control. When I finally did see them, I was a mess. I was just a puddle.

'I had a lot of conversations with Robert Harling, and I felt an obligation to a truth, to explain to the people who would see this movie, "This is true, this is what happened." I felt I had a mission to be just to the woman that she was; yet, at the same time, understand that I was not her, I did not look like her, that my clothes were not the clothes she wore, that this was not a documentary, that I was playing Shelby Eatenton not Susan Harling.'

The first scene Julia had to film in *Steel Magnolias* was by any stretch of the imagination her most difficult. It was the one where Shelby suffers an epileptic fit in the beauty parlour. Julia was terribly frightened before and during filming and thoroughly tired afterwards. 'I was concentrating so hard on what it would be like inside myself – the way my heart looked, the rate it was pumping, all the blood racing through my veins – I got so far down inside my body that as we were coming to the end of the scene a panic went through me. I had gotten stuck down there and didn't want anybody to know. I thought, "I'm never going to get out of here." I finally did, but I sobbed hysterically after it was over. It was the first day and things got too close to what had really happened. Bobby [Harling] flipped out – he had to leave.' Harling admitted that the scene had been a little too close for comfort and he had wanted to hug Julia when she was finished but he became too emotional remembering his sister.

Julia poured the same energy into Shelby's death scene. She was so into her rôle that she refused to sit up in the bed or take refreshments. The crew was shocked by her intensity even though they knew there was nothing really the matter with Julia and the hospital was really a converted gymnasium.

By the time the film wrapped in September of 1988 Julia was engaged to Dylan McDermott. She had a new man in her life and now she wanted a new manager. In October 1988 Mystic Pizza was released and her manager Bob McGowan called her into his office because their contract was due for renewal. McGowan recalls with some sadness in his voice, 'I said "Julia, what's going on with you? Are we going to work together or not?" And I will never forget this, she came over and hugged me and said, "Bob, you started all this. I want you in my life forever." ' Ten days after she wrapped her arms around him, McGowan received a telephone call from Elaine Goldsmith who informed him that Julia no longer wanted his services. Bob McGowan has never seen Julia from that day to this.

Julia was later to explain her decision. 'That was the first completely difficult decision I had to make in my life. Bob had gone to bat for me, but I felt I had to be honest. We'd outgrown each other. There were too many people around me making decisions and I wanted a clearer line between me and the work.

'I'm the show. Elaine and Risa are the business. They take care of the stuff I'm not meant to deal with. If it concerns me, they let me know.'

For McGowan the break-up was difficult but he admits that 'We did sort of outgrow each other . . . I have no hard feelings about it. Julia did a lot for my career. She helped put me on the map. The only thing that bothered me was the closeness and the way it was done . . .'

LOS ANGELES, 1989

Fresh from her completing *Steel Magnolias* and promoting *Mystic Pizza*, Julia returned to Los Angeles. She now had to decide what her next project would be.

She was sent all sorts of scripts including one in which she was to play an inmate of Auschwitz concentration camp. The film was called *Triumph of Spirit* and would co-star Willem Dafoe.[4] It looked to be a worthy vehicle and was certainly different from playing a bawdy pizza waitress and a diabetic Southern belle.

In the end Julia turned down the movie. The reason? She did not want to become bald.[5] 'I was really vacillating. *Triumph of Spirit* was a very good script and [Willem Dafoe] is a great actor, but they wanted me to shave my head. It may seem superficial to say that I can't shave my head, but it would have been five years before I looked like myself again. Willem said it would give me the opportunity to kill the stereotype I have as a glamour girl. I told him I'm not tired of it yet.'

If Julia had agreed to having her head shaved, she would have missed out on the film that made her a household name . . .

---

[4] Dafoe, like Liam Neeson, is reputed to be among the best-hung men in Hollywood.

[5] Going bald did not help Demi Moore in *G.I. Jane* so Julia made the right decision.

6. THE REAL STORY BEHIND *PRETTY WOMAN*

'I'm really against nudity in movies. When you act with your clothes on, it's a performance. When you act with your clothes off, it's a documentary. I don't do documentaries.'

Julia Roberts

HOLLYWOOD, JULY 1989

Julia wanted to appear in the courtroom film *Beyond a Reasonable Doubt* but the studio baulked at the idea because she was regarded as not a big enough star. *Steel Magnolias* had yet to be released. Producer Phyllis Carlyle commented, 'They didn't believe Julia Roberts could carry a film. It's not unusual. In this business a studio gets behind someone once they're established. By the time things had come together, the ship had sailed.'

Following the release of *Steel Magnolias*, Julia's star was in the ascendancy and the producers came cap in hand to ask her to star in the film opposite William Baldwin.[1] Elaine Goldsmith, Julia's agent, refused to allow her client to make the film. In fact, in that period of her life Julia was in the happy position of being able to reject several films offered to her. She later said, 'I turned down more movies that year than I ever thought I'd turn down in my entire life.'

Julia was fully aware that the next film she made would be important to the longevity of her career since so many actors have received plaudits for a movie that has been a perhaps unexpected hit and then chosen a turkey as a follow-up.[2] A script by J.F. Lawton was sent to her. Entitled *3,000* it was the story of a drug-addicted prostitute in Hollywood, not perhaps the most upbeat of stories to receive. The whore meets a wealthy corporate raider who offers her $3,000 (hence the script's title) to spend a week with her. He shows her a world of glamour and excess that she has never experienced before. When the glorious week is up,

---

[1] One of four brothers – Alec, Daniel and Stephen – William Baldwin is best-known for playing opposite Sharon Stone in her post-*Basic Instinct* flop *Sliver* (1993). By all accounts, including their own, they hated each other.

[2] Sharon Stone for one, see above.

he drops her off at the same street corner he found her on and she is back in her sordid world.

Steve Reuther of the film production company Vestron bought the rights to Lawton's script and they renamed it *Off the Boulevard*. Before filming could begin Vestron went bankrupt and *3,000* ended up in the hands of The Walt Disney Organisation. As the world knows Disney is not in the business of making melancholic movies. *3,000* became an uplifting tale in which the businessman falls in love with the hooker and, instead of dumping her back on Sunset Boulevard,[3] he marries her.

Julia said at the time, 'The script changed a lot. It was not a happy or a funny story in the beginning. Then they took it on this journey and turned it into a delightful, funny, extremely different story.'

Garry Marshall was signed to become the director. He had previously created the sitcom *Laverne and Shirley*, an offshoot of *Happy Days*.[4] His sister is the actor Penny Marshall (who starred in *Laverne and Shirley* as Laverne De Fazio).[5]

Vestron knew the actress that they wanted to play Vivian Ward, the hooker in the script. However, Michelle Pfeiffer turned down the part so Vestron turned their attentions to Julia Roberts. For the role of Edward Lewis, the wealthy businessman, Vestron wanted a bankable name such as Al Pacino or Sean Connery or even the pop singer Sting. They all turned it down, as did Richard Gere who opined, 'It just was not the kind of movie that I do. In this film the wild exotic flower was the girl. Usually, I'm the exotic flower.' The chairman of Disney Studios and ex-production chief at Paramount Jeffrey Katzenberg had rung Gere who was then making *Internal Affairs* with Andy Garcia to tell him about the new project for Touchstone Pictures: 'It's a kind of *My Fair Lady* but without the songs.' Katzenberg had hired Gere, whose middle name is the unlikely Tiffany, to star in *An Officer and a Gentleman* and *American Gigolo* and he took a personal interest in Gere's

---

[3] It was on Hollywood Boulevard on 27 June 1994 that Hugh Grant encountered the whore Divine Brown but, unlike the character in *Pretty Woman*, Hugh Grant did not marry Brown. Instead, he made a film with Julia Roberts.

[4] Other offshoots from the show include *Mork and Mindy*, *Out of the Blue* and *Joanie Loves Chachi*.

[5] Other brother–sisters in Hollywood include: Jane and Peter Fonda, Warren Beatty and Shirley Maclaine, John and Ellen Travolta and, of course, Eric and Julia Roberts.

career. Katzenberg had also hired Gere for the monumental flop that was *King David* so perhaps he was trying to make up for that with the new project.

Katzenberg was determined that Gere should take the part. He predicted that within thirty days of the film's release Gere would be 'as important a leading man as exists in our business'.

When Disney picked up the script they wanted another actress instead of Julia. *Steel Magnolias* still hadn't been released and Julia wasn't known to the public or, more importantly, to the studio bigwigs. Julia knew her own mind and she desperately wanted to play the rôle of the prostitute.[6]

She began a campaign to persuade Garry Marshall that she was the right actor for the job. The scruffy actor revealed, 'Garry later told me that half the people at Disney were concerned that you couldn't dress me up – that I could have on jeans and look sort of dirty or whatever but you couldn't dress me up – and the other half were saying the opposite. So Garry was saying, "I don't know" – meaning I absolutely wasn't right [for the part of Viv] no matter what I was gonna do.'

It was at this time that Elaine Goldsmith sprang into action. She had *Steel Magnolias* and *Mystic Pizza* shown to Michael Eisner, the Disney CEO, and David Hoberman, the president of Disney's Touchstone Pictures. Hoberman commented, 'Elaine was like a dog tugging at your cuff who wouldn't let go. She was dogged in her pursuit of the rôle, getting us to believe Julia was right for it.' She also arranged for Julia's friend Sally Field to telephone Eisner and to sing Julia's praises. Julia also had several auditions and screen tests. Still, Disney was loath to hire her and they waited until Richard Gere had signed on the dotted line before agreeing. Elaine Goldsmith also told them that Julia was about to sign for another film. Gere didn't want to play the part of Edward Lewis in the original script and he was not much more enthusiastic

---

[6] In 1992 Kiefer Sutherland would appear in the film *A Few Good Men*, which was written by Aaron Sorkin who in 1999 would write *The West Wing*. In his excellent guide to the series *Inside Bartlet's White House* (London: Virgin Books, 2002), Keith Topping reviews the epsiode 'The Women of Qumar', which was broadcast in America on 28 November 2001 and on Channel 4 on 7 April 2003. One story strand has a feminist telling the White House Deputy Chief of Staff that no girl grows up wanting to be a prostitute. Topping writes, 'It was, in fact, alleged that when the movie *Pretty Woman* was popular in the early 1990s that's exactly what many teenage girls *were* saying.'

about the Disneyfied version. Garry Marshall sent him a copy of *Mystic Pizza* to watch but Gere was still not sold so Marshall flew to New York and went with Julia to persuade Gere face to face at his home in Greenwich Village. It also took pleadings by Jeffrey Katzenberg and Gere's agent, Ed Limato, to persuade him to accept the job. Born in Philadelphia, Pennsylvania, on 29 August 1949 Gere, unlike many in Hollywood, is a deep thinker, perhaps on occasion too deep. A devout Buddhist, he suffers from personal conflicts of conscience between art and business. This was one of the reasons why he procrastinated over taking the part. He disliked the dark side of the original idea. To be fair there was also Gere's ego to consider. He believed that the character of Viv, as written, overshadowed his rôle completely.

When Disney signed Julia, she had been out of work for a year. Deliriously happy, she rang her mother who was back in Smyrna, Georgia. As the phone was ringing Julia realised that her mother might not be that happy that her youngest daughter would be playing a whore in a movie. Deciding that discretion was the better part of valour Julia immediately chose to be economic with the truth. 'My mum works for the Catholic Archdiocese of Atlanta. I mean, my mum's boss baptised me. So I called her at work, and it was like, "Hi, mum. I got a job." She said, "You did? What d'you get?" And I said, "Oh, it's a Disney movie! I gotta go, mum. I'll talk to you later." '

Julia is a Roman Catholic and as such knew little about prostitutes and prostitution so she decided to do some research. She met and talked to prostitutes and was saddened by what she discovered. Despite their world, many of them still had dreams and hopes for the future. One wanted to be a psychologist while another hoped to become Jane Seymour's make-up artist. Julia also visited strip clubs, or titty bars. If anything she was more depressed by the strippers than by the hookers. 'It was real sad. These are girls, not unlike me, who look like your average girl,' she said. 'They have aspirations just like any girl does, except they're in this situation, and they don't really acknowledge it that much. They have a view of life that no one should have to live with.'

Despite the major change to the plot, Disney was still unhappy with the script and so hired writers to jolly up the finished product. Julia was to claim that she spoke to the writers and they used her research. However, since her meetings with the hookers and strippers left her depressed and Viv is anything but depressed it seems unlikely that any of her work found its way into the film.

Under its new title *Pretty Woman*[7] shooting began on 24 July 1989 in Los Angeles.[8] Director Garry Marshall quickly learned that Julia responds well to kindness and is not happy working in confrontational atmospheres. 'Julia needs a lot of holding and hugging,' reported Marshall, 'particularly in the scenes where there's meanness. She performs well when loved, which is why Richard Gere and I took great pains to make her feel comfortable, make her feel loved and make it a pleasant experience – not because we're such nice people, but because we felt it was the best thing for the project.'

The only filming that took place at the Regent Beverly Wilshire Hotel was in its lobby. Marshall filmed at the abandoned Ambassador's Hotel,[9] in the swimming pool of the Westwood Marquis Hotel and on sound stages designed to look like other luxurious places. He insisted, however, on filming on the real Sunset Boulevard. Julia was horrified when Marshall made her wear the regulation whore's outfit – miniskirt, stilettos and skimpy top – in a real red light district. 'I took so much shit for that outfit,' she said. 'In fact at one point there were so many catcalls directed at me I went back to my trailer. I felt hideous and just wanted to hide. I know how to deal with any kind of attention somebody's going to give Julia Roberts, but the attention that Julia got as Vivian standing on Hollywood Boulevard in that outfit was not the kind of attention I'm used to or prepared to deal with. Vivian's clothes were a thousand times more provocative than anything I'd have in my closet. Vivian would say "F*** you! Blow it out your ass!" But I turn red and get hives.'

Julia was not happy with the nude scenes. She was also unhappy about appearing in her underwear but she did not then

---

[7] *Pretty Woman* was the favourite film of Lyle Lovett. He carried a tape of it with him on tour long before he met and married Julia. A friend of his revealed, 'He must have watched it a hundred times.'

[8] The fee had been raised from $3,000 to $4,000 when the film was shot.

[9] On 2 August 1945 aspiring model Norma Jean Dougherty (later to become famous as Marilyn Monroe) went to see modelling agent Emmeline Snively of the Blue Book Model Agency, which was based in the Ambassador's Hotel, Los Angeles. By coincidence Marilyn's sometime lover Senator Bobby Kennedy would be shot dead by Sirhan Sirhan in the same hotel in June 1968.

have the influence to keep her clothes on. When she performed in the bath Garry Marshall closed the set to everyone – including the cameraman. Marshall left the camera running as Julia exited the bath completely alone. She said, 'Garry convinced me [to do the nude scene] thanks to a trick. He instructed me to get into the bathtub with a swimming costume on, then the film crew left the scene but the cameras kept rolling. I took off my swimsuit and walked out of the bathtub quite naturally without the least feeling of shame, because there was nothing in front of me except for a camera lens – it was quite funny.'

Before Julia signed to make the film the nude scene had been the subject of heated discussions between Elaine Goldsmith and Julia. '[Super agent] Sue Mengers comes into the office. I had never met her before, didn't know who she was. She comes in, she sits down and she's got that voice, "Hello, dahling, what's going on?" And Elaine's like, "Uh, we're just having this thing," and Sue goes, "Oh, what's the big deal? We're not talking beaver here." I looked at her. I thought, who is this woman? Why is she saying these things to me? Why is she using that word? And then she's like, "If I had your body, you'd see me in Gelson's going down the frozen aisle naked!" I think I was breaking out into hives. This woman's talking about my naked body . . . Needless to say, I love Sue. Never at a loss for words. But, boy, what a meeting. I'll never forget that for the rest of my life. "We're not talking beaver." Does she not know how old I am?'

Marshall also worked closely with Gere to get the best out of their leading lady. In one scene Edward (Gere) gives Vivian a box containing a fabulous diamond necklace. Vivian opens the box and puts on the trinket. Without telling Julia, Marshall told Gere to snap the box shut as Julia was reaching for it. The snap surprised Julia and she cried out. Marshall was so delighted with the reaction he kept it in the finished film.

Unlike many actors who virtually ignore their co-workers, Julia spent time socialising with the crew.[10] On set she adopted a stray dog, lavishing much love on the pooch. The understanding Garry

---

[10] One leading Hollywood man has forbidden crew members to make eye contact with him unless he specifically addresses them. This can usually be avoided as he is rather on the short side and his eye level is far below others.

Marshall did not object when the dog's barking ruined a scene. He simply waited until Julia calmed the mutt and reshot.

Less calm on set was Julia herself who found it difficult to play the scenes in which Richard Gere or another actor had to shout at her. Remembers Garry Marshall, 'The dramatic scenes where she was going to be very vulnerable were very hard for her too. You're with Richard Gere for six or seven weeks, and suddenly you do this scene where he screams in your face and yells at you. It hurt her. Richard is used to that, but she was devastated by the scene. After each take she was crying, and we'd have to hold her a moment to make sure she was all right.

'In the scenes where she got verbally beaten up by Edward's lawyers and Edward screamed at her, she was playing the vulnerability off camera so she could play against it on camera. So off camera, I had a sobbing mess on my hands. But on camera she fought against it, and I think that worked.'

Later, a journalist asked her about Garry Marshall's kid gloves approach. Julia was unamused. 'Well, wouldn't you think so? You know, some guy comes in and basically says, "I'm gonna f*** you whether you like it it not", and then throws you down on the floor and jumps on top of you, and you're screaming – I think you might feel a little fragile. Garry is a great hugger, a great supporter, he's really right on, but I get thrown on the floor a lot, and it didn't feel so good. I'm not going to pretend like I'm all brave and it's all really easy. I mean, it's fake up to a point, but at some point you're going to get pushed the wrong way, you're going to get hurt.

'Garry is like a dad. He loves to hug and he's really boisterous. All the people on the set are the people he's worked with before and they're like family – so to bring an actor into an environment like that, you're immediately comfortable because everyone knows each other so well. Garry comes from a real place of supporting you with love.'

When Julia's mother visited the set, she saw no examples of her daughter's supposed unhappiness. In fact, in interviews she referred to Marshall as a surrogate father for Julia. Betty remembers, 'It was a very close group, even the crew. When it came time to film the love scene, the crew were shaking like a leaf because they knew how she felt.' When it indeed did come time to film the love scene Julia was physically sick. 'I felt like a twelve-year-old that had never been kissed,' was how she recalled the event.

Julia herself was happy to praise Richard Gere for his on-set kindness. 'He's hysterical. I can't remember anything specifically funny that he did. But take my word for it, he's great. He stayed at the low end in performance terms which is unique to talented people. He made Vivian an interesting character by making Edward show that he found her interesting – otherwise she'd just seem like a whacko. He did it for me; he gave me the opportunities even when it meant he himself was standing back. He is an incredibly generous actor.'

Garry Marshall said, 'I looked for two one hundred per cent beautiful people. But there are a lot of good-looking actors who can't act at all. The chemistry between the two stars was really something quite special.'

The film opened in Britain on 11 May 1990 and in the United States two months earlier on 23 March 1990. It would eventually take more than $500 million at the box office worldwide and it also earned Richard Gere more money than any other film he had made.

Despite the success the film is not without its continuity errors. In the scene where Viv is undressing Edward she takes off his tie, unbuttons his shirt and then in the next shot he is wearing the tie once again. When the couple are eating breakfast Viv picks up a croissant and then takes a bite from a pancake. In the next shot the pancake is whole again. Still on the subject of food, when they picnic in the park Viv removes Edward's shoes and socks only for them to mysteriously reappear in the next shot.

Julia has a reputation for falling for and romancing her leading man. That was indeed how she met her then boyfriend Dylan McDermott on the set of Steel Magnolias. And rumours did indeed surface that she was having an affair with Richard Gere. The rumours reached McDermott who was filming in Morocco. Julia rang him to say that they were not true but McDermott was not placated and flew to the set to confront his girlfriend. Julia had intended to visit McDermott on location but never showed. He assumed that was because she was romancing Richard Gere. McDermott heard of the gossip about the love scene and persuaded his bosses to give him time off to visit Julia. When he arrived in Los Angeles he went straight to the set and did not like what he saw. However, the rumours were wrong. That visit did signal the end of her affair with McDermott, though. It is not certain whether it was his jealousy that caused the end of the affair or if it had simply run its course. Dylan McDermott returned to his film in Morocco but was devastated by the split and reportedly lost a stone in weight.

When filming ended Garry Marshall presented Julia with a diamond necklace and a card that read, 'For my schlumpy girl. Wear this wherever you go and know there's someone who loves you.' Meantime, gossip began to circulate within and without the industry that *Pretty Woman* was going to be a smash hit. *Harper's* magazine described Julia as 'a contemporary beauty' and named her as one of its 'Ten Most Beautiful Women in America'. Julia was ecstatic not because she was overly egotistical but because Campbell High School's library subscribed to the magazine so her former teachers would see it. *Playboy*, which the school library probably doesn't subscribe to, named Julia as the 'Lips of the '90s'. Julia was surprised by that because she has always regarded that her lips were her least favourite part of her body. 'When they're your own lips, you don't really think about them. But there was a time in high school when I felt a little grief because I had an unusual mouth, unlike the other girls who had perfect mouths. But I never have done anything to accentuate my mouth. In fact, I'm really bad at putting [lipstick] on. Every time I've put it on, I've taken it off before I've gone out.'

If Julia was unsure of her looks, she probably wasn't helped by the comments of Bob Mills, the make-up artist on the film, who revealed, 'The hollows in Miss Roberts's cheeks were filled with highlights, as were the eye sockets. The jaw line was also highlighted to broaden it. Shadows were added to slim the nose and contour the forehead. The cheekbone line was lowered to produce a fuller effect. Hidden liners to thicken the lashes were applied, the lips were corrected to soften the very generous quality of her own.'

Of herself Julia opined, 'I think I'm loud and weird. But if you're a real person, people can't help but respond in the same manner. I find myself becoming more and more honest. Still, I know it's a great risk to take. But I found that if I say what I am feeling 90 per cent of the time, any problem can be worked out.'

The marketing poster created by Disney of the opening shot of the film almost certainly did not aid Julia's self-confidence. While Vivian dressed the camera panned up every inch of her body except her face. The reason for this was because the body in question does not belong to Julia but to Shelley Michelle, a model-actress who is a year older than Julia.[11] Nor does the body on the poster, which belongs to model Donna Scoggins.

Three weeks after *Pretty Woman* wrapped, Julia flew back to Georgia for the premiere of *Steel Magnolias* at the Phipps Plaza Cineplex. A gala was held at the Ritz Carlton Hotel to raise money for the Juvenile Diabetes Fund and tickets cost $150 each.

A year after the end of the romance with Dylan McDermott, he plucked up the courage to call Julia and suggest that they be friends if they could not be lovers. Julia agreed to a visit. By the time of the call *Pretty Woman* had been released and Julia was a fully-fledged star who had won a Golden Globe statuette for the film. When McDermott arrived at Julia's house he was shocked. 'The bedroom door was open, and the sheets had rolled off the bed and onto the floor. The Golden Globe was sitting on the dressing room table surrounded by clutter. I felt like a toilet seat.'

Gossip columnist Liz Smith noted in her column, '[Julia Roberts and Dylan McDermott] started having a wild affair and seemed to be very, very much in love. Julia was very sweet to him, very into him. Then all of sudden she dumped him. Her time limit seems to be twelve to eighteen months. As soon as the romance gets serious she can't handle it. She can't seem to handle the reality of commitment.'

---

[11] Aside from her own acting career in films such as *Bikini Summer* (1991), *The Naked Truth* (1992), *Married People, Single Sex* (1993), *Rising Sun* (1993), *Midnight Blue* (1996) and *Ballerina* (2000), Shelley Michelle has also body-doubled for Kim Basinger in *My Stepmother is an Alien* (1988), Catherine Oxenberg in *Overexposed* (1990), Anne Archer in *Nails* (1992) and Claudia Christian in *Hexed* (1993).

7. SATISFIED

'Even though she was just one of the girls [in Satisfaction*] there was something about her that was so sexy and infectious. I decided to keep an eye on her. Then I saw her in* Mystic Pizza. *That was it. That was all I had to see. When I decided to do* Flatliners *she was my first choice.'*

Joel Schumacher

CHICAGO, OCTOBER 1989–JANUARY 1990

About to begin work on *Pretty Woman*, Julia had her next project in her sights. Joel Schumacher was looking for the female lead in his new film which he provisionally entitled *Flatliners*. They met one Sunday in his home and when Julia turned up – in cut-off jeans, T-shirt, face bare of make-up and barefoot – Schumacher was immediately smitten. 'Even though she was just one of the girls [in *Satisfaction*] there was something about her that was so sexy and infectious. I decided to keep an eye on her. Then I saw her in *Mystic Pizza*. That was it. That was all I had to see. When I decided to do *Flatliners* she was my first choice.'

Five days after *Pretty Woman* wrapped Julia flew to Chicago to begin work on *Flatliners*, described by Halliwell as 'hectic fantasy, filmed in a restless manner'. Filming began on 23 October 1989 and wrapped on 23 January 1990. Julia's co-stars were Kevin Bacon and Kiefer Sutherland. Although Julia didn't know the exotically named Kiefer William Frederick Dempsey George Rufus Sutherland it would not be long before they were a hot'n'heavy item, as the American gossip writers like to describe these affairs. Both liked to party, both liked to drink tequila, both came from broken homes, both were four years old when their parents split up, both had fathers who were actors and both found solace in the community created on a film set.

As we have seen Julia can become quite intense when she is working and, as this memory shows, her time on *Flatliners* was no different. Julia says, 'We'd just started shooting, and I didn't know anybody. We were shooting at night, and it was real cold. I had this one easy thing to do, just run up these stairs, looking for the character played by Kiefer. I started talking to Joel, and I'm asking him, "How did I get here? Did I take the bus?" He said, "No, you ran." I thought about how long it would have taken to run there and, all of a sudden, I realised how panicked a situation this was. I'm running and I have to get there for about ten reasons, the biggest of which is to save Kiefer's life, and the least is to tell him it's all right and he's my friend.

'So I get into this place in my mind where I'm breathing really hard and I say to Joel, "Is Kiefer here?" "Yeah, he's in his trailer." So I say I really need to see him, and Kiefer comes out, he doesn't know what I'm doing, he doesn't even know who I am. He came out and I just flailed my preparation at him, tugged his shirt, and I didn't need him to say anything. I just needed him to be there, to be a person. I remember the three of us standing in the cold, and me feeling this support from Kiefer and Joel.'

It was a short time after she received 'this support' from Sutherland that she and he were dating. 'I fell in love with him during some of the most gruesome scenes. There was something about him that was so incredibly old and wise. It seemed to me he was a thousand years older, and yet he's only a year older than me.

'Kiefer has totally captivated me. Two people couldn't be closer than we are. We've hardly been apart since we met. I've found myself weeping when we're separated. He's so knowledgeable and thinks things through.

'We sit at home reading or talking, or I do a lot of needlework. I've nearly worn a hole in my finger but that's the kind of quiet life that we love.'

It has been suggested by psychologists and journalists alike that Julia adopts the film crews with whom she works as her surrogate family. For the length of the shoot Julia had people who were devoted to her, to her needs and to her whims. For the insecure actor this was the ideal situation to be in – safe and secure.

Flatliners was a low-budget movie and as such had to be filmed without too many breaks. Consequently Schumacher did not break for either Christmas or New Year but his beautiful star did not object. She was with her 'family'. Many of the married crew members brought their children and pets to the set and Julia was in her element. 'She had all the kids in her trailer all the time,' remembers Joel Schumacher. 'There was always a line of kids in and out of Julia's trailer. She was feeding them, mothering them.

And, you know, that's unique. A lot of people in Hollywood aren't nice to their parents, let alone their children.'

Once again, Julia buried herself in her work. 'She does her emotional homework before she comes in,' said her director. 'If she has to do a highly emotional scene, she's figured out what she's going to use from her own life and feelings to get there. And she would always let me know, either deliberately or in a more covert way, what the trigger would be from her life. For instance, her father's dead in the film, as well as in real life, and my father's dead, and we'd have that to relate to between takes if she came over to me for help staying in the moment.'

Schumacher will not go into more detail about the conversations he had with Julia during the filming of *Flatliners*, except to say that they were 'poignant and personal'. They became devoted to each other over the course of shooting and became honorary presidents of each other's fan clubs. Schumacher said, 'It's nice to know there's someone like her on the planet. She's brilliant. She's talented. She gets the jokes. She's raunchy. She's the perfect lady.' Julia was equally fulsome in her praise for Schumacher: 'Some directors give you support but they're essentially cool with their flattery because they don't want to give the actor a big head, which I think is poppycock. On *Flatliners* we would do a scene and when it was over Joel would hoot "I can't wait for dailies!" He would just start screaming and make you feel good.'

Back to Schumacher: 'She's quite mesmerising in person. When the camera hits her, it just gets enhanced to a point where it's dazzling. She's really in a class by herself. I've worked with a lot of extraordinary women but Julia is not interchangeable with anyone.'

Once more Julia: 'Joel was so intense and articulate. When we did small scenes, he would give us something basic and then not say anything. When he did say something it was succinct and exactly right. And he'll lead you to things so that the ideas he has become your ideas as well. He created a really happy set, which makes that eleventh or twelfth hour of work worth it.'

Schumacher again: 'She can be funny, sexy, even raunchy and she's a master at telling dirty jokes. But she never seems to come off vulgar in any way, shape or form.

'Like most truly intelligent and enlightened people she has no class system within her. People are people and she doesn't treat the high rollers any differently from the blue-collar people. It's a very enlightening way to live. She adds a great deal of nurturing and support to the communal situation, which is always welcome.'

If everyone on set loved Julia one person loved her more and that was Kiefer Sutherland. Of his future fiancée Sutherland said, 'She comes into rehearsal and she had a really incredible presence just as a person, which made me sit back and take a look. Then we started working together and I got really, really excited because she was one of the best actors I've ever worked with. I mean, she was incredibly giving, incredibly open, and had qualities you can't even articulate when you're watching her work.'

During the filming of *Flatliners*, *Vogue* ran a photo story about Julia that described her as resembling more 'a poetry major than a budding sex symbol'. That was probably due to the way Julia dressed at the time – she favoured hats, five earrings in each ear, spectacles, and huge handbags and kept her house and car keys on a large chain. The article went on to claim, 'She's a free spirit who likes to roam around barefoot, has memorised the entire Elvis Costello songbook, enjoys her privacy and talks endlessly about her "boyfriend" although she never reveals his name.'

Julia told *Vogue*, 'There are times when Hollywood is very unattractive to me. But there was a time in New York when I had nothing but time on my hands. So when Hollywood has no charm and everyone just wants you, you have to be grateful and remember the times when you were sitting in your apartment with nothing to do.'

Julia revealed to the magazine that she intended to take a break from making films after she had completed her next project, a movie called *Sleeping with the Enemy*.

TUCSON, ARIZONA, 14 FEBRUARY 1990
'I was with a friend of mine and I got a call at about five in the morning,' said Julia. 'I was too excited to go to sleep and too tired to get excited. So it was about two in the afternoon and we'd known since early in the morning, but it just hadn't registered with me. Then, I'm watching MTV and all of a sudden I started

giggling. I just couldn't stop laughing.' The 'friend' she was with was Kiefer Sutherland. The call was from her agent Elaine Goldsmith telling Julia that she had been nominated for a Best Supporting Actress Oscar for *Steel Magnolias*. Julia told one journalist that being nominated felt 'like it does when you're walking around on a hot summer day and all of a sudden it starts to rain really hard. It's cold and it feels good, and it makes you want to dance around. Then it stops, and you keep on walking.' Julia was the only cast member to be nominated. She was also nominated for a Golden Globe, which she won. She said, 'I've worked with some really great actors and I hear them talking about structure, and I listen. But mostly I watch. I learned so much from those five tremendous women in *Steel Magnolias*, by watching them do what they do perfectly. I owe them a lot more than I could ever articulate.'

8. OPEN AND VULNERABLE

'My love for Kiefer will last as long as this tattoo.'

Julia Roberts

HOLLYWOOD, MARCH 1990

The odds of Julia winning the Oscar were put at 3–1. She was up against Brenda Fricker for *My Left Foot*,[1] Anjelica Huston for *Enemies: A Love Story*, Lena Olin also for *Enemies: A Love Story* and Dianne Wiest for *Parenthood*. Julia had two major items on her mind in March 1990. There was her Oscar nomination, an honour that would also enable her agents to substantially increase her fees. There was also her burgeoning affair with Kiefer Sutherland. Julia travelled to Cerillos, New Mexico, and Tucson, Arizona, where Sutherland was making *Young Guns II*, 'more pop Western nonsense'[2] with Emilio Estevez, Lou Diamond Phillips, William L. Petersen, Christian Slater and James Coburn. Their romance soon became public knowledge. Donald Sutherland's son bought his girlfriend a 'friendship ring' costing $100,000 'without questions and without response', which was Julia's arch way of saying that Sutherland had not asked her to marry him and they were not engaged. He also paid for her to have a tattoo of a red heart inside a black Chinese symbol, which apparently meant 'strength of heart'. 'My love for Kiefer will last as long as this tattoo,' she told anyone who asked about it. Two years later, after the end of the affair, Julia had the tattoo discreetly removed.

Julia obviously saw the relationship as serious because she bought a secluded, three-bedroomed home in Woodrow Wilson Drive near Nichols Canyon in the Hollywood Hills for a reputed $1.4 million for her and Kiefer to live together in unwedded bliss. She told a journalist, 'I'm what you'd call a decision-action person. I make a decision and I act on it. If I decide I'm gonna have dinner or buy a house I do it. My boyfriend is gonna die when he hears I bought a house. He keeps telling me I got to own things. So first

---

[1] The star of that film was Daniel Day-Lewis, a future lover of Julia, and the winner of that year's Best Actor Academy Award.

[2] Film critics Mick Martin and Marsha Porter.

I bought this car. And then he told me I oughta get a house. I remember telling him, "Why do I need a house?" And he said, "Well you gotta have a place to park the car." '

In fact, the garage was the only part of the house which could be seen from the main road. The garden consisted of a small lawn but the house boasted an outdoor Jacuzzi and the bedroom had a 360-degree view of the Hollywood Hills.

Strangely, in the first three months of her relationship with Sutherland the couple spent fewer than three days there because she was working so much.

Meanwhile, Sutherland began to build a ranch for himself and Julia on a parcel of land he bought in Whitefish, Montana. The idea was for the place to be a bolt hole when the pressures of work or just being in the public eye became too much for either of them.

There was, however, also a problem with Julia's new relationship. Aside from her desire for privacy and hatred of the press, there was another more troubling reason why she was keen to keep her boyfriend's name out of the papers. Kiefer Sutherland was still married to Camilla Kath.[3]

On 15 February 1990 Sutherland filed for divorce from Camilla Kath, a Puerto Rican actress more than a dozen years older than him and the mother of his eighteen-month-old daughter, Sarah.

As Julia went up to receive her Golden Globe she and Sutherland had been living together for some time and were still in the throes of a passionate affair unlike any Julia had experienced before. Dressed in a man's Armani suit, she told the watching audience at the ceremony, 'I want to thank my beautiful blue-eyed, green-eyed boy who supports me through everything and brings so much happiness to my life.' She later commented, 'I have to say the Golden Globes was the most shocking night of my life. I was so unprepared. I heard a recording of my acceptance speech later and I had to laugh. I was such an idiot.'

---

[3] Camilla Kath was born on 10 December 1954 as Camilla Emily Ortiz. Her first husband was Terry Kath, the guitarist from the pop group Chicago. On 23 January 1978 he committed suicide. She married Toto drummer Jeff Porcaro but was divorced again before her marriage in 1988 to Kiefer Sutherland. Sutherland married, for the second time, Kelly Winn on 29 June 1996. They divorced on 13 March 2000.

In mid-March a preview was held for *Pretty Woman* in Westwood that Julia did not attend. Her absence was explained by her publicist saying that she was in South Carolina preparing for her rôle in *Sleeping with the Enemy*. That was not the truth. She was, in fact, in the Sonoran desert with Kiefer Sutherland. *Pretty Woman* opened on 23 March and in its first month grossed more than $150 million. It became the highest grossing film of the year and Disney's most successful ever taking more than $450 million. It also made Julia a star. *Time* magazine film critic Richard Schickel wasn't impressed, however. 'Without taking anything away from Julia Roberts there were doubtless 25 other actresses who could have played the rôle and played it fine. It wasn't exactly a stretch. There was nothing inherent in what she, or Richard Gere, did that pushed the film over the $150 million mark. It took off because the public wanted to plug into the fantasy.'

Director Garry Marshall mused on the delicious irony that the most successful film made by the squeaky-clean Disney company was about a prostitute. 'Walt is somewhere in his grave[4] saying "Pinocchio, no, a nice duck, no, it has to be a hooker as my highest-grossing picture."'

On 26 March Julia went to the Dorothy Chandler Pavilion in Los Angeles for the 62nd Academy Awards. Accompanying her was Kiefer Sutherland and both were wearing identical double-breasted Giorgio Armani suits. Julia told waiting journalists, 'I'm nervous and excited and I just want to sit down.'

The moment of truth came and the 'nervous and excited' Julia became the disappointed Julia when the winner was announced as Brenda Fricker.

ABBEVILLE, SOUTH CAROLINA, APRIL 1990

Julia's next project, or so she thought, was a crime drama called *Class Action*. She was to play a lawyer who found herself opposing

---

[4] On 7 November 1966 in St Joseph's Hospital, Burbank, which was just across the road from the Walt Disney Studios, Disney's left lung was removed because it was cancerous (due to his chain-smoking). Another operation was performed a fortnight later and then he was released. On 5 December he was readmitted to the hospital and died there ten days after his 65th birthday. He was cremated two days later and his ashes interred in the Court of Freedom at Forest Lawn Memorial-Parks, 1712 South Glendale Avenue, Glendale, California 91209. Despite the rumours he is not frozen waiting to be thawed out and rejuvenated.

her father in court. However, Julia was surprised when Twentieth Century Fox turned her down. Although she had been nominated for an Oscar, it seemed that Julia was not then the office draw that she thought. Many actors would have taken the rejection and put it down to experience. Not Julia Roberts. She telephoned Joe Roth, the head of the studio, personally and he still rejected her.

Roth remembers, 'I turned her down because she was too young, and she got mad at me. Two weeks later, I offered her *Sleeping with the Enemy*.' No one had ever called Roth to ask for a job. He offered Julia $2 million to make the film, a considerable pay rise from the $300,000 that she had received for *Pretty Woman*.

In *Sleeping with the Enemy* the lead female character is an abused wife who finally snaps and kills her brutal husband. Kim Basinger had been signed to star as Laura Burney. But then Basinger pulled out of the project to appear in *The Marrying Man* opposite her boyfriend Alec Baldwin, the elder brother of William Baldwin with whom Julia had been scheduled to appear in *Beyond a Reasonable Doubt*. Joe Roth then rang Julia to offer her the part.

Producer Leonard Goldberg had misgivings. 'We thought we might be in real trouble when Kim decided not to do it. Kim was just coming off *Batman* and was on every magazine cover. *Steel Magnolias* was just coming out, and Julia was basically no more than an up-and-coming actress. We were trading maximum star power to work with a near unknown. But Julia seemed really right for the rôle, and we figured we'd end up with a better film, if not a marketable one. Now, of course, we look like geniuses.'

As with many directors *Sleeping with the Enemy*'s Joseph Ruben adored Julia. 'I remember this shy but dazzling smile and her body language. It was a shyness but there was something coming out of her smile. That's the part of what makes her so fascinating on screen – all the contradictions, being both very shy, but very much out there at the same time. She's both very sexual and very innocent too. But she's very vulnerable and there's a private side to Julia. There's an incredibly warm aspect to her, but she can be very cold when she's angry.'

A friend who has known her for years adds, 'She can go from Bambi to bitch in two seconds.' A former colleague said, 'She never got angry with me, at least she never got angry in front of me, but I saw her get angry at other people. You can always tell when Julia's really mad because her eyes narrow down and her chin juts out. Believe me, if she's angry, you know it.'

As we have seen Julia gets very intense when it comes to making films and *Sleeping with the Enemy* was no exception. She involved herself so much that she went down with a case of ringworm during filming.

Julia said, 'I thought it was well-written, very suspenseful and from an actor's point of view very exciting to try to do because it's very challenging. The rôle offered five, ten, fifteen things to play at once, so part of the challenge was that I didn't know if I could do it, if I should do it, if it was the right decision for me at that moment, and so I did it.

'When I read a script what I look for is a cross between thrill and fear. It's more an instinct and sense of emotion than anything specific. The movies I've done have all been scripts I read and felt something at that moment, a sense of being scared and challenged just enough to feel I don't quite want to do it, but realise I have to deep inside.

'[*Sleeping with the Enemy*] was very intense because of the nature of the material and there were very few scenes I wasn't in. So, essentially, I worked nearly every day, six days a week, for over three months. It was very tiring.'

The film saw Julia play Laura Burney, a wife battered – physically and emotionally – by her financial adviser husband Martin (Patrick Bergin) for three years, seven months and six days. One night, believing that his wife is hydrophobic and a non-swimmer, Martin insists that they go sailing with a neighbour. Despite the weathermen's assurance of calm weather a storm blows up and Laura takes the opportunity to fake her own death to escape his clutches. However, she hasn't covered her tracks quite as completely as she should have done and he takes steps to track her down. The scene called for Julia to wear just a bra and knickers. Using her star power she insisted that the crew strip as well. She recalls, 'It was absolutely freezing. I said to [them], "I think we need a little group support here. So drop your trousers. If you're not going to take your pants off, you can't stay in the house." ' Director Joseph Ruben was amused by the request but many of the crew were not and stormed off the set. The remainder did as their star bid and Julia took some pictures of the trouserless crew. One of them was pantless as well as trouserless and appears in the pictures with a towel protecting his modesty. Ruben, who also stripped to his underwear, recalls, 'I was at a low ebb and Julia was so cold and having such a hard time and somehow her request did not seem unreasonable. With the benefit of hindsight, I think it was very unreasonable.' Julia commented, 'It had nothing to do with acting and everything to do with just getting everybody as naked and cold as I was. And I think everybody was silently thrilled by it. It was the bonding thing, you know.'

In another scene Bergin has to hit Julia because she has displeased him. The slap was to send Julia hurtling to the floor and, because it was in close-up, she couldn't use a stunt double. A cushion was placed on the floor to break Julia's fall but on the first take she flinched as she hit the floor. On the second take she flung herself down and missed the cushion hitting her head on the hard floor.

'I really fell and my head bounced like a basketball on the marble floor. I can't tell you how much that hurt. I'm hysterical with pain. I'm crying. It's gone too far. I cracked the floor so hard I have a black eye, but that's what made the take so exciting, cracking my head like that.'

Unfortunately for Julia, her woes in the scene were not over. Co-star Bergin was supposed to aim a kick at Julia as she lay prone. A sandbag was put near Julia for the Irishman to kick but in his excitement he missed and kicked her.

Back to Julia. 'Anyway, I'm in pain, and lying there when the actor comes to kick me, and misses the sandbag and kicks me in the leg. It can't get any worse. By now I'm just a blithering idiot. I can't even see straight.

'When the take was over the director came up to me and said, "I wanted to call 'Cut!' when I saw what happened." And I said, "If you'd called 'Cut!', I would've wrung your neck – 'cause I'm not gonna do that scene again." '

Despite their on-screen animosity, Bergin claimed that they gelled away from the cameras. 'There was nothing we weren't able to do, from love scenes to violence. It was never a question of mistrust,' he recalls. Yet Julia was not so sure as was evident by her referral to him as 'the actor' in the above anecdote. 'We weren't necessarily friendly towards each other. When you come to work and someone kicks the shit out of you for three hours, you really don't feel like finding out where he is and saying "Goodnight".' Away from the cameras the pair practised him beating her up. Director Joseph Ruben was worried by what he saw. 'They knew they were in control,' he said, 'but I didn't.'

Julia was used to putting her soul into her work but she found the rôle of the abused wife to be the hardest she had ever taken on. 'Every emotion that you see in the movie, that you feel or think about from one moment to the next, I probably went through drastically. It was physically exhausting. By virtue of size, it was the biggest part I've ever played, as far as hours spent working. And I did get hurt.'

It seems that Julia hurt emotionally as well as physically. 'It was an emotionally harrowing experience. There were whole weeks where I'd have to arrive on the set at 5 a.m., start crying and be the victim of those terrible fights.' Using the Method style of acting she dredged up incidents from her own past for her performance. Often, she left herself in tears. Ruben commented, 'It's as if she has the thinnest skin imaginable. There's a vulnerability there that knocks you out. She's got two things going on. There's something that happens photographically with her, that star quality you hear about. And she's got this emotional vulnerability that lets you see and feel everything that's going on with her. And the two of them together? Bam!'

For her own part, Julia told *Playboy* that the most annoying cliché about actors is 'that they are temperamental and have to be coddled and have their egos stroked. I guess you have to treat some people as if they were fragile. But speaking for myself, I don't need to be treated that way. I don't need to be treated badly. I don't want to be abused for the sake of a performance because I'll find my performance. But I don't have to have people tiptoeing around me, either, trying not to hurt my feelings. If my performance is bad, the best thing you can do is tell me and not in a cruel way, "That was not good."'

A more disturbing incident happened on location. *Sleeping with the Enemy* was set in Cape Cod, Massachusetts, and in Cedar Falls, Iowa,[5] but was filmed in Abbeville and Spartanburg in South Carolina. One day Julia went to a restaurant called Michael's with a crew member who was black, and was horrified when the man was refused service. She complained to anyone who would listen, telling *Rolling Stone* in August 1990, 'The people [in Abbeville] were horribly racist, and I had a really hard time . . . I didn't feel like I was on location. I didn't feel like I had a job.'

Abbeville didn't take the controversy sitting down. Disc jockey Mike Gallagher of WFBC-AM, the local radio station, drew up a petition denouncing Julia. The community also paid for a quarter-page advert in *Daily Variety* headlined PRETTY WOMAN? PRETTY LOW!

Joe Savitz, the mayor of Abbeville, joined the argument. He called Julia naïve for patronising 'a real redneck type place in Abbeville that does not allow black customers. No self-respecting person would want to go there.'

Julia realised that labelling the whole of the South racist was probably not that smart a move and had her publicist issue a statement. 'I was born in the South so in no way am I trying to create a stereotype. I was shocked that this type of treatment still exists in America in the nineties – in the South or anywhere else.'

As she had with Joe Roth, Julia rang the mayor to make her displeasure known and to clarify her comments claiming that she been 'a little misquoted' by *Rolling Stone*. The mayor said, 'She said she was talking about one person she met, but the magazine made it sound like she was talking about the whole town. I think the residents were a little upset – I think anybody would be upset if somebody said something like that about their town – but it was really a big flap over nothing. I think everybody has kind of forgotten what she said.'

Julia's mother leaped to defend her daughter. She told *People* magazine, 'Julia grew up in the South and is not naïve about the fact that there's prejudice. But she was very shocked. I am proud she spoke up. Julia has never picked friends by colour. She always

---

[5] For trivia buffs, the house that Laura/Sara rented was at 408 Treemont, Cedar Falls.

had a lot of black friends in school. What happened is she became friends with a crew member; they went to a place of business; her friend was black and they were refused service. Julia was shocked. She had never seen that happen in Smyrna or Atlanta. I think she saw enough [racism in Abbeville] that she thought it was condoned.'

During the filming of *Sleeping with the Enemy*, *Pretty Woman* was released nationwide on 23 March with the result that her star rose and Julia went from being a successful but relatively unknown actress to being a big name. 'You could definitely say the phone has been ringing,' said Elaine Goldsmith. 'The reaction we've gotten has been incredibly positive. People really feel she's one of a kind. She's going to take a break now. If people want her now, they're going to want her a year from now.' Meanwhile, back on location Julia was also enormously cheered by the occasional visits from boyfriend Kiefer Sutherland and her mother and half-sister. Even Eric Roberts turned up occasionally to see his sister but it was Sutherland's visits that Julia most looked forward to.

One crew member said, 'They were very playful together. There was a sense of mutual support. I think they both like to cut through the bullshit factor. I think they make each other laugh. They both know the kind of pressures they're dealing with, and they both have the same uncompromising attitude about their work, so they can be supportive and respectful of each other.'

The final scene of *Sleeping with the Enemy* took five days to film and left Julia exhausted. 'I've spent the last year and a half making movies and giving, and giving, and giving. There would be nothing left but I'd find one more thing, so I'd give that. But there comes a point where you're losing sleep, and it takes a long time to get anything back from all that giving.

'When you have family, friends and there's love in your life, and you give to that, you can see instant gratification. You can see somebody smile or just pick somebody up or something. It's a lot easier to give that way than it is to be giving to the [cameras and sound equipment].'

Director Ruben added, 'She's incredibly talented. There's an ease about her acting, something real and very deep about her acting. Everything comes through her – through her body, her eyes, her face, her smile. That's very rare and because of it the audience makes a tremendous connection with her. She's one of the most sympathetic actors to come along in a long time. She's the real thing. There's nobody quite like her. She's an original.

'Julia is a force of nature. She's so full of life. Most people go through life with a very dim wattage and they let out only a small part of their light. But not Julia. She just blasts it out. You get everything from her – the whole range of what she's feeling. If something pisses her off, she expresses it and goes on. If something hurts her, she expresses it and goes on.'

Producer Leonard Goldberg commented, 'Everything she's feeling you see in her face and her eyes. Her eyes are like a tunnel right into her soul. I thinks that's why the audience identifies with her so much. She is beautiful. There are a lot of beautiful actresses but she is vulnerable and so open they can readily identify with her and associate with her because she is not much different from [the way] they are.'

9. DYING AT THE BOX OFFICE

*'This was the first time a star had ever asked me to direct, and I don't think
I would have made that particular movie if Julia hadn't asked me. I'm in
love with Julia. She's a combination of many things which is why she's so
fascinating on screen: sexy but ladylike, guileless yet sophisticated, fragile
but strong. She's street smart rather than educated, but extremely
well-read.'*

Director Joel Schumacher

LOS ANGELES, OCTOBER 1990

While Julia was filming *Sleeping with the Enemy* Kiefer Sutherland
was busy. While Patrick Bergin was beating her up, Kiefer
Sutherland was organising her home in Nichols Canyon. When
Julia left for Abbeville, South Carolina, the place was a mess. Julia
disliked the décor of the previous owner but did not have the time
to do anything about it. This is where Sutherland came into his
own. While Julia was busy working, he was arranging for her
possessions to be moved from her Venice apartment to Nichols
Canyon and put into some kind of order.

'There were books and papers scattered all over my apartment,
the house needed a paint job, and it was just too much. I had so
much in storage that my girlfriends and I joked about a whole
town called Storage, California. You know, "Where's your stuff?"
"In Storage." But while I was gone Kiefer took care of the whole
thing. I came home to find the house all ready. Even my clothes
were hanging in the closet,' remembers Julia.

The couple had spent three months apart and in the movie
world there are many temptations. Some actors away from home
and on location resist the blandishments of a sexy new lover but
many do not and succumb. Indeed Julia herself had met and
would meet some lovers on movie sets.

Julia and Sutherland had agreed that if one was working the
other would not and would stay at home and play housekeeper.
However, following *Pretty Woman* Julia found herself much in
demand and that situation has remained ever since. In short, she
was and is a much bigger star than him. Although that has been
excellent for Julia's bank balance and insecurities it was not good

for her relationship with Kiefer Sutherland. She was sent numerous scripts but managed to stave off her workaholic tendencies – at least for a while. When *Sleeping with the Enemy* wrapped the couple spent a few months partying. Nightly they went dancing in clubs and nightly they were hounded by paparazzi.

The idyll ended in October 1990 when Sutherland was offered and accepted a rôle on the film *Article 99*.[1] The film was being shot in Kansas City and Julia, ever the faithful girlfriend, went with her man. However, her determination to stand by that man only lasted a short time. The short time it took to offer Julia and for her to accept a job making a new film called *Dying Young*. To be honest, Julia was also bored by life in Kansas City. The opportunity to make a film was too good to resist.

She said, 'Acting is a true love of mine but it's not *the* true love. There are times when I get so bogged down by the politics of this business that I just have these great domestic fantasies. Being at home and being quiet, and reading, and having a garden, and doing all that stuff. Taking care of a family. Those are the most important things. Movies will come and go, but family is a real kind of rich consistency.'

MENDOCINO, CALIFORNIA, NOVEMBER 1990

Julia excitedly flew to Mendocino, California, to make *Dying Young*. The film was actually set in New England but northern California was a cheaper option to film in.[2] The film's interiors were shot in San Francisco and studio Fox also built a 7,000 sq ft sound stage. Julia was signed to play Hilary O'Neil, a nurse who was hired to care for Victor Geddes, a rich and handsome leukaemia sufferer. Geddes was played by Campbell Scott, the son of George C. Scott. The C stood for Campbell.

Julia was very keen to make *Dying Young* not only because she believed in the script but also because she thought it would give her the opportunity to play a really meaty rôle.

The genesis of *Dying Young* began in 1988 when Julia's mentor Sally Field bought the rights to the novel on which the script was

---

[1] The film co-starred Ray Liotta and had overtones of *M*A*S*H* which, of course, starred Sutherland's father, Donald.

[2] *Murder She Wrote*, the crime drama starring Angela Lansbury,was also set in New England (Cabot Cove, Maine, to be precise) and filmed in Mendocino.

based. She pitched it to Twentieth Century Fox with Julia in mind to play Hilary. However, at that time Julia was unknown. *Steel Magnolias* had not been released so the studio believed a 'name' was needed to sell the film, especially one with such a grim subject matter. 'I told [Fox that] I had this girl, Julia Roberts, who would be wonderful but they wanted someone better known.'

Two years later, *Pretty Woman* was released and took $450 million at the box office. With this success Sally Field went back to the studio honchos and pitched again. 'By then we had a script, I went to Fox and said, "I repeat. There's this girl I know who would be wonderful for this part." The good thing was I didn't have to say, "You don't know her yet."'

Julia had another ally in Joe Roth, the Fox chairman, still impressed by her chutzpah in calling him and yet more impressed by the performance she turned in after he took a chance in casting her in *Sleeping with the Enemy*.

'When you have Julia's name on the marquee,' said Roth, 'you have the biggest female star in the world who can open a picture simply because she's in it.' Roth also offered Julia $3 million for the film, one million dollars more than she received for *Sleeping with the Enemy*.

In the pre-publicity Julia made a point of thanking Sally Field. Asked by a journalist if she thought there were few good rôles for women in Hollywood, Julia said, 'I haven't been affected by [that problem] as a lot of people have, but I know it exists. I also think that women are starting to develop projects and characters and scripts for themselves that give them a part that they want to play. *Dying Young* is from a book Sally Field developed for me – a great gift because it's an incredible part to play.'

As if Hollywood wasn't already queuing up to praise Julia, Fox offered her another bonus – the director they hired, on Julia's recommendation, was Joel Schumacher, her old friend from *Flatliners*.

The disappointment of another person in showbusiness was a stroke of luck for Julia. Schumacher had been hired to work on another project. 'I was going to do *Phantom of the Opera* with Andrew Lloyd Webber,' he recalls, 'then he postponed the production. A dream had ended and I needed to move on.

Emotionally, I couldn't afford to be attached to it any longer. I didn't want to get disappointed again.'

On Julia's offer to work, Schumacher commented, 'This was the first time a star had ever asked me to direct, and I don't think I would have made that particular movie if Julia hadn't asked me. I'm in love with Julia. She's a combination of many things which is why she's so fascinating on screen: sexy but ladylike, guileless yet sophisticated, fragile but strong. She's street smart rather than educated, but extremely well-read.

'Julia and I early on worked out a symbiotic emotional dance. We don't talk a lot. We discuss maybe in one sentence what the scene is. She has some preparation she does emotionally, then I have some preparation to help, some things we do that are private. There are ways we talk, not about the scene but about something from our past or current lives that is relevant to the emotional fibre of what is going on. Sometimes we don't talk at all, we just look at each other.'

Given that the subject matter was not exactly a laugh a minute, it was perhaps not that surprising that shooting was also a little depressing. During filming, which began on 12 November 1990, Julia told a reporter, 'Yesterday I shot a scene with Campbell that was very sad and I didn't anticipate it being that sad. That's the hardest part of doing things like this: you don't appreciate how much it will really happen.'

Schumacher was also unhappy with the movie. His previous work had featured casts in which the major rôles were widely spread. *Dying Young* needed just two lead characters. He said, 'I had always done ensemble movies using six or seven points of view to tell a story. Making a movie is like building a 747 while you're flying it. You invent as you go along and it is never what you think it is. I didn't realise the relationship between Julia and Campbell would lessen the need for other elements. We didn't realise on paper how strong the two of them were going to be.' In order not to weaken unnecessarily the lead rôles Schumacher had to dilute the rôles of the supporting cast. Colleen Dewhurst, at one time Campbell Scott's real-life stepmother, found her part diminished and Vincent D'Onofrio was relegated to a bit part even though in the original book he formed one third of a love triangle involving Hilary and Victor.

The love triangle may never have happened on screen but many thought that Julia and Campbell Scott might have become an item off screen. It never happened. Julia was too wrapped up in her affair with Kiefer Sutherland to fall for the undoubted charms of George's son.

He said, 'I think Julia's handling this whole [fame] thing unbelievably well. As an actress she has beautiful presence. People find her identifiable and accessible.'

But the film was not a success. Speaking two years later to the popular and anything but sycophantic *Movieline* magazine, Schumacher tried to explain the flop. 'I was blinded by my passion to be around her, and I wasn't thinking clearly. This is still a disturbing subject for me.'

When filming wrapped on 8 February 1991 Julia had made seven films in less than four years – *Satisfaction*, *Mystic Pizza*, *Steel Magnolias*, *Pretty Woman*, *Flatliners*, *Sleeping with the Enemy* and *Dying Young* – and decided to take a break. 'People have done a lot of things for me but I do things for everybody too and right now it's a lot. I think it's time for me to go away for a little while. I just want to slow down.'

Julia later remembered, 'We weren't trying to make a hit. We were trying to make a good movie, tell a good story. It was also just released at the wrong time – everyone connected to the movie will attest to that. Certainly, I don't regret making that movie. I really enjoyed making that movie. The movie that we made I was very proud of. The movie that I ultimately saw didn't move me the way the film we had made did.'

Her next project was to be a movie called *Renegades* in which she would co-star with Mel Gibson. The devoutly Catholic New York-born Australian met Julia at the offices of his agents, ICM, to discuss the film. Julia was at her most shy that day and few words were exhanged between the two. Hollywood was excited by the prospect of the film and expected a big return at the box office. Not so Mel Gibson. He withdrew citing other commitments as his reason for not making the picture. Enter Kiefer Sutherland as Gibson's replacement. It would be a great opportunity for Sutherland to work with his girlfriend. *Renegades*, a romantic Western set in the 1800s, was a love affair between a bounty hunter (to be played by Sutherland) and a Red Indian (Julia) who robs banks – 'a sagebrush Bonnie and Clyde' was how one journalist described it. Julia said that the part was 'a dream opportunity for me'. The pay packet was something of a dream too. For her work on the film she was to be paid $7 million while Sutherland would trouser $2.5 million. But Julia decided not to make the picture. 'I don't have to do anything I don't want to. Your life is as pressure-filled as you allow it to be. Sometimes I feel people try to make it more difficult, to see how absolutely taxing they can make your life.'

HOLLYWOOD, DECEMBER 1990

It was while Julia was working on *Dying Young* that her agents Risa Shapiro and Elaine Goldsmith decided to leave the William Morris Agency and head for the fresh pastures of International Creative Management. The William Morris Agency was once the natural home of Hollywood's biggest stars but by the end of the twentieth century many had left for other agencies including Creative Artists Agency (CAA), which was founded by Michael Ovitz and Ron Meyer. It seemed likely that if Julia were to leave William Morris her natural home would be CAA, especially since the agency already represented Kiefer Sutherland, Sally Field and Joel Schumacher. However, CAA had its fill of agents and although it wanted Julia, then the fastest rising female star in Hollywood, it did not want to take Goldsmith and Shapiro. Julia showed a remarkable loyalty – a quality not always in evidence in Tinseltown – by staying with Goldsmith and Shapiro and spurning CAA. When her agents joined ICM so did Julia. She said, 'I heard "Your agent is never your friend", but it's a complete and total f***ing piece of shit lie. I also heard that "All producers are scumbags", which is also untrue of the producers I've worked with. So everybody was wrong. But my brother told me something that was true, "You have to remember that this is showbusiness not show friendship."'

'William Morris is a fine company but I wasn't so much a company man as a client of Risa and Elaine. They're smart. They care about me. If they told me they were forming Elaine and Risa, Inc. I would have said OK.'

Not everyone was happy by Julia's arrival at ICM. The company also represented Kim Basinger (who was due to play the Julia role in *Sleeping with the Enemy*), Daryl Hannah (Julia's co-star in *Steel Magnolias*), Holly Hunter and Meg Ryan, and their representatives were worried that Julia would be offered all the best jobs. Elaine Goldsmith tried to allay their fears. 'Julia's arrival is great for the actresses here. I read all the scripts and she can't do everything. We expand rather than contract their possibilities.'

In 1991, a year after she sang the praises of Risa Shapiro, Julia sacked her as her agent while retaining the services of Elaine Goldsmith. Away from her business activities it was said that Goldsmith performed many personal tasks for Julia such as collecting clothes that Julia had bought,[3] overseeing her investments and dogsitting her basset hound.

---

[3] Goldsmith may have collected the clothes but Julia bought them and still had her own unique style, i.e. she dressed like a man – much to the horror of Tinseltown's fashionistas. Nolan Miller, who designed the outfits worn by Joan Collins, Linda Evans et al. on *Dynasty*, commented, 'In person she looks worse than anything on the street. She looks like she dresses from the Salvation Army. Who wants reality? I want a movie star.' Bitchy Mr Blackwell named Julia on his infamous Ten Worst Dressed List calling her style 'schlumpy'.

10. THE END OF A FINE ROMANCE

'I've known many actors, including myself, who've been tortured by having gone out with somebody they've worked with. It doesn't matter if you go out with them for two years because people will still call it a location romance. Give me a f***ing break. Who am I going to go out with? I don't work at a pet store.'

Julia Roberts on her romances and the press

WHITEFISH, MONTANA AND HOLLYWOOD, CALIFORNIA, MARCH 1991

Julia and Kiefer Sutherland were Hollywood's latest ideal couple. They seemed to spend every waking and sleeping moment together. Shirley Douglas, Sutherland's mother, has only ever given one interview on her son's romance with Julia. She said, 'They help each other not to take things too seriously. At Julia's age it's remarkable to see someone not dithering.'

Julia and Sutherland went trekking around their home in Montana with their dog, Jack, a Border collie, and Sutherland showed his lover where he grew up in Canada. It was a romantic time for the pair of them and at the time Julia said, 'I have goals, real simple things that are hard to attain. I want to have a family, raise kids, be in love – all those things come way before work.' Julia's first biographer, Aileen Joyce, disputes this. She comments, 'Despite the rhetoric, however, Julia is a woman in love with the idea, not necessarily the daily realities of being in love, whether she realises it or not.'

However, something was changing within Julia. Wherever she and Sutherland went they were followed and snapped by the paparazzi. Julia, for one, was unhappy. 'I hate being photographed,' she moaned. 'I get so nervous – my heart starts to pound and I flip out.' This is remarkable when you consider that at one time Julia considered modelling as a potential career.

Julia also loathed what she regarded as press intrusion into her private life. '[Kiefer and I are] just real[ly] happy. I've been lucky to find someone whom I not only like and is my best friend, but whom I so admire and respect and have fallen madly in love with. I've been immensely blessed in the discovery of this person.

'It's bizarre to deal with reports in the press about my romantic life. Why the f*** would anybody care?

'I've known many actors, including myself, who've been tortured by having gone out with somebody they've worked with. It doesn't matter if you go out with them for two years because people will still call it a location romance. Give me a f***ing break. Who am I going to go out with? I don't work at a pet store.'

Julia quickly became further irritated by the media's interest in her relationship with Eric. 'People seem surprised that Eric and I act so differently. Well, we're two different people. We share the same last name but that's about it. We also have a sister in between us, Lisa, who's an actor, who's at the stage now where she's looking for representation and doing plays, and she's as different as we are. Who'd want us to be the same? That would be boring.'

The situation deteriorated further and by January 1992 Julia never mentioned Eric publicly and asked that he adopt a similar moratorium where she was concerned. What was unknown except to their closest intimates was that by that time Julia and Eric were not speaking to each other at all.

Julia was with Kiefer Sutherland when she learned that she had been nominated for a second Oscar, as she had been when she learned of her first nomination. Her previous nomination had been Best Supporting Actress for *Steel Magnolias* but this time it was the big one: Best Actress for *Pretty Woman*. At the ceremony on 25 March 1991 Julia had more to do than just get nervous about whether she had won. She had been asked to introduce 'I Love to See You Smile' by Randy Newman, from the film *Parenthood*, one of the nominations for Best Song. The song didn't win. Julia was also a loser that night. Kathy Bates picked up the award for playing Annie Wilkes in William Goldman's adaptation of Stephen King's book *Misery* about a spinster who rescues her favourite author, Paul Sheldon, after he is involved in a car crash and then imprisons him. Daniel Day-Lewis, who would soon play an important part in Julia's life, presented the gong to Bates.

Julia did an interview with the doyenne of American television Barbara Walters that was broadcast the night of the Academy Awards. In the television show Julia was asked about her relationship with Kiefer Sutherland. She said that she believed that she and Sutherland would be together forever. 'Forever love. I believe in that and I believe this is it. We live together and we are happy and we are in love with each other – and isn't that what being married is? He is the love of my life. He is the person I love and admire and respect the most in the world. Kiefer is probably the most wonderful, understanding person I have ever met.'

Julia's contempt for the media was growing. 'When they completely fabricate something, it really blows your mind. I have seen years of my life summed up in five sentences, but it sounds like it all took place over the course of a wild weekend. I've read flat-out lies so hideous they made me cry. But I stopped because I wasn't going to let those people get to me.'

The media hit back at the criticism. The Hollywood Women's Press Club nominated her for a Sour Apple Award. But why was Julia falling foul of the press so often? What had happened to the hippyesque actor who wandered barefoot, chain-smoking Marlboro Lights? It seemed that all was not sweetness and light on the home front.

The press hinted that Sutherland was having difficulty coming to terms with having a more successful girlfriend. A gossip column hinted that Sutherland was not finding it that easy to get work and that of the films that he had made in the previous year – *Flatliners*, *Chicago Joe and the Showgirl* (which co-starred the lovely but troubled British actor Emily Lloyd), *Flashback* and *Young Guns II* – only *Flatliners* was a success and in that his co-star was Julia Roberts.

The *Los Angeles Times* published an article that echoed the gossip column snippet and went further, claiming that Julia was so in love with Sutherland she was determined for the relationship to work even though he was not exactly inundated with work. Further press speculation hinted that Julia insisted that her boyfriend sign a prenuptial agreement.

The couple determined to put a stop to what they claimed was unfounded and malicious gossip. On 30 April 1991 their respective publicists issued a statement that the two thespians would be married on 14 June.

Hollywood went into overdrive as celebrities and journalists queued up to fete the engaged couple. Joel Schumacher said, 'If God said, "Design the daughter you want", it would be Julia.

'Julia's an original, in a category all to herself which probably explains how she's captured everyone's attention so quickly. She's a brilliant actor – her presence lights up a room, yet there are these delicious contradictions. She's not really a sex symbol, but she's very sexy. She's got great comic timing but she can also make you cry. She seems very wise for her age sometimes, yet she's totally guileless, unpretentious.'

Of her fiancé Schumacher commented, 'He left home when he was fifteen and so did I. What happens is that you either grow up very fast or you don't. And so Kiefer is very, very, very overly mature and responsible for his age. He had no time to be a kid. He left home very young, had a child very young and got divorced very young. If there's such a thing as an old soul, he has one.'

1 VIRGINIA STREET, WAPPING, EAST LONDON E1; SOUTHEAST COAST AVENUE, LANTANA, FLORIDA 33464-0002, AND HOLLYWOOD, MAY–JUNE 1991

America does not have a 'tabloid press' in the same way that Britain does. Their newspapers – broadsheet or tabloid – are deadly earnest and often, it has to be said, deadly dull. This is in no small part due to the vastness of the country and that so many newspapers are full of local news. A recent trip by this author to a major American city saw him buy a huge newspaper and in the reams of newsprint find just one article of interest – a book review, although sadly not for one of his books.

What America does have is the so-called 'supermarket tabloids' although they are sold in newsagents as well. Among this stable are *Star*, *Weekly World News*, *Globe* and the most famous of the lot *National Enquirer*, which is based in Lantana, Florida, a swampy town eighty miles north of Miami between the Everglades and Palm Beach. Lantana is an evergreen shrub.

As we have seen, American newspapers are earnest and so the supermarket tabloids originally attracted a different kind of journalist – hard-drinking former Fleet Street hacks and no doubt equally hard-drinking Australians, the former keen to escape the grey London skies and the latter after the money and the experience.

The *National Enquirer* at its most notorious was the brainchild of Generoso Pope Jr, whose godfather was Frank Costello, a real-life mafioso godfather. Costello bought the *Enquirer*, then a Long Island local paper, for $75,000 from Randolph Hearst and handed it to his godson. Gene Pope moved the offices of the *Enquirer* to upstate New York and then to Lantana in Florida. In the early 1970s the *Enquirer* decided to hire new recruits from the former motherland because most American journalists were and are unable to write 'tabloidese'. There were also rumours that under Gene Pope the *Enquirer* was a money-laundering organisation. Since Pope's death the company has come under new management and there is no suggestion that they operate anything other than a fully honest business.

In May 1991 the *Sun*, Britain's biggest-selling tabloid and a cash cow for its owner Rupert Murdoch, published a kiss'n'tell story alleging that while Julia was away Kiefer Sutherland went out to play. Specifically to play with a long-haired stripper called Amanda Rice who performed under the stage name Raven. Rice claimed that she and the actor had been an item since January. On 14 May the *National Enquirer* went into bat with the story and featured photographs of the actor and the stripper at Disneyland and contained details of Sutherland's alleged gripes over Julia. Rice reported that Sutherland had supposedly said that Julia was too thin and her skin was too pale. Julia was also apparently unhappy with her body and sexually she was 'a cold fish' and it was like having sex with 'a corpse'. The stripper also said that after *Pretty Woman* Julia had metamorphosed into an 'ice princess'.

The *Daily Express* then ran a story reporting that Donald Sutherland was furious at his son's behaviour and said that 'if Kiefer doesn't sort his love life out, Julia will probably walk out on him and he will lose the best girl he's ever had.'

Sutherland's publicist, Annett Wolf, who would marry the *Knots Landing* actor Ted Shackelford and who also represents Richard Chamberlain, issued a statement admitting that he did know Amanda Rice but denying that theirs was anything other than a platonic friendship.

As with all kiss'n'tells, details become hazy and what is a seemingly indisputable fact to one is argued over by the other. Only two people know what really happened if anything.

On 22 January 1991 Sutherland moved out of the home he shared with Julia and moved into the $105-a-week St Francis

Hotel on Western Avenue and Hollywood Boulevard, a less than salubrious area populated by prostitutes, pimps and drug addicts. He stayed there supposedly to research a rôle in a film, *In From the Cold*, a film that would never be made. Across the road from the hotel was a pool hall – the Hollywood Billiards Parlour which, established in 1928, was the oldest in Los Angeles.

In the hallowed halls of the pool club was where Sutherland met the curvaceous Amanda Rice. She told the actor that she was a dancer at Crazy Girls, a club on La Brea Avenue in Hollywood, and insisted that he should visit the 'joint' to see her. Sutherland took her up on her invite and did indeed go to the strip club on two or three occasions. The assistant manager of the club, Marwan Khalaf, remembers, 'He always came in just before closing, and I saw them leave together.' Sutherland also took her out for breakfast at an all-night diner on Sunset Strip, played pool with her and several friends and took her, her young son and his daughter to Disneyland. Another stripper from the club claimed that she double-dated with Sutherland and Rice. Interestingly, Rice never visited or rang him at the St Francis. In the time he was there – a fortnight – Sutherland received just two calls: one from Julia and the other from Michelle Pfeiffer who never got through and left a cryptic message: 'Remember, there's always a rainbow after the storm.' However, Sutherland may have rung Rice from the hotel. We know that she neither visited him nor rang him because the St Francis requires every visitor to sign in and the switchboard takes all calls. Outgoing calls are made from lobby payphones since none of the rooms are equipped with telephones.

On 5 February Sutherland checked out of the St Francis and returned to the home he shared with Julia. His lover, Julia that is, came back home on 8 February and soon after the couple visited Sutherland's 300-acre ranch in Whitefish, Montana, a town in the northwest corner of the state and populated by about 5,000 people. It was at Whitefish that Julia learned that she had received an Oscar nomination for *Pretty Woman*. If the couple had been having problems, the issues were resolved by the time she returned from Mendocino or she and Sutherland would not have gone to Montana.

On 13 May Julia began work on *Hook*, a film that would not be a happy experience for her. The *National Enquirer* story broke the next day and, two days later, using a fake name, Julia entered the Cedars-Sinai Medical Centre suffering from 'a severe viral infection, headaches and a high fever'. The Hollywood rumour mill went into overdrive. Some said that it was Sutherland's behaviour that had caused the breakdown in Julia's health. Others alleged that she had a heroin habit and she was going cold turkey at the medical centre. Julia finally put the record straight. 'I was exhausted. I had a fever, a bad fever. That was the worst symptom. It was like 104 [degrees]. That's why I was in the hospital so long. People should be allowed to be sick without enduring takes that they've got a needle stuck in their arm. I had the flu. I was sick. F*** off!'

The rumours of drug abuse began because Julia, preternaturally slim, looked more emaciated than usual. 'I don't nor have I ever done drugs. I'm just naturally thin. I guess it's boring in Hollywood to be a young actor and not have a drug problem. Well then I'm boring, but that's OK because I've got clear skin and clean arms.'

As if the reporting of her boyfriend's supposed infidelity wasn't bad enough word leaked out from the set of *Hook* that all was not well. The dailies had been poor and Julia's performance under par. Tinkerbell was wan, drawn and unhappy. It was a film in which Julia would be nick-named Tinkerhell by the crew.

Julia stayed in hospital for five days and Sutherland was by her side the whole time. He helped her when she was discharged on 21 May. The legendary Hollywood reporter Army Archerd said in *Daily Variety* that the couple were out on the town at The Moonlight Tango Club celebrating their engagement and Julia had led the conga. The couple then retired to The Great Greek Café where they also danced up a storm into the early hours of the morning. Julia was back at work the following Monday.

On 2 June Elaine Goldsmith threw that most American of traditions, a wedding shower for her client. The party at which the future bride is 'showered' with gifts was given at Goldsmith's Marina del Rey home. The attendees included Julia's mother and 25 other guests who gave the bride saucy lingerie.

By this time in early June the cake had been ordered – a four-tiered effort, twenty inches across with white icing and pale green ribbons also made of icing sugar and, replacing the traditional bride and groom, were violet icing flowers. The wedding dress had been bought at a cost of $2,500 from Tyler-Trafficante on Melrose Avenue. The bridesmaids' footwear had been ordered – four pairs of $260 Manolo Blahnik pumps made from white satin that had been dyed green to match their dresses.

The food was ordered, the flowers – roses, Julia's favourite – were readied to be picked, the cutlery and crockery was in place and the ice sculptures were commissioned.

The happy couple's intention was to marry in their own home surrounded only by a chosen few family and friends. But when Joe Roth, the head of Fox, heard about this plan he immediately announced that he would pay for the nuptials. Soundstage 14 on the Fox lot would be transformed into a verdant paradise like the antebellum home in *Steel Magnolias*. Guests would be served by 150 specially trained waiters and the studio spent $100,000 on security guards to ensure that no paparazzi would be able to gate-crash the event. Guests would include Emilio Estevez, Sally Field, Michael J. Fox, Richard Gere, Daryl Hannah, Shirley Maclaine, Garry Marshall, Demi Moore, Dolly Parton, Lou Diamond Phillips, Joel Schumacher, Charlie Sheen and Bruce Willis. The whole wedding was to cost Twentieth Century Fox in the region of $500,000.

On 5 June Sutherland flew from his ranch in Whitefish, Montana, back to their home in Los Angeles. The couple intended to spend at least part of their honeymoon there so Sutherland was making it suitably romantic. Two days later, 7 June 1991, Julia and some female friends supposedly went on her hen weekend to the exclusive and expensive Canyon Ranch Spa in Tucson, Arizona. The women returned to Los Angeles on 10 June and Julia had a short telephone conversation with her fiancé. However, that night she did not return to their home. Julia and her mother stayed at the Marina del Rey home of the faithful factotum Elaine Goldsmith.

Early the next morning Sutherland received a telephone call from Goldsmith telling him that the wedding was off. She then rang Pat Kingsley of PMK, one of the most powerful publicists in

Hollywood, and had her announce to the media that the wedding was cancelled. It was 11 June 1991, twenty years to the very day that Julia's parents had separated. The story of the non-wedding made front page headlines the world over. The question on everyone's lips was 'Why?'

The rumours ran the gamut of every possible Hollywood excess. It was caused by Sutherland's refusal to sign a prenuptial agreement. It was caused by Sutherland's out-of-control drinking. It was caused by Sutherland's affair with Amanda Rice. It was caused by Sutherland's jealousy over the disparity in their careers. Lest the reader think that all the rumours were about Sutherland, *Newsweek* magazine, a normally reputable publication, ran the completely unfounded rumour that Julia had a secret lesbian lover. Another title claimed that the wedding was not really off at all and it was a cover story to put off the press and avoid a media circus such as the one that had accompanied Madonna's wedding to the volatile actor Sean Penn.

Most of these can be discounted immediately. Sutherland liked a drink like many young men the world over and had neither increased nor decreased his intake in the time he and Julia were together. Further, Sutherland's father was one of the most famous actors in the world and was well aware of the vagaries of Hollywood in which one moment a career is on track and is then derailed but is soon back on track. Julia and Sutherland had been together for long enough to discuss money so that a last minute refusal to sign a prenuptial agreement seems unlikely. Publicists for both actors denied that there had ever been such a document – the only fact that they all agreed on.

A friend of Sutherland went into bat for him. 'Kiefer supported Julia in everything. He's been the best thing that ever happened to Julia. He took a year off so they could focus on one of their careers. I know of at least two movies out now that he turned down. He's the reason she agreed to do *Hook*. Julia's decision to call off the wedding had nothing to do with their careers or money.'

Another friend agreed: 'The problem was not money or other women. The problem was Julia. Every time she gets close, she just shies away.'

On 19 June 1991 Amanda Rice spoke out and denied telling the *National Enquirer* that Sutherland had been unflattering about Julia and her body image. She also denied having a sexual relationship with Sutherland. 'Kiefer is a friend. We have not had an affair. Everything that has appeared about us in print has been manufactured and blown out of proportion.'

On 22 November, Julia gave an interview to *Entertainment Weekly* in which she made it crystal clear that she did not believe Amanda Rice's denials. 'I mean, this had been going on for a really long time. So then I had to say, "Well, I have made an enormous mistake in agreeing to get married. Then I made an even greater mistake by letting it all get so big. I'm not going to make the final mistake of actually getting married." At that point I just realised that this had all turned into an enormous joke, and that it wasn't going to be respectable, it wasn't going to be honest, it wasn't going to be simple. And it could have been all those things.' Further, the information about Julia's poor body image was too accurate for the magazine to have made up. 'Only my wardrobe people know how sick and paranoid I am about this,' said Julia. 'With them I go bananas: "I'm not going to wear that! Let's get one thing straight. These are the body parts I have a problem with. These are the ones we will hide, we will conceal, we will make look better. This is your job. This is your task."'

Finally Amanda Rice spoke out again. 'Yes, we had a relationship. I don't know that what Kiefer and I had would be categorised as an affair. Julia gave him a ring but as far as he was concerned they were not engaged. He said that being with her during the last six months was hell. I believe that Julia wasn't as upset about my relationship with Kiefer as she was about the criticisms he had levelled about her to me. For instance, he told me that she was too skinny, and too pale, that she was unresponsive and self-conscious when they made love. That's hard for a guy to put up with.'

It was Julia's 'people' who rang all the guests to tell them that the wedding was off and cancelled all the arrangements. Sutherland's publicist, Annett Wolf, also sprang into action giving her client's side of the story, such as it was.

Sutherland spent the rest of that day trying to contact his ex-fiancé but she refused to take his calls. A friend of the actor's said, 'He was despondent. When someone you spent three years of your life with, someone who goes on every talk show and tells the world how much she loves you does something like this, how could you not be upset?'

The press reports of the time had Julia sobbing her heart out but, in fact, Julia was not unhappy. Her mother remembers, 'I took Julia to her agent's house where we thought we'd be safe. But [when] we looked out of the window in the morning we could not believe it. There must have been 150 photographers ringing the house. They were flying over in helicopters. I went out there and said, "C'mon you guys! All she did was break off the engagement. People are starving in the world, y'know. Go home."

'These people from the *National Enquirer* would call the house and lie about where they were from. One even said it was the London *Times* calling. But we checked and there was no such person there. Once they said [they were from] the US News Agency but there is no such thing. Anytime you get a British accent from a Florida area code it's a tabloid.'

Her mother fended off press inquiries. 'Julia's been working very hard. She's been under a tremendous amount of pressure and stress. I think she feels she should allow a little more time before making such an important decision as marriage.

'Julia did not ask my advice about Sutherland and I wouldn't have had the vaguest idea of what to tell her if she had. Julia knows that I respect her decisions – that's why we're so close. She's handled this whole thing with maturity. She's ignored the press.'

On the morning of Wednesday 12 June the 'wedding set' on Soundstage 14 was dismantled. The next day Julia posed for publicity pictures for her latest film, *Hook*. She was, according to an assistant who was there, in fine fettle. Posing alongside director Steven Spielberg, Julia wore a baseball cap bearing the legend 'Notre Dame'. It was later learned that the Irish Catholic actor Jason Patric was a huge fan of American football and his favourite team was . . . Notre Dame. After the pictures were taken Julia drove to Jason Patric's home on Stanley Street in West Hollywood where she stayed the night. The next day – which should have been her wedding day – she was seen eating turkey burgers with

Patric at the Nowhere Café on Melrose Avenue. Kiefer Sutherland spent his 'wedding' day moving his belongings out of the Hollywood Hills home he had shared with his now ex-fiancée. That night he spent playing pool at the Hollywood Billiards Parlour.

On Saturday 15 June Julia and Patric flew to London and then caught an Aer Lingus flight to Ireland where they booked into separate $250-a-night rooms at the Shelbourne Hotel in Dublin and then went to Eddie Rocket's Diner for burgers.

The waitress who served them was Siobhain Burgess, now 34 but then just 22. She remembers, 'They sat chatting away for over an hour. She said she was over here on a break. I asked her about Kiefer and said I was sorry. Julia said, "I don't want to talk about him at the moment. I am over here for a break from all that." '

The next morning they left at 4.45 a.m. and reportedly stayed at the home of Adam Clayton, the bass player of the rock group U2, in Galway. Back in America Sutherland spent the day – Father's Day – with his ex-wife and their daughter.

The media had a new interest. Who was Jason Patric and how had he captured the heart of Hollywood's pretty woman? He was born on 17 June 1966 in Queens, New York, the son of Pulitzer Prize-winning playwright-actor Jason Miller and grandson of Jackie Gleason. Miller persuaded his son to use his middle name as his acting surname. An intensely private, some might say reclusive, man, Patric rarely gives interviews and dislikes talking about himself.

He lives in genteel poverty even though he is wealthy. His apartment at the time had sheets rather than curtains at the windows. The furniture was nondescript. The actor Jami Gertz said, 'He doesn't live in a palatial place. There's an old, used couch. I go in there and I'm disgusted.' To add to the air of decadence Julia gave her new boyfriend a present, a pot-bellied pig called Ferguson. She told neighbours not to be alarmed if they heard screaming. It would be her giving Ferguson a bath.

Patric once stayed unemployed – by choice – for eighteen months because he could not find any worthy projects. The media began to stake out his West Hollywood home and trained telephoto lenses on his windows. The braver hacks knocked on his front door hoping either he or Julia would answer.

In the year before he began dating Julia, Patric gave a rare interview in which he told the journalist, 'I don't want to be photographed, I don't want to be a celebrity.' His relationship with Julia made this statement the antithesis of reality.

In July 1992 he was caught on camera by a television crew. In the scuffle Patric was bitten on the arm by the cameraman as he tried to wrest the camera from her. The police were summoned but Patric refused to press charges against the woman.

In their time together Julia began dressing like Jason Patric. Like many women, including Jane Fonda, Julia adopts the persona of whomever she is involved with. With Kiefer Sutherland she wore Armani but with Jason Patric she often looked as if her wardrobe came from Oxfam or War on Want. Sutherland liked a drink whereas Patric was fascinated by organic health foods. Sutherland was a party animal, Patric preferred more cerebral pursuits. During their time together Julia tried to give up smoking and capuccino and began working out early in the morning alongside Patric and his personal trainer. Both eschewed socks and Julia often went barefoot even when driving her Porsche Targa.

Jason Miller said of his son, 'He's a very solid guy. I've seen him with two girls he loved and he's like a knight errant from medieval times. He believes in chivalry.'

And at this time in her life a knight in shining armour on a trusty charger was just what she needed . . .

11. HOOKED INTO TINKER-HELL

*'She's very young. She's incredibly shy and not confident meeting strangers.
She doesn't have the wit or the confidence to parry with a Dustin Hoffman
or a Robin Williams, so instead of even trying to get involved with the cast
and crew, Julia retreated to her trailer, staying pretty much on her own.'*

Studio spokesman explaining Julia's
seemingly offhand behaviour on *Hook*

HOLLYWOOD, CALIFORNIA, 1990–91

On most of her films Julia has enjoyed a great rapport with both
the crew and her fellow cast members. Not one to throw tantrums,
she is happy to muck in and joke with the grips or play cards with
the best boy or laugh with the lighting rigger. Things were very
different on *Hook*, Steven Spielberg's version of Sir J.M. Barrie's
classic *Peter Pan*. Dustin Hoffman played Captain James S. Hook
while Robin Williams was the grown-up Peter Pan, called Peter
Banning,[1] and Julia played Tinkerbell.[2]

Like many children's stories, *Peter Pan* is not a wholly innocent
tale. Barrie was a strange man who never grew above five feet tall,
didn't shave until he was 24 and never consummated his
marriage. He virtually adopted the sons of Sylvia and Arthur
Llewelyn-Davies and wrote the story for them. Authors have tried
to analyse Barrie and are split between describing him as asexual
and a pædophile. Originally written as a play, *Peter Pan* was first
performed on 27 December 1904 at the Duke of York's Theatre
and Captain Hook was played by Sir Gerald du Maurier, the father
of the novelist Daphne du Maurier. His portrayal was so fearsome
that many children had to be carried out of the auditorium after
fainting. Barrie continued to work on *Peter Pan* and he turned the
play into a novel and a screenplay. In the original version Peter is

---

[1] In April 2003 the respected magazine *Vanity Fair* published an article by Maureen Orth that
claimed that bewigged pop star Michael Jackson paid $100,000 to a witch doctor to put a spell
on his enemies who included David Geffen and Steven Spielberg, who was to be 'punished' for
not casting the increasingly mad Jackson as Peter Pan in *Hook*.

[2] Possibly one of the most unusual jobs that anyone could put on their CV was one held by a crew
member on *Hook*. His job at a salary of £2,000 was to wash Julia's feet and keep them clean for
the duration of filming. It was thought that under no circumstances should Tinkerbell have dirty
feet.

a Londoner who escapes from the real world and travels to Never Never Land where he meets fairies and other children who have been forgotten by their parents or misplaced by their nannies. All the boys live together in a tree house, sleep in the same bed and, with the Picanniny Indians, fight Captain Hook and his band of pirates. On his travels to London, Peter befriends Wendy Darling and her two younger brothers and persuades her to go with him to Never Never Land where he wants her to become his mother. Captain Hook has the same idea and kidnaps Wendy. Peter rescues her and Hook jumps into the sea where a crocodile bites off his hand. As Wendy grows up she returns to London unable to communicate with Peter and the 'Lost Boys' but Peter stays forever locked into this fantasy land. In later versions Peter kills fourteen pirates and chops off Hook's hand and feeds it to a crocodile.

In the early 1980s following a conversation with his young son, screenwriter James V. Hart created the story of the grown-up Peter Pan. In his version Peter is Peter Banning, a mogul too concerned with his business life to notice his family life. Wendy is a nonagenarian philanthropist looking after one of the Lost Boys. When Banning visits London for a banquet to honour Wendy's philanthropism, Hook kidnaps Banning's son and daughter because he wants a final confrontation with his 'child-hood' nemesis. With the help of Tinkerbell, Banning 'relearns' his childhood imagination and rescues his children in the nick of time.

Hart sold his script to the director Nick Castle who showed it to the producers Craig Baumgarten and Gary Adelson. When Steven Spielberg showed an interest in the project Nick Castle was dispatched and the script fell into the hands of Sony and CAA. Dustin Hoffman caught wind of the script and expressed a desire to be involved if the part of Captain Hook was beefed up. When Spielberg learned that Nick Castle had been dismissed because of his (Spielberg's) involvement, he claimed to be 'horrified'. In the kind of machinations for which Hollywood is renowned the rights were then bought by TriStar. These included the rights owned by Barrie's legatee, the Great Ormond Street Hospital for Sick Children and its nominated producer, the playboy Dodi Fayed. In the final version of the film *Hook* Baumgarten, Adelson, Fayed and James Hart all share 'Executive Producers' credits.

The budget was set at $40 million and Great Ormond Street received £300,000 plus net profit points. Since few films ever officially make a profit – and *Hook* was certainly in that camp – the hospital didn't receive any more money.

The film was made over nine soundstages at Culver City including Stage 27. Spielberg was particularly pleased by this because Stage 27 was where the Emerald City scenes of *The Wizard of Oz* had been filmed. The producers hired 150 extras to play pirates but the additional cast members were not recognised actors but locals who were kept very separate from the expensive talent when they were not needed. Some famous names including Glenn Close (in a beard), Phil Collins and Quincy Jones made uncredited cameo appearances. Carrie Fisher wrote Tinkerbell's dialogue. Spielberg also refused to let Robin Williams ad-lib, a mistake the director readily admits. 'I should have released Robin and let him go in all directions. I contained Robin.'

The budget rose to $75 million and Julia's contract ran out so Sony arranged to pay her $75,000 a day and left it to the insurance companies to work out who actually paid her salary.

The crew did not for the most part take to Julia, nor she to them. For someone who temporarily 'adopts' film crews it must have been terribly upsetting for Julia that she was unable to bond with them. Some crew members said that Julia was 'hell to work with' and often burst into tears for no apparent reason.

A studio spokesman attempted to diffuse the tension by saying of Julia, 'She's very young. She's incredibly shy and not confident meeting strangers. She doesn't have the wit or the confidence to parry with a Dustin Hoffman or a Robin Williams, so instead of even trying to get involved with the cast and crew, Julia retreated to her trailer, staying pretty much on her own.'

Julia originally agreed to make *Hook* in the autumn of 1990. She was eager to work with Steven Spielberg. However, not long after she began production on *Dying Young*, she had second thoughts and had Elaine Goldsmith inform Spielberg of her change of heart. The film was due to begin shooting in January 1991 and Julia believed that she was not physically up to the challenge of making another film so soon after she finished one movie. '[I thought it was] better to pull out than go in half-hearted and let everyone down.'

In late December of 1990 Julia changed her mind and had Elaine Goldsmith ring Spielberg, his agent, Mike Ovitz, who headed CAA, and producer Kathleen Kennedy. So what made Julia alter her decision not to be involved in the film?

Money.

According to some sources Julia was paid $7 million for her work on the film – more than all her previous films added together – and earned every cent. (One of Spielberg's biographers, however, lists the figure at $2.5 million.) She also probably realised that she had made a huge mistake. She spent much of her working day wearing a contraption she described as 'industrial bicycle shorts' to which was attached the wires that allowed her to 'fly'. Julia also claimed that the 'flying' made her dizzy and that Steven Spielberg wanted to fire her. USA Today reported, 'Don't be surprised if Julia Roberts is dropped from Steven Spielberg's in-the-works movie Hook.' The newspaper added that Julia would be replaced by Meg Ryan or possibly Annette Bening and if not her then Michelle Pfeiffer. It was only a matter of time. The film's on-set publicist denied the story as did Julia's personal PR flack Pat Kingsley: 'It seems too silly. I keep hearing about Meg and Michelle – and Julia keeps going to work.'

It was time for action and Spielberg took it in an attempt to diffuse the situation. He rang the veteran gossip columnist Liz Smith and told her, 'Julia is not acting up and is performing well. Julia was my first and only choice for this rôle from the moment the movie began production eleven months ago. She has remained my only choice. No other actress has ever been in the running, and no other actress will replace her. Julia is doing a great job. She's been hard at work, very professional – no problems whatsoever . . . [but] when stories about Julia's so-called misbehaviour or her replacement in my film begin to appear in what I consider legitimate print and TV news venues, I think it's time to speak up.' Still the rumours continued and many of the media either ignored Spielberg's denials or disbelieved them. Finally, Spielberg took Julia to the gates of the studio and staged a press conference there and then.

He told the assembled press, obliquely referring to her non-marriage and the untrue rumours of a drug problem, 'Julia was going through hell at the time for reasons I won't go into. The last thing she needed was to read in the papers that I was going to fire her. I called a couple of reporters and told them the truth but the stories kept appearing in print. Coming here says in effect, "See, we love each other." '

In fact, Spielberg was being economic with the *actualité*. Although he was never going to sack Julia, neither did he feel much affection for her. One day on the set Julia became fed up of waiting for a scene to begin and testily said, 'I'm ready now.' Spielberg looked at her and merely said 'We're ready when I say we're ready, Julia.'

Of her time on the film, Julia remembers, 'Robin and I worked together sometimes and I met Bob Hoskins once. I was also off camera one time for Dustin Hoffman. But I spent 90 per cent of the time on a stage by myself with no other actors anywhere to be seen. It was me, Steven, and the crew, because most of the time I was on the blue screen.'

The reports of disquiet began almost as soon as filming commenced on 19 February 1991, continuing until 8 August 1991. During this time Julia was supposedly planning her marriage to Kiefer Sutherland and many cast and crew members put her behaviour down to pre-wedding nerves. A friend said at the time, 'Her insecurities are at an all-time high right now. She's just overwhelmed by everything in her life. Julia's at her wits' end. She's a wreck and she's taking it out on the cast and crew. No one will be happier when the wedding is over than the people she is working with.'

A crew member added, 'Dustin and Julia are probably both getting the star treatment but maybe . . . she felt that she needed a little more attention than she was actually getting.'

The late Herbert Ross, her director on *Steel Magnolias*, couldn't resist putting his oar into the water. 'Julia is timid, frightened and inexperienced, but a talented young actress. Her sudden tirades and infrequent overbearing actions could be the result of over-work. She's had a lot to deal with this year.'

Julia herself said, 'I'm a normal person. If I sit in my trailer for six hours doing nothing, I'm going to say, "What the f*** is going on?" I don't think that's an outrageous question. I don't think that's temperamental either. I don't think I'd do a search and destroy for other parts like this, to be hanging on a wire.'

As we have seen, Julia failed to connect with the crew, the people she most relies on when making a film. Her sense of isolation was exacerbated by this seeming breakdown in 'normal' relations. If she had established a rapport with them, then she might not have found *Hook* to be such a demanding and unsatisfying job. If she had managed to befriend Steven Spielberg, she might have enjoyed the film. But she couldn't and she didn't. Spielberg was either not willing or not able to indulge Julia in the way that Garry Marshall or Joel Schumacher had.

On 11 December 1991 the main cast traipsed up to Century Plaza Hotel to face the press on a promotional junket for *Hook*. Julia was asked about her preparations for playing Tinkerbell. 'I don't know. She's just this sort of thing that happens. And who wants to know anyway how Tinkerbell came about? It's like knowing a magic trick. If people enjoy it, it doesn't matter how hard it was or how easy or anything.'

For twenty minutes Julia, Robin Williams, Steven Spielberg and Dustin Hoffman answered the press's questions varying between patience (Spielberg), humour (Williams), philosophising (Hoffman) and barely controlled boredom and irritation (Julia). Then came the question Julia had been dreading: was she on drugs? 'It's just absurd. It's ridiculous. I guess people are really bored with themselves.'

The press was not finished with her yet and asked how she coped with negative publicity. 'I don't concern myself with it. I don't follow it. When it follows me around, that's when I sort of react to it. I just wish the public at large would concern themselves with their own lives, with their own personal business and affairs. And then probably divorce rates would be lower, there wouldn't be so many fractured families and troubled people, and things would be a lot easier for everybody.'

When she was asked by a journalist if she was happy to be at the press conference, she replied, 'I've learned the hard way to be more frugal with words around people like you which is not necessarily a bad thing to learn. You just sort of figure things out as you go along, I guess. I've made plenty of mistakes and everyone's made sure that I've known about them.'

Later that month following *Hook*'s release on the 11th, the day of the press conference (the film took just $14 million from 2,197 cinemas across America on its opening weekend), Steven Spielberg appeared on the prestigious and long-running news magazine *60 Minutes*. He was asked by reporter Ed Bradley if he would ever work with Julia again. After what seemed an interminable pause, Spielberg finally said, 'No.' Watching at home Julia was horrified by Spielberg's comment. She later told *Premiere* magazine that she was 'on the verge of tears' when she heard Spielberg's words. 'People disappoint me. It's too bad. Steven and I had an enjoyable time. The last day on the set, a friend shot a video of my last day filming on *Hook* for me as a wrap present and it was very funny. I was up on a picnic table with these gigantic mushrooms doing my thing and Steven and everybody were way down below and he kept going up and talking into the video camera and going, "You are just the greatest Tinkerbell . . . I love you. And you were fabulous. You dealt with all the crazy technical blue-screen isolation", blah, blah, blah. It was so nice. I didn't leave *Hook* on bad terms with Steven. We hugged and kissed and did the whole goodbye thing in what I felt was a genuine way. It was so nice.

'Then to turn on my television unknowingly and watch him on *60 Minutes* . . . that's surprising. He obviously missed some aspect of me as a person.

'Is this the same man I had whipped cream fights with on the set? Is this the same man who said that he couldn't wait every day to get to our stage because it was more fun than the big stage and more relaxed and easier and, even though it took nine hours to set up a shot, that I got it done so fast and I kept everything moving and was always good-humoured and didn't complain? I guess sometimes it's too tempting to be in the majority. To have him even say that it was difficult for me to be going through a personal experience like that while making a movie – well, yeah, it is. But did I do it with as much ease as anyone could ever do it? Yeah. Do I feel like I inconvenienced him with my personal life in any way, shape or form on the set? No.

'You can only find disappointment in an expectant mind, and I don't really expect anything from Steven.'

Julia was tired with her life, hurt at what she saw as Spielberg's betrayal, confused that she had been unable to reach out to the crew and depressed at her non-wedding. She turned to Jason Patric but the actor was not able to provide a complete support system.

A family friend did not help matters by telling one reporter at the time, 'Julia is all f***ed up. She doesn't know what's what. She's still not normal. Every time she thinks she's finally OK, someone will ask for her autograph and she can feel herself ready to burst into tears. It's a good thing she got $7 million for *Hook* because with the way she is feeling it may be her last film.'

To add to her woes *Dying Young* was released on 21 June 1991 and received poor reviews from virtually every film critic. Martin Grove of the *Hollywood Reporter* opined, 'They said Julia Roberts could open any film. They said she could open a phone book. *Dying Young* proved they were wrong.'

Time magazine said, 'Perhaps what *Dying Young* really proved is that you don't call a picture *Dying Young*. Roberts's rapid ascendancy taught Hollywood that she could sell innocence, glamour, pluck. But not even the movies' most reliable female star since Doris Day could peddle leukæmia – particularly not to a summertime audience that wants only the bad guys to die. So *Dying Young* did just that, and Roberts's pristine rep got terminated too.'

It was time for Julia Roberts to take a break from film-making. Time for her to get her life back on track. She couldn't do that while in the public eye. As a temporary parting shot, she told a reporter from the *Los Angeles Times*, 'They say I've had it easy but "easy" based on whose account? True, I haven't slept in the park. I haven't struggled to the bone. But this is my journey, so who's to criticise or judge? Making movies, to me, is the best thing in the world. But at the risk of sounding ungrateful, it's very, very hard.'

12. JULIA ROBERTS: THE WILDERNESS YEARS

'In Hollywood it is not unusual for a star or a director to say, "I'm not working for the next year or until the spring." No one thinks that's strange. But with Julia Roberts, it was odd because about every three months I'd get a call from Elaine, asking if I had any projects for Julia. I'd send out the scripts and Julia would reject them all. Then, like clockwork, Elaine would call and the cycle would start again. This was strange, even by Hollywood standards.'

Hollywood producer on Julia's working practices
during her 'sabbatical'

'I have not learned unfortunately, in my 25 years, how to create the balance of my work and of my personal life. I have at times lent to that imbalance and I have at times not dealt with that imbalance well. But the greater aspect of it is people's inability to accept that one is private and one is public . . . I can make jokes or whatever, but I don't have to make jokes and I don't have to deal with crap because regardless of how many things have been written about me in the last two years I haven't said anything.'

Julia's view on her 'sabbatical'

HOLLYWOOD, CALIFORNIA, 1991–93

1992 was the first year since Julia's career began in earnest that she did not work. She did an unenjoyable promotional tour for *Hook*, a film she intensely disliked but not as much as the critics, and then went into virtual seclusion. She would remain out of public view for almost two years.

In December 1991 she accompanied Jason Patric to the première of his film *Rush*. Later that month the couple holidayed in Stowe, Vermont, where they spent Christmas in their rented home and also visited local attractions such as the Ben and Jerry Ice Cream factory in Waterbury. The following month Julia went back to Smyrna where she visited her high school where her half-sister Nancy was studying. She also stopped for a chat with David Boyd, who had been one of her favourite teachers. Boyd later said that Julia was in a good mood and seemed happy to be back in familiar surroundings. In May 1992 she was once again back in Smyrna and went to a local bar, Miss Kitty's, to watch one of her favourite bands. Julia was dressed all in black and sat upstairs in the middle of the balcony overlooking the stage. However, on this occasion she seemed a little disjointed and when she was approached by the public for an autograph and a chat she and her party left the club. It was her third visit to Smyrna in six months. Oddly, in 1990 she had told the *Atlanta Constitution* that she had 'no great desire to return to Smyrna'.

In June 1992 Julia and Jason Patric celebrated his 26th birthday with a five-day cruise to Cabo San Lucas in Baja, California. The trip confounded the rumours that were gaining popularity in Hollywood that the couple had split up. In the following month Julia went house-hunting in California. In August 1992 she went on holiday to Hawaii with Elaine Goldsmith and Susan Sarandon. Not long after her return the trade press announced that Julia would be starring opposite Denzel Washington in the film version of John Grisham's novel *The Pelican Brief*. The film would begin shooting in May 1993. In September she attended the christening of Miles Guthrie Robbins, the son of Susan Sarandon and Tim Robbins. On her left shoulder Julia sported a bandage where she had had laser treatment to remove the tattoo proclaiming her love for Kiefer Sutherland. She was not accompanied by Jason Patric, which once again gave rise to rumours that the relationship was in its final throes. Later she attended – alone – the première in Beverly Hills of Tim Robbins's film *Bob Roberts*. Then just when Hollywood had convinced itself that Julia and Patric had split up the pair were seen at an American football game between Notre Dame and Michigan in South Bend, Indiana. On 22 September 1992 Julia and Jason Patric attended the taping of the MTV Unplugged concert starring Bruce Springsteen. At the after-show party Julia became engrossed talking to Bon Jovi guitarist Richie Sambora who was then in the midst of a passionate affair with Oscar-winning actress and singer Cher. Patric decided he had had enough of the night and wanted to leave. When he failed to attract Julia's attention he began to throw pieces of liquorice at her. After Julia ignored him he stood up and walked over to her and took her hand and began to pull her away. Julia took her hand back and told him crossly, 'You don't own me.' Sheepishly, Patric stood and waited while Julia and Sambora finished their conversation. The following night the couple attended 'The Boss's' concert at the Los Angeles Forum although Patric returned alone for the next three performances. Apart from those rare public appearances Julia was keeping a very low profile.

To disappear in Hollywood is an unusual move and the gossip began with the word that Julia was on drugs – heroin to be precise. Julia gave an interview to *Entertainment Weekly* in November 1992 in which she bared her arms to the journalist to show him that she had no track marks on her arms, thus confirming that she had heard the rumours that she was addicted to heroin, which one usually injects, rather than cocaine, which one usually inhales. In an interview a year later Julia again brought the subject back to drugs. 'Probably 80 per cent of [press stories about my life are] just pure fiction. So people walk in with these preconceived notions and these rumours in their heads and I think that you can't help but look and say to yourself, "Oh yeah . . . she does look a little bit *thin*." Thin equals drug use! Doesn't everybody know that? But they say I'm thin for all kinds of reasons. Then if I wear a baggy dress, I'm pregnant. You just can't win with these people. It's just silly. The fact is that I don't use, nor have I ever used, drugs.[1] I'm scared of drugs. I'm a big chicken. That's why I can have a sense of humour about all this, because I know that deep down inside I'm a chicken. I have this great energy anyway and I always think that my head would blow off my shoulders or something. I mean, I'm curious about it. I've talked to people about it. I've heard other people's drug stories and am fascinated by them. I'm around people who have done [drugs] but I'm not really around a drug scene. When the rumours first surfaced I was just shocked because it was so ridiculous. Then it just became absurd. Then it went into a kind of surreal thing which took on a life of its own that didn't have anything to do with me. The fact is that I don't know why people want to think that I'm good or bad or a drug addict or whatever. Finally, though, why protest it? What is the point of saying, "No, you're wrong." Who cares? If they want to believe it, they'll believe it. If

---

[1] These words were spoken before Julia was photographed smoking a joint (in December 2001).

they don't want to believe it, they won't believe it. I'm not out to change anybody's mind.' Another word at the time had it that she had retired permanently; a third had her suffering from a nervous breakdown.

The columnist Liz Smith commented, 'I think the luckiest thing that ever happened to her was to cancel her marriage, although she was totally discombobulated by it. But I don't think it's calming when you're rushed from one love affair to the next. I think it would be great if she concentrated on her career and not the men in her life.'

The director Joel Schumacher said, 'I think it was one of the smartest, healthiest, most self-protective moves she could have made. Celebrity is a bucking bronco but I think she's very firm in the saddle. She's not impressed by it and she's not obsessed by it. She has a real mum. I'm not worried about Julia at all. She's got what it takes to deal with whatever life has to offer.'

But not everyone was so sure that Julia would be able to make a comeback even if she wanted to. One producer said, 'It's not that the bloom is off Julia Roberts, it's just that she's going to have to gain momentum again. Hollywood really is a town of who is flavour of the month. With each passing month there is less and less demand for her services. I still think of her as bankable. But how long are the studios going to risk huge budgets on an unproven?'

'Her private life has become a movie in itself,' said another executive, 'and that is difficult for anyone to handle. She pulled back and didn't do anything and the media wrote so much about it that she became a celebrity. She went from being an ingénue to a celebrity. Now she has to come back and be a serious actress. I think she's still our homecoming queen. She may have broken up with the captain of the football team, but she's going to go on and graduate with honours.'

Interestingly in an interview she gave during her 'sabbatical' Julia claimed that it was Kiefer Sutherland who had cancelled the wedding and not her. 'I had returned from a trip to Arizona intending to tell Kiefer that I thought it would be best for both of us not to get married. But the next time I talked to Kiefer [was when] he called me on the telephone. The only thing I said was

"Where have you been?" And he proceeded to tell me what I was going to tell him, which is that he did not want to marry me. He did not want this to happen.' Julia said that she called him a few hours later and then she told him that she did not want to get married either.

It is often said that there are three sides to every story: my side, your side and the truth. In this interview Julia was open and accommodating but her version of events does not tally with everyone else's.

Yet when the reporter asked about Patric the shutters came down heavily. 'I think that at this point the things I am choosing to discuss are things that I am willing to give to the public. I choose at this moment not to speak about Jason for the reason that it is far more dignified and deserving of respect than to put it out there and to allow people to give their opinion on it at lunch.'

In her wilderness period she did make one film – a brief cameo rôle in Robert Altman's *The Player*. 'I'm not into mocking myself. I have great respect for myself, and I have great respect for what I try to achieve. I don't think that's what the circumstances provided in that period of time. I don't think I'm mocking myself in *The Player*,' said Julia. 'I think I'm going "Get it?" And there's a difference. Not that mocking oneself is bad. I just think that, with the circumstances I was given over that period of time, it was really a great opportunity to be able to show that I wasn't dragged down by all this crap – that I maintained my sense of humour.' Julia's part was an in-joke on her bankability, i.e. any film that she was in was guaranteed to make money at the box office. However, the great irony at the time was that her presence in a film did not guarantee its financial success. In fact, both *Dying Young* and *Hook* had been flops. Hollywood loves a winner and there you are only as good as your last film. The talk of the town one day is often the next day's forgotten figure. To adapt an old saying a producer says, 'Who is Julia Roberts?' then 'Get me Julia Roberts', followed by 'Get me a younger Julia Roberts' and finally 'Who is Julia Roberts?' However, with Julia the situation is different. Hollywood still wanted her despite the two failures. But it seemed that Julia didn't want Tinseltown. She also, it appeared, failed to tell her agent, Elaine Goldsmith. Goldsmith continued her attempts to get work for Julia even though Julia didn't want it.

A producer said, 'In Hollywood it is not unusual for a star or a director to say, "I'm not working for the next year or until the spring." No one thinks that's strange. But with Julia Roberts, it was odd because about every three months I'd get a call from Elaine, asking if I had any projects for Julia. She'd tell me, "She wants to work. Have you got a comedy, a drama?" I'd send out the scripts and Julia would reject them all. Then, like clockwork, Elaine would call and the cycle would start again. This was strange, even by Hollywood standards.'

Among the stuff of Hollywood legend is just how many people have turned down leading rôles in films that have gone on to become smash hits. Julia was offered the rôle of Diana Murphy in *Indecent Proposal*, the story of a woman who is offered $1 million to sleep with billionaire John Gage (Robert Redford), a part that went to Demi Moore. Julia also turned down the part of Annie Reed in *Sleepless in Seattle* that made Meg Ryan a star.[2]

During her 'Wilderness Years' Julia's affair with Jason Patric also ran its course. It ended when Julia became involved with another man, another actor, another co-star, albeit a putative one. Julia signed to appear opposite Daniel Day-Lewis in a low-budget film for Universal to be called *Shakespeare in Love*. The film was to be produced by Edward Zwick who co-helmed the hit television series *thirtysomething* and the Oscar-winning *Glory*. The movie was to be a romantic comedy based on a script by Marc Norman. In it William Shakespeare falls for the actor playing Romeo in a new production of his tragedy *Romeo and Juliet*. The bard is relieved to find out that the actor is, in fact, female.

---

[2] James Cagney turned down the title rôle in *The Adventures of Robin Hood* that went to Errol Flynn. James Booth, Laurence Harvey, Anthony Newley and Terence Stamp all rejected the part of *Alfie* for which Michael Caine was nominated for an Oscar. Kim Basinger turned down the part of Catherine Tramell in *Basic Instinct*, the film that made a star of Sharon Stone. Axel Foley in *Beverly Hills Cop* was originally offered to Sylvester Stallone before Eddie Murphy signed on the dotted line. Robert Redford was in the frame for the part of the assassin in *The Day of the Jackal* that was played by Edward Fox. Sigourney Weaver turned down the rôle of bunny boiler Alex Forrest in *Fatal Attraction* that went to Glenn Close. Originally offered the rôle, Anthony Hopkins passed on the title part in *Gandhi* that won an Oscar for Ben Kingsley. Robert Redford and Warren Beatty both passed on the part of Michael Corleone in *The Godfather* that went to Al Pacino along with an Oscar nomination. Redford also turned down the part of Benjamin Braddock in *The Graduate* that went to Dustin Hoffman. Henry Winkler was due to play Danny Zucco in *Grease* before John Travolta assumed the quiff and *L.A. Law*'s Susan Dey was due to play Sandy before Olivia Newton-John.

The road to the cinematic altar was fraught. On 12 June 1992 *Screen International* reported that the *Robin Hood, Prince of Thieves* director Kevin Reynolds had signed to direct Day-Lewis and Julia. A fortnight later, the trade paper reported that *Shakespeare in Love* was in limbo because Julia was refusing to commit herself to the project. Due to Julia, Day-Lewis was instead to appear in a new TriStar film to be called *Probable Cause* or *At Risk* about a lawyer who is fired from his law firm after they discover he has Aids. Less than a week later Julia was reported to be on board and Day-Lewis was also back with the project.

In mid-September the *Hollywood Reporter* said that all systems were go on the film and announced that Julia would be making her comeback in *Shakespeare in Love* at a salary of $4 million. The report quoted Julia as 'lov[ing] the script' and was just awaiting final confirmation from Universal.

Within a month it was all over. It transpired that Julia was awaiting 'the word' not from Universal but from Daniel Day-Lewis. He, however, did not even receive a firm offer until the start of October and within 72 hours had declined. On 6 October 1992 *Daily Variety* announced that he was to work with Jim Sheridan once again[3] on a film based on the reminiscences of Gerry Conlon, a member of the Guildford Four.

Julia's alleged affair with Day-Lewis ended when he decided not to make the film. Day-Lewis was, in any case, not free to be seeing Julia. At the time he was dating the French actress Isabelle Adjani. It was a very on-off relationship. She obviously forgave him because on 9 April 1995 she gave birth to his son Gabriel-Kane. She said, 'I felt incredible sadness and disappointment.' (Day-Lewis went on to marry Rebecca Miller, the daughter of the respected playwright Arthur Miller and the Magnum agency photographer Inge Morath.)

When Day-Lewis dropped out of the film, the producers looked for a replacement and the name of Sean Bean came into the frame. Other names considered were Colin Firth (later to be Mr Darcy in *Pride and Prejudice* and Mark Darcy in *Bridget Jones's Diary*) and, ironically, Ralph Fiennes (star of *Wuthering Heights* and then

---

[3] They had previously worked on *My Left Foot*.

married to the future *ER* actor Alex Kingston whom he would leave for the much older Francesca Annis).

As the leading lady Julia had the final say on who her leading man would be and she turned down all the suggestions. Then Julia decided that she didn't want to appear either. On 20 October 1992 at 10.30 a.m. Terry Clegg, the line producer on *Shakespeare in Love*, assembled the 200-strong crew on B Stage at Pinewood Studios and told them that the film was closing down. As he spoke Julia had already left London and was back home in Los Angeles. Four days later Julia was in New York where she attended a taping of *Late Night with Letterman* and then went to see *A Few Good Men*,[4] which starred Tom Cruise, Demi Moore and Jack Nicholson and restarted the career of Kiefer Sutherland. On neither occasion was she accompanied by Jason Patric. Professionally, Julia was fast finding herself in a no-man's-land. The longer she stayed away from films the more difficult it would be to return – both in terms of finding suitable projects and having the requisite self-confidence to get behind the cameras. Julia decided that she needed someone she trusted to get her back on track. The call went in to Joe Roth, the former chairman of Twentieth Century Fox, who was now running his own Caravan Pictures under the auspices of the Walt Disney Organisation. On 3 December 1992 Julia formed YMA Productions and signed a two-year non-exclusive contract with Roth's company. Under the terms of the deal Roth would personally develop films for Julia to star in or produce under her YMA banner. She announced, 'I have the utmost respect for Joe Roth and I trust his creative instincts. I am delighted to be working with him again, and to be affiliated with his new company. I am equally pleased to be returning to the Disney Studios.' Not long after it was announced that Julia would star in a comedy called *I Love Trouble* before the repeat announcement that she would appear as the Tulane law student Darby Shaw in the film version of John Grisham's novel *The Pelican Brief*. Of Darby Julia said, 'She's clever and complex and I find her very admirable in her ways and choices. It's nice to see a woman of

---

[4] The film was written by Aaron Sorkin who would later receive great acclaim for the multi-Emmy Award-winning television show *The West Wing*.

strength and, regardless of the paralysing situation she finds herself in, she is never without strength. Regardless of how doomed she feels, she always hangs on. I find that very noble.' Julia used her clout to get Denzel Washington hired as her co-star. He was not Warner Bros' first choice to play Gray Grantham. In fact, in Grisham's book his character is white but Julia insisted that she wanted him not because she wanted to show how politically correct she was but because he was suitable for the rôle.[5] 'Who cares? White or black – who cares? I just wanted the best man for the part. Who gives a shit? [If there had been miscegenation] then I would give a shit. But this movie is not about who's black and who's white, who's the girl and who's the boy. This movie is about intrigue. It's beside the point who's doing what, who's wearing what colour of skin while they're doing it. Who cares? It's about time we stopped casting rôles by colour.'

Joe Roth opined, 'There is a non-threatening appeal to Julia. She's boldly vulnerable. It's unbelievable that someone so physically beautiful could also have this "everyman" quality about her, but that's exactly why she's a movie star. It's the same quality that Costner has.'

Meanwhile, back at *Shakespeare in Love* things were not good. To lose one star on a film project was unfortunate, to lose both was a much more serious problem. And the producers didn't take Julia's defection lightly. The sets had already been designed and built and costumes fitted for Julia. The film had been budgeted at £20 million and a goodly portion had already been spent. One studio executive commented, '[She] has definitely gone beyond the range of normal movie star behaviour. We've reached the point where a lot of people are wondering just what in the world is going on with her.'

Julian Belfrage, Daniel Day-Lewis's agent in London, immediately went into damage limitation mode. He told the *Evening Standard* that although the producers had been after his client since July it was only in October that he had received a firm offer and then took just three days to decline. 'He has behaved entirely honourably. Julia's reason for not doing it is that she adores Daniel

---

[5] There is no romance between Gray and Darby in the film but in the book they *do* fall in love.

and doesn't want to do it without him. I think she thought that by leaving she might persuade him to reconsider.'

In La-La Land Elaine Goldsmith said that Julia dropped out because she was not happy to work with the actors who were suggested as Daniel Day-Lewis's replacement. 'I think the frustration comes with everyone wanting to go forward with this project and not being able to find the right person once Daniel Day-Lewis passed.' She added that Day-Lewis dropped out because of scheduling conflicts with his IRA drama *In the Name of the Father*.

The romance with Daniel Day-Lewis was no more than a fling but it was enough to kill off Jason Patric's love for her. On 1 December 1992 the *New York Post*'s Page Six column reported, 'Although *Rush* star Jason Patric should have realised his *Pretty Woman* Julia Roberts's track record with men isn't exactly marathon material, Patric is one lost boy over stories that Roberts has dumped him for hawk-eyed playboy Daniel Day-Lewis.' Delores Robinson, Julia's manager, said, 'I don't know a thing about it. I just try to stay on the career side and let the personal side take care of itself.' In the middle of December 1992 *USA Today* asked, 'Has Jason Patric become the *Last of the Mohicans* on the trail of Julia Roberts? Are Roberts and Daniel Day-Lewis a new twosome?' Julia's publicist Nancy Seltzer stated, 'She and Daniel are friends, professional friends. They met when they were discussing doing *Shakespeare in Love*. To make more out of it is not fair.' The poorly informed press were out of the loop. The couple had split in November after a furious row but had reunited in December. At Christmas 1991 Jason Patric had given Julia a mint condition 1968 Volkswagen van. At Christmas 1992 she returned the sentiment by presenting him with a top of the range Landcruiser. The couple saw the New Year in together more in hope than expectation that the relationship still had legs.

On 10 January 1993 Julia accepted a Screen Actor's Guild Lifetime Achievement Award on behalf of Audrey Hepburn from Gregory Peck. Miss Hepburn was at her home in Tolochenaz, Switzerland, unable to travel because of the colon cancer that would kill her just ten days later on 20 January. Gregory Peck gave a speech recording Miss Hepburn's life and humanitarian achievements as an ambassador for Unicef before Julia's words accepting

Julia in 1977: the winning smile was evident even then.
(Rex Features)

The stars of *Mystic Pizza* (1988). From left: Annabeth Gish,
Lili Taylor, Julia Roberts. (The Kobal Collection/Samuel
Goldwyn Co.)

Her role in *Steel Magnolias* earned Julia a Golden Globe in 1989. (The Kobal Collection/Tri-Star/Rosenthal, Zade)

Body doubles were used for Richard Gere and Julia in the publicity for the 1990 hit *Pretty Woman*.
(The Kobal Collection/ Touchstone/Warners)

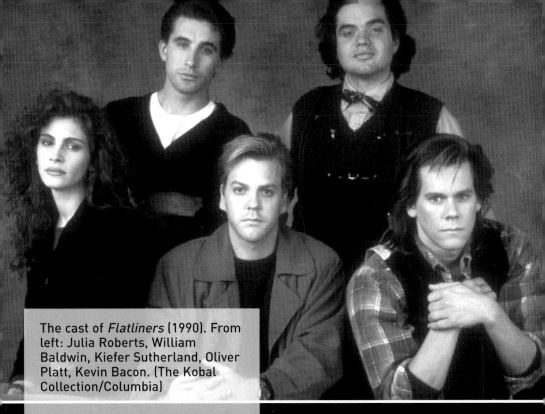

The cast of *Flatliners* (1990). From left: Julia Roberts, William Baldwin, Kiefer Sutherland, Oliver Platt, Kevin Bacon. (The Kobal Collection/Columbia)

With fiancé Kiefer Sutherland. Julia called off the wedding just three days before the ceremony in 1991. (Steve Granitz/Retna USA Ltd.)

ABOVE: Julia with first husband Lyle Lovett. The marriage lasted less than two years but the pair remain firm friends. (Joe Major/LFI)

BELOW: Julia and Jason Patric in 1991. The couple was together straight after Julia jilted Sutherland. (Randy Bauer/Rex Features)

ABOVE: With former lover Liam Neeson in *Michael Collins*, 1996. (Pat Maxwell/Rex Features)

BELOW: With co-star John Malkovich in box office flop *Mary Reilly* (1996). Director Stephen Frears found out the hard way that the public didn't want to see a glum Julia Roberts. (The Kobal Collection/TriStar)

ABOVE: With boyfriend Pat Manocchia in 1996. (Alex Oliveira/Rex Features)

BELOW: Julia's surprise wedding to cameraman Danny Moder made headlines all over the world in 2002. (Oscar Davis/Retna Ltd.)

Julia's role as super-star actress Anna Scott in 1999 box office smash *Notting Hill* was part of her return to the A-list. (The Kobal Collection/Polygram/ Coote, Clive)

Julia as Erin Brockovich. (The Kobal Collection/Universal/ Marshak, Bob)

ABOVE: Oscar night 2001: a triumphant Julia with soon to be ex-boyfriend Benjamin Bratt. (© AllStarPL.com)

the trophy. However, Nancy Seltzer had insisted on a news blackout of the event apart from CNN and the three main television networks ABC, CBS and NBC. When officials from the Guild protested Seltzer threatened to withdraw Julia's participation. SAG then had to inform all the invited press that there had been an 'adminsitrative error' and that they were all disinvited. A SAG spokesman said, 'If it were up to us the press would be there. We'd welcome as much coverage as possible.' Was the demand a decision by Seltzer who wanted to maintain her client's mystique or was it from Julia who wanted to demonstrate her ego and power? The question remains unanswered.

On 18 January 1993 Patric's neighbours were awakened by shouts and screams from his Stanley Street apartment. Then his door burst open and the couple spilled out onto the street. They continued shouting at each other. Witnesses later said that the subject of the argument was Daniel Day-Lewis. One bystander said, 'Jason was almost falling down drunk, and he kept accusing her of having slept with Daniel Day-Lewis, yelling, "You f***ed him. I know you f***ed him." Then Julia yelled back at him, "I can f*** anyone I want to!" '

Julia then jumped into her Porsche and drove off. She was never to set foot inside Jason Patric's home again. Julia took the break-up in her stride but her ex-boyfriend was distraught. According to a close friend he slept on the settee, unable to face sleeping in the bed he had shared with Julia.

According to *US* magazine he even went to Julia's house in search of love letters supposedly written to her by Daniel Day-Lewis. Patric later told *Time Out*, 'It was for me the ultimate nightmare. Relationships have their own problems, and the attention [of the press] didn't help.'

In an episode reminiscent of her break-up with Kiefer Sutherland, Julia had her faithful factotum Elaine Goldsmith call Jason Patric to tell him that it was all over. But what did happen between Julia and Day-Lewis? Many believe that they did have an affair although some claimed that it was no more than one meeting to discuss *Shakespeare in Love*. It was much more than that but it is likely that Day-Lewis did not want to make a film with Julia. When he left, Julia lost all interest in the project. Her main interest it was said had been the handsome Day-Lewis.

In March 1993 Julia 'spent a fortune on flights from Hollywood to Ireland' but no one had a picture of the lovers together. A photo opportunity did arise on 30 May 1993 when Julia and Day-Lewis spent three cosy hours together in the Wren's Nest of the Strawberry Beds pub in the Chapelizod area near Kilmainham. The couple arrived in a red Mercedes with a chauffeur. Both were casually dressed in jeans and while Day-Lewis quaffed Guinness Julia supped lager. Francis Heffernan, the barman at the pub, remembers, 'They were having a great craic, she was all over yer man. If you did not know them you would have thought they were boyfriend and girlfriend. There was a lot of laughing and whispering going on.'

Six years later, Joseph Fiennes, the younger brother of one of the actors suggested as a replacement for Daniel Day-Lewis, and Gwyneth Paltrow were happy that in the autumn of 1992 Julia and Day-Lewis had chosen not to make *Shakespeare in Love*. But in the summer of 1993 Julia had other things on her mind . . .

13. MARRIED LIFE – THE FIRST TIME AROUND

'Julia always wanted a traditional wedding without all the fanfare and glitz of Hollywood. She's a Southern girl at heart, and Lyle's a down home Texas boy. They worked together to plan the quiet ceremony.'

A friend of the bride on her unusually un-Hollywood wedding

MARION, INDIANA, 27 JUNE 1993

On 21 June 1993 Julia attended a press conference to promote *The Pelican Brief*[1] which was then still shooting and sat alongside Denzel Washington and director Alan J. Pakula. The gathered press corps were surprised that the Julia they had come to know, someone for whom fashion appeared unimportant and who was content to adopt the fashion persona of a bag lady, seemed happy, relaxed and confident. She was even cracking jokes with the hacks. One reporter asked if she was rusty having not appeared in a film for almost two years. 'I don't feel rusty. Do I look rusty? I think I came back with renewed vigour . . . I've been giddy.

'Maybe the press will focus on the work instead of me and how many times a week I do my laundry.' It was too good a feed for Denzel Washington to ignore. 'How many times a week *do* you do your laundry?'

Julia laughed along with the rest of the fourth estate members. But unbeknown to them she had something to smile about. She had a new man in her life. They had been dating for less than a fortnight and she had managed to keep his identity secret.

A few days before the Washington junket Julia had been interviewed by Jeannie Williams of *USA Today* and was in a buoyant mood. Talking about her self-imposed hiatus from Hollywood, Julia said, 'I got to spend time with my friends, visit with my family, and travel around and just have a quiet time. I had lots of nice days that were nothing more interesting than anybody else having a nice day.'

---

[1] During filming in Louisiana Julia lived in a rented house on Robert Street and patronised Robert's Bar. Both establishments were fewer than a couple of blocks from Tulane University where almost thirty years earlier her father was educated and her mother worked in a bookshop to support her studies.

It would be fair to say that on 27 June 1993 Julia surprised Hollywood in particular and the world in general by her marriage and by her choice of husband. With all due respect to Lyle Lovett, he was not stereotypical Julia Roberts boyfriend material. One magazine described his hairstyle as a 'thatch of nuclear-radiated alfalfa sprouts' and another said he was not 'conventionally studly'.

Virtually unknown outside America and inside huge parts of it before his marriage to Julia, Lovett was born in Klein,[2] Texas (some sources say that he was born in Houston and raised 25 miles away in Klein) on 1 November 1957 (a Scorpio like his new bride), making him almost exactly ten years older than Julia. An only child, Lovett, the son of retired Exxon employees William and Bernell, grew up in a large but loving extended family with six uncles and aunts living within half a mile of his home. He is remembered by locals as shy and sensitive. His main residence is still in Klein and he is a regular worshipper at his local Lutheran church.

He was educated at Texas A&M University where he studied journalism and German, a language he had learned as a child. Lovett graduated in 1980 but decided to forgo the pleasures of being a member of the fourth estate. 'I don't think I had what it takes to be a journalist. Journalists have to tell the truth. And I don't know if I could have worked that hard. What I do mostly is have fun. I get to do for a living something I would do for fun. I get to travel to interesting places, meet interesting people, eat in great restaurants and sing and play my guitar. I get to think about life and turn it into music. What could be more fun than that?' He began writing songs in the late 1970s and performed in the unlikely settings of Germany and Luxembourg. In 1984 he signed to MCA Records and his first album, the eponymously titled *Lyle Lovett*, came out in 1986 but it took another trip to Europe before he received recognition in his native land. Even after four more albums many in the country establishment still regard Lovett as, not to put too fine a point on it, not one of them.

In October 1989 he met Allison Inman, a student at Tennessee Tech University and they quickly became so serious that he asked

---

[2] Klein was named after Adam Klein, a German immigrant, who was Lyle Lovett's great-great-grandfather.

her to marry him. They finished the relationship just a few weeks before he married Julia. However, Inman was not free to become Mrs Lovett if it meant becoming part of the showbusiness world. 'I don't like the phoniness and I don't like to be nice to people I don't like. I just [am] not comfortable in that lifestyle. I love Lyle dearly but we had too many problems and it just wasn't worth it. Lyle and I were emotionally exhausted. We'd gone through a lot . . . So I can see why either of us would be vulnerable to fall in love with someone in a matter of weeks. I don't feel betrayed. I understand.' Her understanding was helped by a telephone call made to her by Lovett on 25 June, two days before he married, to explain that he was seeing someone although the relationship was only just over a fortnight old but that it was serious. She was also impressed by the suddenness of the gesture. 'I'm proud of the old guy because I've never seen him do anything spontaneous. I have to applaud a woman who can get him to do something like that.'

The same year he met Allison Inman, Lovett won a Grammy as Best Country Male Vocalist. In 1993 he won a second Grammy nomination for his album *Joshua Judges Ruth*. In the previous year Lovett appeared in Robert Altman's film *The Player*,[3] the only

---

[3] Despite rumours and a story put out by her publicist Nancy Seltzer, Julia did not meet Lovett on the set of *The Player*. They worked on the project on different days and the movie was shot in the summer of 1991, two years before the couple married. And anyway, Julia was dating Jason Patric at the time in the aftermath of her break-up from Kiefer Sutherland. Robert Altman later said, 'I thought there was a 50-50 chance Julia wouldn't show up [for filming]. She was emotionally distraught. The press was after her. She had to poke fun at herself. She would have been perfectly justified to not show up, but she did it. She was very gutsy.' In an interview with the *Los Angeles Times* published on 22 July 1993 Lovett confirmed that he had only met Julia in early June 1993, a few weeks before their wedding. 'Meeting her is unlike anything that had happened to me before. She's so wonderful. It was one of those immediate things that you hear about.' Some believed that one of the contributory factors to the ending of the affair with Sutherland was that both were fighting for film rôles. With Lovett there was no such competitiveness. Although he had had a bit part in *The Player* he professed he had no desire to do anything other than sing. Perhaps being married to Julia unearthed latent ambitions in him because he went on to appear in Robert Altman's *Short Cuts* (1993) with Andie MacDowell, Bruce Davison, Jack Lemmon, Julianne Moore, Matthew Modine, Anne Archer, Jennifer Jason Leigh, Christopher Penn, Robert Downey Jr, Tim Robbins, Lily Tomlin and Lori Singer; Altman's *Prêt-à-Porter* (1994) with Sophia Loren, Marcello Mastroianni, Tim Robbins, Kim Basinger, Stephen Rea, Anouk Aimée, Lauren Bacall, Cher and Sally Kellerman; the Anjelica Huston-directed *Bastard Out of Carolina* (1996) with Jennifer Jason Leigh, Ron Eldard and Christina Ricci; in 1998 he again appeared opposite the gorgeous Christina Ricci in *The Opposite of Sex*. He again linked up with Robert Altman to appear in his *Cookie's Fortune* (1999), which starred Glenn Close, Julianne Moore, Liv Tyler, Chris O'Donnell and Patricia Neal.

movie that Julia made during her self-imposed Hollywood exile. As a result Lovett became a close friend of Tim Robbins and his girlfriend Susan Sarandon. 'You've got to admire someone who can rhyme ice water and fly swatter,' said Robbins. 'He's a real Texas gentleman. His songs may be twisted, eccentric and dark, and I was expecting the same in his personality, but he is totally egoless and his music is art.'

Country singer Tanya Tucker said, 'I think Julia's tired of the Hollywood pretence. Maybe she's ready to be treated like a goddess, which Lyle will do.' Lovett had been a fan of Julia's for some time before their meeting. Watching a television chat show he saw her asked who her favourite country singer was and was more than pleasantly surprised when she said his name. 'I thought that she was really something and I wanted to write her a note, but I was too chicken,' he said. In May 1993 Lovett toured America promoting his album *Joshua Judges Ruth* and met the journalist Terry Tomalin. The hack mentioned that he had been on holiday in Costa Rica with his sister and one of her friends and the pal had the complete canon of Lovett's work in her possession. The sister was Susan Sarandon and her friend, of course, Julia. This time Lovett plucked up his courage and rang Julia.

The couple met for the first time on 8 June 1993 in New Orleans, Louisiana, on the set of Julia's film. Lovett stood quietly by watching her work during the day. That night they went for dinner with six others at the Cafe Brasil and listened to the New Orleans Klezmer All-Stars, an acoustic band whose *métier* was Jewish folk music with a funky rhythm. Julia wore a loose cotton dress and had no make-up on her face and was also barefoot. Julia and Lovett danced to the music oblivious to the stares from other patrons.

Four days later, Julia attended Lovett's concert in the Mud Lane Amphitheatre in Memphis, Tennessee, but stayed in his dressing room for most of the show. On 20 June Julia and several members of the crew from *The Pelican Brief* went to see Lovett's gig at Wolf Trap Farm Park in northern Virginia. During the concert Lovett dedicated the song 'She Makes Me Feel Good' to 'Fiona'. The audience and even Julia's co-workers were unaware that her middle name is Fiona. Two days later, Lovett appeared at the

Paramount Theatre in New York and again dedicated the song to Fiona. He announced, 'Fiona likes to think that I wrote this song for her and, well, I won't tell her any different. I love you, Fiona.'

Five days later, Julia and Lovett were married in Marion, Indiana, a suburb of Indianapolis and home to fewer than 40,000 people. Marion became incorporated as a city in 1889 and was named after General Francis Marion (1732–95), one of the heroes of the American Revolution. Marion, the city not the man, is located 28 miles northwest of Muncie, on the Pennsylvania, Chesapeake and Ohio, New York Central, and Toledo, St Louise and Western railroads. It has its own airport and nearby are situated oil wells and gas pockets. Indiana is also one of the few places in America where there is no waiting period to get married and where neither blood nor Aids tests are required. One requisite is that all women under the age of fifty must prove that they have been immunised against German measles.

The happy couple presented themselves at the County Clerk's office to collect their marriage licence at 11.45 a.m. for their 1.30 p.m. nuptials. The clerk of the Grant County court, Karen Weaver, arrived at her office in her Sunday best having just been to church. Julia and her soon-to-be husband were sitting in the front row of a large tour bus. The clerk climbed into the bus and asked 'Are you the real Julia Roberts?' Julia said that she was and produced her German measles immunisation certificate. Later Weaver was to say that the couple were 'nice people. I was very impressed but not awestruck. I was awestruck when I met [Vice-President] Dan Quayle.'[4]

The weather was wet, hot and humid when Julia finally married at 3 p.m. in a twenty-minute ceremony conducted in the St James Lutheran Church by Pastor DeWyth Beltz, Lovett's childhood minister, and the Reverend Mark Carlson in whose church the wedding took place. There was no confetti but the centre pews were decorated with small bouquets of purple, red and yellow flowers. In the second pew sat Julia's mother Betty, and half-sister Nancy. The chief bridesmaid was Lisa Roberts and the other

---

[4] J. Danforth Quayle was vice-president when George Bush was in the White House (1989–93). He was not highly regarded by political commentators and was renowned for his verbal gaffes long before George W. Bush made an art of presidential double talk.

bridesmaids were Elaine Goldsmith, the actresses Deborah Good-rich Porter, who described Julia as 'ecstatic, giddy and excited', Susan Sarandon and Paige Sampson, Julia's closest friend from Campbell High School, who had arrived from Chicago, Illinois to see her old pal married.

As the bridal party made their way to the altar led by Eva Amurri, the eight-year-old daughter of Sarandon, and Alexandra Porter, the five-year-old offspring of Goodrich Porter, scattering flowers, the music was Bach's 'Jesu, Joy of Man's Desiring' which segued into Mendelssohn's more orthodox 'Wedding March' ('Here Comes the Bride').[5] The actor Barry Tubb gave the bride away.

'Julia always wanted a traditional wedding without all the fanfare and glitz of Hollywood,' said one friend. 'She's a Southern girl at heart, and Lyle's a down home Texas boy. They worked together to plan the quiet ceremony.'

The bride's sister-in-law, Eliza, commented, 'Julia wouldn't be getting married unless she planned on staying with Lyle for the rest of her life.'

Julia commented, 'It's funny. We were both just giddy and wanted to get together and get married. Certainly as an after-thought, you go "Let's do it now! We love each other. We want to spend our lives together." This way things are calm and quiet and we can do it the way we want to do it without any influences from anybody else. The only downside to it was that I have a handful of really good friends and I didn't have time to arrange for them to come. That, I'll always be sorry about. But you can only do so much when you have limited time. But heck! We'll just keep getting married.'

Unlike the aborted wedding to Kiefer Sutherland, at this one there were no expensive designer pumps, no co-ordinated outfits, no studio backdrop, no hundreds of guests. The bridesmaids chose their own outfits and a red rose corsage was the only decoration that allowed them to stand out from the other female guests. In total there were 75 guests. Notably absent was Eric. He

---

[5] In fact, far from being played as the bride walks to the altar, the 'Wedding March' is played in its original form in *A Midsummer Night's Dream* as the bride is getting undressed for her marital bed.

later told the press that he was not invited because Julia feared he might cause upset although what the upset might be was never identified. Earlier that year Eric had split up with his girlfriend, Kelly Cunningham, and fought for custody of their daughter, Emma, who was born in Los Angeles on 10 February 1991. Julia had taken the side of Cunningham which unsurprisingly had infuriated Eric. The brothers-in-law were never to meet.

The bride wore a long white sheath dress that Lovett had bought for a reputed $2,000 from the New York shop Commes des Garçons. Julia was also barefoot.[6] One of Lovett's cousins thought the attire unsuitable for the solemnity of the occasion. 'It looked more like a slip that should go under a wedding dress. You could see her bellybutton,' he complained.

The groom wore a dark suit and was supported by his best man, Wayne Miller, who had directed several of Lovett's music videos. It was Larry Chandler, Lovett's tour bus driver, a resident of Marion and a worshipper at the St James Lutheran Church, who suggested the venue.

Halfway through the service Julia was overcome by emotion and burst into tears to be soon followed by Lovett. As the couple were pronounced man and wife Francine Reed, a backing singer for Lovett, sang an a cappella version of 'The Lord's Prayer'.

As they left the church to pose for the wedding pictures the rain began to fall more heavily and Lovett held a protective umbrella over his new bride who was still barefoot. At 5.30 p.m. the reception began in a large green and white striped tent outside the Deer Park Music Centre Amphitheatre. The guests ate shrimp, turkey and prime rib and drank champagne and munched on the five-tier wedding cake. When Julia threw her bridal bouquet it was caught by her spinster agent Elaine Goldsmith who had

---

[6] Julia's feet have often featured in stories about her. In her early days in New York she would often wander around barefoot, something that many journalists picked up on. She drove her Porsche barefoot and even married her first husband with nothing on her feet. In November 1996 Julia's feet came second in a Gallup poll for the Society of Chiropodists and Podiatrists to find out which celebrity feet men would most like to fondle. The top five were: 1 Joanna Lumley, 2 Julia Roberts, 3 Ulrika Jonsson, 4. Martine McCutcheon, 5 Elle McPherson. The women's votes for men's feet they would like to get their hands on revealed the following result: 1 Sean Connery, 2 Tom Cruise, 3 Brad Pitt, 4 Keanu Reeves, 5 Ross Kemp. Further, Julia is pictured barefoot on the cover of the video and DVD of *The Mexican*.

arranged the whole event. Breaking with tradition, there was no first dance and nor were there any wedding presents. The speed with which the ceremony was arranged made the buying of gifts difficult if not impossible. Besides both bride and groom were wealthy enough to buy whatever they needed for themselves.

The one thing that the ceremony did have in common with other celebrity weddings was that it was arranged in the utmost secrecy. The guests were telephoned on Friday night (25 June) and told to be near a phone on Saturday when they would be given the final instructions. Some guessed that the ceremony would take place in Cleveland, Ohio, where Julia and Lovett were staying on the Saturday night at the Ritz-Carlton Hotel, having spent the Friday night in Detroit, Michigan. At 10 a.m. on Saturday 26 June a telephone call was made to Lyle Lovett's relatives telling them to board a private jet in Houston on the following morning.

Wanda Hill, the groom's cousin, remembers, 'It was like "Boom, let's do it. You're here, I'm here. Whoever can come can come." Our whole side was saying, "Oh Lord, please don't let her back out because that'd break his heart." '

The ceremony was delayed for nearly two hours to accommodate the late guests but the spectacle of three limousines and five tour buses outside the small church no doubt made sure the locals knew something big was about to happen. Then Susan Sarandon arrived from Memphis, Tennessee, where she was filming *The Client*, the film version of yet another John Grisham novel. Tim Robbins flew via Learjet from Mansfield, Ohio, where he was making *The Shawshank Redemption*, a movie based on the Stephen King novella.

Not long after 8 p.m. at the Deer Park Amphitheatre Julia walked onto the stage and into the spotlight. Peering into the audience, she announced, 'Ladies and gentlemen, my husband . . . Lyle Lovett . . . and his Large Band.'

Julia left the stage to a rapturous ovation from 10,000 fans of her new husband and then almost immediately reappeared when Lovett played the old Tammy Wynette classic 'Stand By Your Man'. As Lyle Lovett and his Large Band played Julia stood behind her husband and then moved to his side where she moved in time to the music. As the song finished the audience cheered and Lovett said, 'Thank you very much and welcome to the happiest day of my life.' When Julia left the stage Lovett and his Large Band continued with their set. Julia made a reappearance for the last song, 'Pass It Not Gentle Saviour' and she took her husband's hand and even managed to persuade him to dance with her thus making up for missing the traditional first dance at their wedding several hours earlier. When the applause finally died down Lovett and Julia left the stage and he put a large white Stetson on her head.

'I'm afraid I'm going to wake up and this will be all just a dream,' said the deliriously happy but cautious bride.

After the exertions of the concert the newlyweds went back to their honeymoon suite which was in the $250-a-night Omni Hotel in nearby Castleton, Indiana. The suite had a king-sized bed, a living room, luxury *en suite* bathroom with TV and telephone and a bar although Lovett ordered a bottle of Dom Perignon from room service. On 28 June the couple gave lunch for a select group of friends and more Dom Perignon was quaffed and lobster-filled pasta and veal cutlets were eaten.

In the meantime the world's press had to be informed of the good news and so Julia's publicist Nancy Seltzer rang the Associated Press (AP), the American version of Britain's national Press Association. However, the staffers at AP were on their guard and refused to believe Seltzer when she told them that Julia had married Lyle Lovett. They were convinced that she was trying to perpetrate a massive hoax. 'I could not prove to them who I was. The AP asked me to name my clients so I did. Then I said, "What about Julia's agent, Elaine Goldsmith? She's right here." But then we couldn't prove who she was either.' In the end Susan Sarandon came to the phone and she spoke to several people at AP before the news agency finally decided to put the story on the wire.

Late on 28 June the happy couple went to the airport where he kissed her and then he went to Kettering, Ohio, and she flew to New Orleans. Lovett had dates to complete on his tour and Julia had to finish filming *The Pelican Brief*. In an ultimately successful bid to avoid the press, Julia and Lovett left the hotel via the kitchen and the back door.

The media began to cover the wedding and, in the days before big celebrity buy-ups prior to the event, had to make do with what they could put together. *People* managed to secure the exclusive rights to the wedding photographs. The ingenuity of the press knows no bounds and the downmarket *Globe* took a still from Julia's screen wedding in *Steel Magnolias* and cropped out her former fiancé Dylan McDermott's head and replaced it with her new husband Lyle Lovett's! Not wishing to be left out the psychologists and psychiatrists just had to have their say. It could almost be said that psychologists and psychiatrists have never met a media outlet that they didn't like. First up to the microphone was Dr Irene Kassorla who opined, 'I call these whirlwind relationships "Velcro Attachments" [because] they are easily attached and easily separated.' Beverly Hills psychiatrist Carole Lieberman said, 'Because showbusiness is so precarious, sometimes people panic and want to reach out for a quick feeling of security. The quest for fame can be so stressful that in a period of vulnerability you may impetuously reach out and grab someone. I think that's what Julia did.'

Back on the set of *The Pelican Brief* Julia was greeted by cast and crew wearing T-shirts bearing the legend 'Welcome back Mrs Lovett' on the front and 'He's a lovely boy . . . but you really must do SOMETHING about his hair!' on the back. Julia said, 'If you spend any time with him, his hair isn't as big as everybody makes it out to be. I've seen some pictures from a few years ago, and that picture is high. But now, it's pretty normal. He's really good-looking.'

Director Alan J. Pakula told the press on 29 June, 'There is not a single crew member who does not wish Julia a lot of happiness.' Pakula played a kind trick on his star. One scene called for Julia to talk on the telephone to John Heard but when the call was made Pakula had arranged for Lovett to make it and speak Heard's lines. Julia recognised her husband's voice – luckily – and played the scene until Pakula shouted 'Cut!' Julia let out a gleeful yell, 'That's my husband.'

Filming was uneventful. Julia was in the first flush of post-marital happiness and Denzel Washington was as good as gold. Usually Washington can be difficult to work with if he feels his needs are being left unmet. In between scenes and make-up Julia spent her entire time talking to Lovett on her mobile. On Friday 2 July Julia again appeared on stage with Lovett and again he placed a Stetson on her head.

To all around them it seemed as if Julia was happy and finally had found a man she loved who loved her back and with whom she could be content. But how long would it be before all the old insecurities came racing to the top?

One friend said, 'Lyle is a very shy, very sweet and sincere fellow. He's very humble and very un-Hollywood, and not terribly ambitious. He just wants to do his music. He's also not great-looking, which can only enhance her security. So Lyle is a safe bet. He's not going to be leaving her. He's not going to compete with her.'

But would Julia be competing with herself?

14. I LOVE TROUBLE – AT WORK AND AT HOME

'From the moment I met him, we sort of gave each other a hard time and naturally we got on each other's nerves. While he can be completely charming and very nice, he's also completely disgusting. He's going to hate me for saying this but he seems to go out of his way to repel people.'
Julia speaking about her *I Love Trouble* co-star Nick Nolte

'It's fascinating to listen to someone speak with such authority about me when I wouldn't even have known what she looked like except when I saw her on TV talking about me. There's your exclusive authority interview.'
Julia on her sister-in-law Eliza's decision
to become the unofficial family spokesman

HOLLYWOOD, 1993–94
The Pelican Brief opened on 17 December 1993 and received great acclaim with many reviewers saying that it was the film that had restarted Julia's career. *Variety* called her performance 'sensational' and said that the film was 'a cracking thriller' with a 'long, prosperous box office flight'. The *Los Angeles Times* was not quite as fulsome in its praise. It opined, 'Roberts and Washington do what is expected of them quite nicely and manage a pleasant on-screen rapport'. If only Julia and her next co-star Nick Nolte could have managed that rapport.

I Love Trouble is a romantic comedy about a pair of rival newspaper journalists in Chicago. It was written by the producer Nancy Meyers and her husband director Charles Shyer who was responsible for *Baby Boom* and *Father of the Bride*.

Joe Roth commented, 'This is a very Spencer Tracy–Katharine Hepburn kind of film, very *Pat and Mike*-ish. Julia Roberts in a romantic comedy. I think it might work.'

Roth was wrong. The film did not work.

Julia by this time was a star very much in the ascendancy and one of the perks of being a star very much in the ascendancy is the right to choose your leading man (or woman). Julia chose Harrison Ford, 25 years her senior and who would later date Calista Flockhart, the star of *Ally McBeal* and 22 years Ford's junior.

There was one problem. Harrison Ford did not want to appear in a film with Julia Roberts. By this time Ford had been successful for more than fifteen years, appearing in *American Graffiti* (1973), *Star Wars* (1977), *Force Ten from Navarone* (1978), *Apocalypse Now* (1979), *The Empire Strikes Back* (1980), *Raiders of the Lost Ark* (1981), *Blade Runner* (1982), *The Return of the Jedi* (1983), *Indiana Jones and the Temple of Doom* (1984), *Witness* (1985), *The Mosquito Coast* (1986), *Working Girl* (1988), *Indiana Jones and the Last Crusade* (1989), *Presumed Innocent* (1990), *Patriot Games* (1992) and *The Fugitive* (1993) so he, too, could have his pick of co-stars. Harrison Ford is a private man compared to most Hollywood stars. One of his biographers described him as guarding 'his private life with a passion bordering on the obsessive, resulting in an unwelcome reputation for being a complicated man, an actor whose personality is a veritable maze of which journalists never have and never will find the true centre.' Ford has never revealed why he turned down the opportunity to work with Julia. Perhaps he felt the script did not pass muster; perhaps he had heard about Julia from his friend Steven Spielberg. We simply do not know.

To replace Ford the producers cast one of his contemporaries. Nick Nolte was born in Omaha, Nebraska, on 8 February 1941 (although some sources list 1934 as his natal year). He is known as much for his tumultuous private life as his respected professional one.

Julia played Sabrina Peterson, an enthusiastic reporter not too dissimilar from Teri Hatcher's Lois Lane in the ABC television series *The New Adventures of Superman*. Nolte played Peter Brackett, a seen-it-all, done-it-all and drank quite a lot of it, hardbitten news hack who decided to chase girls rather than stories – à la Henry Davenport in the Channel 4 sitcom *Drop the Dead Donkey*. Both are assigned to cover a train wreck but that is just the start of their adventures.

Unfortunately, off screen the two stars simply did not gel. Julia found Nolte to be a boor. She objected to his crude, macho behaviour and to his swearing, even though she was no stranger to blue language herself. She threw more than the occasional strop and Nolte gave back what he received from her. When the film was released on 29 June 1994 the normally staid *Los Angeles Times* ran a large story about the feud between the two actors. Julia's press flack Nancy Seltzer denied that there had been anything other than sweetness and light on the set and criticised the respectable newspaper for running what she believed was an extended and untrue gossip item. Julia refused to speak to the *Los Angeles Times* but she did grant an interview to the *New York Times* that inadvertently backed up the West Coast story and refuted Seltzer's damage limitation. 'From the moment I met him,' recalled Julia, 'we sort of gave each other a hard time and naturally we got on each other's nerves. While he can be completely charming and very nice, he's also completely disgusting. He's going to hate me for saying this but he seems to go out of his way to repel people.'

By this time a veteran of Hollywood, Julia realised that the public wants to believe that everyone in showbusiness loves everyone else and so when she gave an interview to *Entertainment Weekly* she played down the disharmony between her and Nolte. 'We had a great, erm, high-spirited needling of each other, trying to get a rise out of each other.'

Even Jim Wiatt, Nolte's agent, got in on the act admitting that his client and Julia did not get on but put it down to the 'typical spats' that Hollywood stars often become embroiled in.

The feud also tried the patience of the studio's marketing department. They had originally intended to sell the film as a feel-good summer romance movie but, because of the obvious lack of affection between the pair, it became a murder mystery.

That still did not sate the critics. *US* opined, 'Even a microscope couldn't detect a chemical reaction between Roberts and co-star Nolte.' Kenneth Turan of the *Los Angeles Times* said, 'The repartee is mostly lacklustre . . . the comedy aspects . . . are not especially entrancing despite the star power.'

The feud with Nolte seemed to reignite the simmering hostility between Julia and Eric. The media reported that Julia had sided with Eric's ex-girlfriend (from before his marriage) in a child custody battle and had even paid her legal bills. Eric's wife, Eliza Rayfiel Roberts, told *Redbook*, 'Eric takes responsibility for the separation [from Julia]. He's a wonderful guy who, when depressed, can be short-tempered and impatient. When that happens, feelings get hurt. Julia was not going to be hurt again and again by somebody she cared about.'

Julia came back with, 'It's a private matter that for some reason he and his wife have decided to make more public than I think they should. Eric tells his stories, and his wife tells her stories. What I find most fascinating about Eric's wife and what she says about me and how I feel about things and what I do about things is that I've never even met her.

'It's fascinating to listen to someone speak with such authority about me when I wouldn't even have known what she looked like except when I saw her on TV talking about me. There's your exclusive authority interview.

'It's too bad. My brother knows specifically what our problems are. He's very clear. He can choose to relay them however he sees fit. I've just decided to take the Nancy Kerrigan approach. There's always more respectability in being quiet as opposed to Tonya Harding's "Look at me, I'm here, I'm here. I'll tell you anything".'[1]

TROUBLE AT HOME, 1995

I Love Trouble was released two days after Julia and Lyle Lovett celebrated their first wedding anniversary – or they would have celebrated had not she been in New York publicising the film and he 3,000 miles away in Los Angeles shooting the video for his album *I Love Everybody*.[2] Julia and her husband would not have the opportunity for a second.

On 28 March 1995 Julia and Lovett issued a joint press release

---

[1] Tonya Maxene Harding was the 5 ft 1 in ice skater who engineered an attack by her bodyguard at the Cobo Ice Arena in Detroit, Michigan, at 2.35 p.m. on 6 January 1994, on her main rival, 5 ft 4 in Nancy Ann Kerrigan, to ensure an Olympic gold medal for herself. Poetic justice saw Harding fall, break a shoelace and fail to win a medal at the Lillehammer Games (the gold went to Oksana Baiul, Kerrigan picked up silver). On 16 March, Harding escaped jail by pleading guilty to a felony count of conspiring to hinder the prosecution in the case. She was sentenced to three years' supervised probation, a $100,000 fine and forced to resign from the US Figure Skating Association as a result. She was also told to create a $50,000 fund for the Special Olympics, reimburse the DA's Office $10,000, serve 500 hours community service and undergo psychiatric evaluation and treatment. Harding, who measured 36C-25-37 after plastic surgery, later sold stills from a hardcore porn movie of herself and her husband, Jeff Gillooly, purportedly on honeymoon, to *Penthouse*. Gillooly was released from prison on 13 March 1995 eight months into a two-year sentence. On 16 February he petitioned the Multnomah County Circuit Court to change his name to Jeff Stone.

[2] Jim Kerr of Simple Minds and Julia both supplied backing vocals on the album.

that signalled the end of their 21-month marriage. As is the norm in these matters, they affirmed their mutual respect of each other but, as with much of their marriage, they were apart when the announcement was made. In fact, they were in different countries. Julia was in London working on *Mary Reilly* while Lovett was nursing a broken collarbone in a Houston hospital having fallen off his motorbike.

The press release was timed to coincide with the Oscars in the hope that the razzmatazz occurring at the ceremony would cause the press to ignore the break-up of the star marriage. No such luck. *People* put the story on its next issue front cover relegating the Academy Awards to an inside spread.

The couple had been so effusive in their admissions of love for each other that the break-up announcement took many by surprise. Robert Altman said of the marriage, 'It's a true romance. It'll survive long after the trashy media bandwagon has moved on.' But perhaps the split should not have caused so many ripples. Absence does not always make the heart grow fonder and Julia and Lovett spent very little time together. In their entire marriage they had rarely been together for more than a week at a time and during their first eight months of married life they spent just ten nights under the same roof. She was making four films, he was touring. They even maintained separate residences – her apartment in Gramercy Park,[3] New York, his cabin in his home town of Klein, Texas.

In September 1994 Lovett spoke at length of his desire to become a father. 'We have been discussing having a child after Julia finishes *Mary Reilly* – the Jekyll And Hyde movie she's been making in England with Stephen Frears. She really wants children and so do I. But both our lives are so busy at the moment that we think we're gonna hold off for a while. Of course, it's pretty difficult for us to get together at all at the moment, let alone start having babies. Julia has been busy with new movies and I've been working on my new album and now I'm touring.'

He also discussed the media intrusion into their lives and, unlike many celebrities, did not whinge at people doing their jobs.

---

[3] Julia bought a duplex penthouse in 1993 with views over the private garden in the square. Since then, she has snapped up four other flats in the 24-unit block.

'All the press coverage has very little bearing on the reality of our life. The things written are so removed from what's really happening in my life that it's really funny. Dealing with the tabloid press has been a real experience. And not that unpleasant. It can be inconvenient, but it's interesting to watch. It's like having the best seat in the house. All the speculation about the state of our marriage would be difficult if Julia didn't handle it so well. As long as things are straight between her and me, the other stuff doesn't really matter. It's something to deal with, but as long as she and I are together, those things don't matter. OK, we have to spend a lot of time apart, but that's the way it works. I've been over to see her several times this summer. And Julia came to our show in Iowa when she zipped over for 22 hours. When I started to record a new album, I chose Los Angeles because Julia was going to be there making a movie, so I could spend the autumn there with her.'

In February 1995 they were spotted holding hands in the Champs-Elysées in Paris while they were filming Robert Altman's *Prêt-à-Porter*. When they were apart, they often flew to where the other one was to spend some time together. In December 1994 Lovett turned up on the set of *Something to Talk About*, the comedy in which she played the cuckolded wife, Grace, to Dennis Quaid's Eddie. On occasion Julia would visit her husband on the road when he would stop rehearsals so they could be alone. The signs were there, however.

In April 1994 Mr and Mrs Lovett were in New York at the same time but, oddly, they stayed in separate hotels and did not socialise together. It was around this time that Julia stopped wearing her wedding ring. On 27 April after Lovett had left Julia in New York to fly to Paris to film some more scenes on *Prêt-à-Porter* she had dinner with the actor Ethan Hawke, who would marry another tall, slim actor, Uma Thurman. Julia's people explained the meal as a business occasion at which the actors discussed the making of *Pagan Babies*, a film that never materialised. One report had Julia paying for the repast with Lovett's credit card. The next day pictures of the pair appeared in the *New York Post*. *Time* reported that Julia was staring 'dreamily' into Hawke's eyes and that they were 'dancing, hugging and amorously holding hands'. Nancy Seltzer announced somewhat sarcastically,

'I'm so glad Julia and Ethan went out dancing because, prior to this, I had no idea dancing was a crime.' She also added that the two actors were 'friends, just friends'. With a touch of *schadenfreude Time* noted that Seltzer had used the same description 'friends, just friends' a few days before Julia married Lyle Lovett.

On 29 April Julia rang *Vogue* to explain the *Post* pictures and said, 'I have a deep, tremendous love for Lyle. I think he is one of the poetic geniuses of our time.' The reporter to whom she spoke then asked if Julia believed in monogamy. Julia answered but asked that her reply be considered off the record.

In August 1994 Lovett flew to London for a concert tour. He met up with Julia for dinner but they left the restaurant separately, twenty minutes apart.

Julia has always had a healthy sex drive and it seems that sex may have driven a wedge between her and Lovett. At the start of their relationship, Julia told friends that Lovett was the best lover she'd ever known. But over a period of just months, the spark of passion was snuffed out. 'That was OK with Lyle,' says Richard DeVille, a family friend of Julia. 'He could have gone on like that, as long as he knew he had Julia.' But it was confusing for her. Though Julia had always valued her sexuality, during her marriage she began losing track of it. 'She knew it wasn't healthy,' says DeVille. 'But, still, she was happy because Lyle was a good man. It was a confusing time. Do you end a valuable relationship just because it's not sexual? Or, as she put it, "Maybe I can live without having orgasms, as long as I feel loved. Why not?" ' So why was such an arrangement acceptable to Lovett? 'I think he began to think of her as a daughter – even though there is only a ten-year age difference between them,' says Thomas Caldwell, a close friend.

Julia chose to leave Lovett. 'I just hope you know what you're doing,' Lovett reportedly told her. 'Great sex often lapses, but what we have, people spend decades trying to achieve.' 'But I want more,' Julia told him through her tears. 'I need to be loved.' 'When the couple agreed that any further intimacy between them was impossible, that's when Julia knew it was over,' said a source.[4]

---

[4] In April 1997 Julia revealed where she had the best sex of her life – on a Los Angeles bar-top with a cocktail waiter.

On 4 August 1995 *Something to Talk About* was released and provided some much-needed respite from the woes that were troubling Julia. The film was about Grace Bichon who supposedly has a perfect life. She is a successful equestrian star who gives up her dream for her husband (Dennis Quaid) and her daughter. It is only when she discovers that Eddie has been serially unfaithful to her that her world falls apart. Robert Duvall plays Grace's father, Wyly King, while Gena Rowlands is her mother, Georgia, and Kyra Sedgwick is her sister.

As Grace's marriage fell apart on screen, Julia's had disintegrated off screen. Certain unscrupulous journalists took this to mean that her rôle was autobiographical. This then gave them the opportunity to pry into Julia's private life. Julia denied the film was autobiographical which it plainly wasn't and spoke in general rather than specific terms about her own failed romance.

'The timing [of my separation] and the filming of the movie aren't parallel as everyone seems to think because it makes for a little juicier lunch conversation. It wasn't this symbiotic everybody-breaking-up-at-the-same-time sort of thing,' she said.

In the film Grace and Eddie's break-up is anything but friendly. Julia's split from Lovett was just that and they have remained friends. She said, 'I felt like I was sincerely lucky with the situation I found myself in, the joy I felt within that situation. And the ultimate demise of the marital structure – the outcome of it – it's actually ridiculously amicable. You'd think people who could be that nice to each other would probably be a couple, but it just sort of wasn't the way it was intended to be. We found our little niche and then overstepped it a little bit. In fact, I think it can just as often be the weaker choice to stay.'

However, at the New York première Julia was interviewed by Oprah Winfrey. Julia told Winfrey that her marriage to Lovett was a sham and never really stood a chance. 'I have understood since childhood that marriage was something you're supposed to do. When Lyle came along I was pretty swept away. It was like he put some voodoo spell on me.'

On *Something to Talk About* Julia once again adopted the cast and crew as her surrogate family. It was a situation that she revelled in especially after the unfortunate experiences that were *Hook* and *I Love Trouble*.

Kyra Sedgwick recalls, 'After the second day on the set she knows everyone's name. She comes in every single morning, smile and says "Hello, so-and-so" to every member of the crew. She's constantly cracking jokes, even in the midst of a huge crying scene. She feels she needs to let everyone off the hook for a minute. It's a responsibility she doesn't need to take on but it makes her feel comfortable knowing everyone is OK. Julia is physical – she touches you a lot in a really nice way. From the moment Julia saw [Haley Aull, her on-screen daughter] on the set she went straight to her, kneeled down to her level and started talking to her.'

Julia was happy on a set again although the film only received fair notices. *Newsweek* said that it was 'nice to see Roberts working with good material again'. No doubt a reference to *I Love Trouble*. *Something to Talk About* was a reasonable summer hit taking $50 million at the American box office.

15. MARY, MARY, QUITE CONTRARY

'She was a movie star, so undoubtedly people were concerned. But she just bewitched Stephen [Frears]. She's an extraordinary creature. I remember her walking past me on the way to the set. You just wanted to put your arms around her and say, "It's going to be all right." She just exudes vulnerability and a need for affection in this rôle.'

Producer Norma Heyman

PINEWOOD, EDINBURGH AND IRELAND, SUMMER 1994–AUTUMN 1995

In 1886 Scottish author Robert Louis Stevenson published his novel on the duality of human nature. *The Strange Case of Dr Jekyll and Mr Hyde* was based on the life of Edinburgh town councillor Deacon William Brodie. By day Brodie was the epitome of genteel respectability. By night he was a thief and the leader of a gang of vicious robbers. Brodie was finally apprehended and hanged on 1 October 1788. Stevenson's tale became a bestseller and was eventually made into several movies including a 1971 Hammer House of Horror version with a twist – *Dr Jekyll and Sister Hyde*, which starred Ralph Bates and Martine Beswick.

Yet another new version was created and called *Mary Reilly*. It proposed to tell the tale of the fiendish double life from the point of view of Dr Jekyll's maid, Mary Reilly. She slowly discovers the doctor's dark secret. Like many ideas, it seemed a terrific idea on the storyboard and the 1990 novel by American writer Valerie Martin on which it was based was very successful. TriStar had bought the rights soon after its publication.

Christopher Hampton who had written the Oscar-winning *Dangerous Liaisons* wrote two drafts of the story for Tim Burton who was to be the director. Burton dropped out when he clashed with the studio over his film *Ed Wood*. Shortly afterwards Stephen Frears was hired to replace Burton. Hampton recalls, 'Paradoxically, I have never handed in a script greeted with such ecstasy and a feeding frenzy. Directors and actors pursued it hard. Julia's people called all the time about her playing Mary.'

Other elements from *Dangerous Liaisons* came on board including producer Norma Heyman, and John Malkovich as Jekyll and

Glenn Close as a brothel keeper. However, Hampton was constantly asked for rewrites. 'The script expanded to half its length again, from 85 pages to 130. It was the sort of rewriting that destroys all rhythms. Then the film gets made, it's too long, it's cut down and you lose all cohesion in the process.'

The teamwork that had made such a success of *Dangerous Liaisons* came apart at the seams. Frears had brought in Ned and Nancy Tanen, two American producers whom he felt could protect him from studio interference. Hampton remembers, 'I gather Ned was keen to have me fired and I can't say I ever agreed with anything Nancy thought needed doing to the script.

'For a time, it seemed [the studio] were asking me to write three new endings a week. Eventually they shot three of them.'

There was an immediate problem that no one at TriStar seemed to spot. Julia was America's 'Pretty Woman' and here she was being paid a reputed $10 million to look dowdy. As one critic wrote, 'Roberts plays Dr Jekyll's homely maid, swathed in long-sleeved, high-necked servant gear with a bonnet atop a scraggly wig. Without make-up or even eyebrows.[1] Her celebrity presence vanishes and she becomes a humble, rather unremarkable looking waif.'

For her part Julia was happy with her look as it gave her a chance, she thought, to prove she could act without relying on her grin or beauty or girliness. 'This rôle does not call for any ounce of glamour I could ever possess. I was thrilled to pieces to get to do something where no one at any point was going to say, "Could you just give us a smile?" '

The backroom staff were initially reluctant to cast Julia. Norma Heyman remembers, 'She was a movie star, so undoubtedly people were concerned. But she just bewitched Stephen [Frears]. She's an extraordinary creature. I remember her walking past me on the way to the set. You just wanted to put your arms around her and say, "It's going to be all right." She just exudes vulnerability and a need for affection in this rôle.'

In May 1995, as filming progressed on *Mary Reilly*, the *Hollywood Reporter* published its list of Hollywood's most bankable stars. Julia was listed as twelfth with Demi Moore at fifteen,

---

[1] She bleached them.

Sharon Stone at seventeen and Michelle Pfeiffer at nineteen. The highest ranking woman, at ninth, was Jodie Foster, who tied with Michael Douglas and Sylvester Stallone. Heading the list was Tom Hanks – riding on the success of *Forrest Gump*, he tied for first place with Tom Cruise, Harrison Ford, Mel Gibson and Arnold Schwarzenegger. Clint Eastwood followed, with Kevin Costner and Jim Carrey jointly in seventh place. Julia's future leading man Hugh Grant entered the list at number thirty thanks to *Four Weddings and a Funeral*.

Filmed in England, *Mary Reilly* had a large contingent of British actors and crew. One of them was Kathy Staff who is better known for her rôle as Nora Batty on the long-running television sitcom *Last of the Summer Wine* and as Doris Luke, the woman who cared for Benny Hawkins in *Crossroads*. She recalls Julia as being superb to work with. She remembers, 'We didn't always finish at the same time after our scenes together. Stephen would do close-ups of Julia, then she'd leave and he'd do close-ups of me, but even when Julia had finished for the day and changed into her normal clothes she absolutely insisted on coming back to give me the correct eye-line. Well, I've not known that before. It's normally done by a stand-in. But she said, "No, Kathy must have the correct eye-line." I thought Julia was absolutely wonderful, a lovely girl. It was her husband's birthday while we were filming and she bought him a big Victorian musical box, about the size of a television. She kept it in her dressing room and she had us all in listening to it. It was beautiful, it really was. And every morning she was there at 7 a.m. with the rest of us. In fact, she was so professional that you forgot how young she was. The only time she became a girl was when they brought in these electric buggies to take us to the set, because it was hard to get into cars with our costumes on. Oh, and she used to go screaming around in them as fast as she could and you thought, "Yes, she is only young." '

Julia exercised daily on the exercise bike in her dressing room at Pinewood, which was painted pale blue and white. No doubt to keep in character, she developed a taste for Murphy's milk stout. Reportedly, she kept her refrigerator stocked with pints of the drink.

For *Mary Reilly*, Julia wore an elaborate wig designed by the best hairpiece-makers money could buy. When the five months it took to film the movie in Ireland were over, she cut her own hair into the same scraggy style. She even continued to bleach her eyebrows when she returned to New York. She was able to laugh at her image. 'I looked like some kind of bizarre, mad alien. My friends were like, "What the hell has happened to you?" Then, when I went and got myself all pasted together, my eyebrows coloured in, I felt like Groucho Marx.'

In December 1995 Julia was spotted walking down a Parisian street with Lorenzo Slavan who for a time was her bodyguard. It was the first time they were seen as an item in public. The press speculation reached fever pitch because on her right hand Julia wore a heart-shaped ring. However, if there was a romance between the pair it was a short-lived one. On 28 January 1996 Julia appeared on the television sitcom *Friends* in the episode entitled 'The One After the Superbowl, Part 2'. She played Susie Moss who went to junior school with Chandler Bing (Matthew Perry). When they were both nine years old Chandler had pulled up Susie's dress in front of the whole class. Having not seen each other since school, they bump into each other and Susie flirts outrageously with Chandler, virtually asking him out on a date. One night as they go out she persuades him to wear her knickers. In the restaurant she seductively tells him to go to the comfort station and take his clothes off. She comes in and then steals his clothes leaving him naked apart from her G-string. Revenge is indeed a dish best served cold for Susie. For fans of Julia's feet, she was barefoot in a scene in the bathroom. For a short period after she appeared in the long-running comedy, Julia and Matthew Perry were an item. In an interview Julia stopped short of calling their relationship a love affair, but insisted that despite reports of other flings it was her most serious since the end of her marriage to Lyle Lovett. 'I wouldn't classify [it] as a relationship. We were friends. We are friends. Went out on a bunch of dates, had fun, but the "love affair" never existed. For that to happen, I think people being in love with each other probably helps.' However, she did once send him a saucy note that read, 'I love a man who can fax me five times a day.' For his part Perry was less than gentlemanly and echoed the comments of a previous boyfriend, Dylan McDermott, who had made unfavourable remarks about her tidiness. Perry said, 'She leaves her panties on the bathroom floor and toothpaste all over the sink.'

However, what Perry also did not like was Julia's continued closeness to Lyle Lovett. 'Matt became enraged one night when, after an argument, he caught her crying and whispering on the telephone to Lyle,' reveals a close friend. 'He thought her attachment to her ex-husband was unhealthy and told her as much. Julia became so upset that she took off – in Matt's brand new black Porsche – and didn't return until the next day.' When the relationship between Julia and the star of America's hottest comedy first became public, some thought it was a publicity stunt, but close friends disagree. 'Matt really liked her and she felt the same about him,' says one. 'Of course he had to get used to the untidy side of Julia – a common complaint of all of her boyfriends. He said that there were always diet drinks cans leaking their contents all over her carpet, and crumpled up scripts everywhere. Matt told me, "People ask what it's like to be with America's sweetheart. And I'm thinking, my God, if only you knew what a slob she is. Julia won't lower herself to pick up a duster and what's more, she can't cook. But what can I tell you? I love her, anyway." 'Matt is insatiable,' says Tracy Martin, who dated Perry before he met Julia. 'I'm sure he kept Julia very happy. Through mutual friends, I heard that Julia finally had to tell him, "Down, boy. Give a girl a chance to breathe!"'

'Julia and Matt Perry have never lost touch with one another,' says Thomas Caldwell. 'They do care about each other.' In the spring of 1997, Julia was in Los Angeles when she called Perry and asked to see him. She had heard on the Hollywood grapevine that he had become worryingly thin, and wanted to find out how he was. Even though Julia rang at all hours, there was never an answer. Finally Julia telephoned Perry's co-star, David Schwimmer, to find out what was going on. He said that he believed Matt was 'having some sort of drug problem'. 'She freaked out,' says Thomas Caldwell, 'and decided that she was going to see him, no matter what. Then she just dropped in on him. When he opened the door, she couldn't believe her eyes.' Perry was thin and spaced out and in dire need of sleep. 'I don't know what she said to him in there, but I know she has no time for drugs and she probably let him have it,' says Caldwell. 'Then they made plans to meet for dinner.'

Julia arranged to have dinner with Perry at the Four Seasons hotel after Julia finished a television interview. Julia and Lisa went to the hotel and waited for three hours for the *Friends* actor but Perry never showed. Thomas Caldwell reveals that the next day Julia went to Perry's home to find out what had happened. He looked in even worse shape than before. Julia insisted that Perry get help for his addictions. Three weeks after that conversation, Perry checked himself into the Hazeldon Clinic in Minnesota.

While Hollywood is often unable to recognise a surprise hit – hence their industry nickname 'sleeper' – word often leaks out when a film is going to be a stinker. Many words leaked over *Mary Reilly*. There is one thing Hollywood hates more than a flop and that is an expensive flop. *Mary Reilly* was reputed to have a budget of $50 million. TriStar had heard the word and decided to delay the film's release.

The company showed *Mary Reilly* at two test screenings to American audiences. It was not well received and the studio took *Mary Reilly* away from Frears and re-edited it. What happened next is dependent on whom you ask, but it appeared that test audiences liked the studio cut even less than Frears's. TriStar begged him to return and Frears agreed, but only on the condition that he had the final say.

It missed out on the lucrative Christmas market in 1995 and did not see the light of day until 23 February 1996. The film took an abysmal $5 million at the box office. Three weeks after its opening, TriStar effectively stopped supporting it with advertising or publicity. It fared no better when it was released in the United Kingdom on 26 April 1996. Blockbuster films can command 250 cinema screens, but only forty prints of *Mary Reilly* circulated in Britain. 'We're not releasing it with a huge advertising spend,' said Jon Anderson, TriStar's marketing director in London. 'Taking the US release as an indicator, it wouldn't be wise. I have to say I think we're starting from behind the blocks on this one.'

The author of the original novel Valerie Martin said, 'It's better than I expected but it's still uneven and incoherent. It looks as if it was made by people who were tired.'

The critics were no kinder than the studio had been. Mick Martin and Marsha Porter noted that the film was 'Murky, mushy, glacially slow and devoid of suspense, with one-note performances from the stars. Roberts, unable to deploy her trademark smile, cowers like a scared rabbit, while Malkovich inexplicably plays Jekyll and Hyde as looking and sounding almost exactly alike.' Christopher Tookey of the *Daily Mail* echoed that point:

'There is no sexual chemistry between the leads and director Stephen Frears mishandles the cast, atmosphere and special-effects climax so badly that he creates no suspense or horror. By far the most horrific aspect is the acting. In a role which demanded forbidden, sado-masochistic passions, Julia Roberts behaves like Bambi on tranquillisers. As for John Malkovich, he is so obviously the same man whether playing Dr Jekyll or Mr Hyde (to play the monster he simply shaves and puts on a Max Wall wig), it's impossible to understand why his domestics don't spot the similarity. Direction and screenplay are so appalling through-out that it is hard to imagine why it wasn't abandoned after the first day's rushes.'

Liese Spencer of the *Independent* said, 'Recounting the tale of *Dr Jekyll and Mr Hyde* from Roberts's point of view, this prurient slice of Victorian Gothic has all the taste of Madame Tussaud's Chamber of Horrors. The film has a deliberately claustrophobic feel, but every time Roberts steps out for an errand, the streets seem to be awash with blood as some leering working-class type guts a cow carcass or symbolically skins an eel. A trip to the local knocking shop (run by Glenn Close's Cruella de Vil madam) reveals a lurid salon stuffed with further bad meat. Imagine *Seven* mixed with The Jack the Ripper Experience and you get the idea.' The *New York Times* said that Julia was 'solemnly repetitive without much spark.'

Newsweek noted that Julia's Irish accent came and went 'between Dublin and Dixie' and said that although she 'gamely deglamoris[ed] herself' she did not have the 'technique to plumb this character's psychosexual depths'.

In her next outing Julia already had the sexual measure, if not of her character, then certainly of her co-star.

16. NOT SLEEPING WITH THE CO-STAR

'The love triangle is a historical fact; that it fizzles on screen is also a fact. The fault lies both with the rather wan Roberts and with Jordan's failure to write her a part: all we know about Kitty is that she always shows up wearing a new and improbably smashing outfit . . . Mary Reilly and Michael Collins proved [that] Roberts was not meant to time travel.'

Newsweek's review of *Michael Collins*

DUBLIN, IRELAND, SUMMER 1995–96

One can only imagine the conversation in Liam Neeson's home in 1996 when he told his wife, Natasha Richardson, about his latest film project. *Michael Collins* was the story of the Irishman who was one of the founders of what was to become the IRA. In 1907 Collins moved to London where he joined the Irish Republican Brotherhood. In 1916 he took part in the Easter Rising but was imprisoned. In December 1918 he was elected as Member of Parliament for West Cork but, like Sinn Féin representatives in later years, he refused to take his seat at Westminster. He and the other Irish MPs set up their own parliament – the Dail Eireann – in Dublin. Collins was appointed minister of finance and head of intelligence of the IRA. On 22 August 1922 he was killed, aged 31, in an ambush in Beal-na-Blath, County Cork.

The rôle of Michael Collins was given to Liam Neeson. The same Liam Neeson who had, of course, been Julia's live-in boyfriend between 1987 and 1988. Julia was signed to play his love interest Kitty Kiernan although there was a love triangle between Kitty, Collins and his best friend Harry Boland (Aidan Quinn).

However, as with much of Hollywood's output, fiction mingled with fact. According to an authoritative book, *Michael Collins and the Women In His Life* by Tipperary-born historian Meda Ryan, the Irishman died a virgin – despite tales of his legendary prowess with women. Ryan claims that Collins was too involved with Irish independence to fall in love with a woman. Social mores of the time also prevented Collins from consummating his affair although he was engaged to Kitty. Rumours of an affair with an

English socialite Lady Hazel Lavery were fanciful nonsense spread by his enemies in Dublin who claimed the romance had undermined his rôle in treaty negotiations with Britain.

The film was directed by Neil Jordan who commented, '[Liam and Julia's] love scenes are tender, warm and very sexy. It helped the film enormously that they had once been an intimate couple. They were playing lovers and so they didn't have to go through that awkward stage that actors usually do of getting to know each other.'

Ever thoughtful, Julia had Jordan ask Neeson if he or Natasha Richardson would object to her playing his screen lover.

'I was sure Liam wouldn't be embarrassed by my being his leading lady because we've remained the best of friends over the years. And it was all a long time ago. What also helped was the fact that Natasha and I are great friends. I think they are the perfect couple.'

Neeson was unusually tight-lipped for an Irishman. 'Julia and I are actors who happened to once have had a relationship. But we are first and foremost actors and we were able to make the old relationship work to our benefit in the film. In fact, I've managed to remain friends with most of the women I've dated. But I'd rather not talk about that. I don't want to be a public relations agent for my past girlfriends.'

At the time of the filming Julia was dating Pasquale 'Pat' Manocchia, a fitness trainer and herbalist. She said at the time, 'We are dating exclusively now. I go out only with him and he with me. But he's not my personal trainer. He owns a centre for preventative medicine and we met socially some time ago.'

Hollywood always wants all its output to be a success and to make money and to be critically acclaimed. Julia needed a hit more than most. Her recent films had left a lot to be desired. She had not got on with Patrick Bergin and alienated the crew by making them strip in *Sleeping with the Enemy*. *Dying Young* was written off as too depressing. *Hook* had been a personal and professional flop. *The Pelican Brief* had been acceptable but that was followed by the execrable *I Love Trouble*. *Something to Talk About* had been satisfactory but was by no means a smash hit. *Mary Reilly* was slated so an awful lot rested on *Michael Collins*.

Neil Jordan said that he had to cast Julia because there were no Irish actors suitable for the rôle. 'I couldn't find somebody in Ireland who was luminous enough to play the part of Kitty Kiernan. There were some wonderful women actors there, but they were all in their thirties. I couldn't find somebody in their twenties. So I started to look abroad. Julia called me and we met. She was unique among all the American actresses because she knew the period and she knew the song ["She Moves Through the Fair" which she sings in the film]. So there and then I said, "If you want to do it, you've got the part." '

Once Julia had received assurances that Natasha Richardson was happy with her playing the part Julia accepted the rôle of Kitty. The part was 'a perfect balance of complexity and simplicity. She came from an interesting family, and when she became involved in the lives of Michael Collins and Harry Boland, it brought out an untapped source of strength and compassion. And certainly she was no fool. She had both of these men in love with her and I think she enjoyed that. But I think that ultimately she was truly and deeply in love with Michael Collins. It's almost unbelievable how much she loved him. I don't think you see that very much in films – a love based on something so pure and simple. She loved him for her whole life.'

Despite her insight into the film and the part, much of what Julia filmed ended up on the cutting room floor. The film chronicled a bloody period in Irish history and does not spare the death toll – reaching about 5,000, mostly Irish.

Neil Jordan stated, 'I have never lost more sleep over the making of a film than I have over *Michael Collins* but I'll never make a more important one. This story is more about history than any political statement. Collins wasn't a proponent of terrorism. He developed techniques of guerrilla warfare later copied by independence movements around the world, from Mao Tse-tung in China to Yitzhak Shamir in Israel.

'He fought the British Empire in Ireland with the only army available to him – the Irish Volunteers, bands of poorly armed peasants and working-class youths. Collins would never be a proponent of contemporary terrorism as practised today. He was a soldier and a statesman and, over time, a man of peace.

'Even though Collins lived only about 75 years ago, much of the information we have about him is as mysterious as the existence he maintained. I have made choices about certain events based on my own extensive research into his letters and reported speeches. I want to make this story as accurate as possible without killing it dramatically and I think I have. It is a very true film.

'I have had to combine a few of the minor players into composite characters – most notably a double agent named Broy, who dies in the movie on the night of Bloody Sunday. Though the real Broy survived these events, two of Collins's associates, Dick McKee and Peadar Clancy, were tortured to death in Dublin Castle that night. For purposes of dramatic unity, I have combined all three characters.

'With regard to the murky circumstances surrounding Collins's death, I have made several assumptions. One was that Eamon de Valéra was in the vicinity at the time, which is true. Two, that Collins was trying to arrange some conciliatory meeting with those on the opposing side in the Civil War, which is also true. Three, that Collins was ambushed and shot by a renegade band on his way to a meeting, which I believe to be true. Out of this I have constructed the drama of the last ten minutes – Collins's attempt to meet de Valéra, de Valéra's inability to deal with the issues, and the young nameless go-between, who sets up the ambush on his own initiative and becomes Collins's assassin.

'There are those who call this a pro-IRA movie but I believe that this inaccurate description is being used simply to inflame an already contentious situation.'

The film opened on 11 October 1996 and the reviews were mixed. The Irish-born critic and biographer Alexander Walker said in the London *Evening Standard*. 'All told, *Michael Collins* is both a surprise and a relief: a more powerfully affecting film than even I, an Irish-born Protestant from the north, could have imagined; yet far less inflammatory about the past than I expected, given it was made in a country that has preserved for too long its baleful love of opening graves, as well as its ruthless ability to fill them.' *Newsweek* added, 'The love triangle is a historical fact; that it fizzles on screen is also a fact. The fault lies both with the rather wan Roberts and with Jordan's failure to write her a part: all we know about Kitty is that she always shows up wearing a new and improbably smashing outfit ... *Mary Reilly* and *Michael Collins* proved [that] Roberts was not meant to time travel.' In its initial run in the United States the film grossed just $10 million.

It was also the first film in which Julia had sung on screen. It was an experience she was to repeat in her next film, *Everyone Says I Love You*, in which she also took a small rôle. 'It's just a coincidence that two things I was asked to do that I liked and wanted to participate in were smaller parts in these two films. You can do a big part that's crappy, and then it's just a big, crappy part. It always comes down to the quality of what you're doing.'

Julia did put to rest the minds of people who were worried that she would release an album of her singing. 'Don't count on it. I could not have been more terrified, getting up and singing in front of groups of people. I wanted to do these songs justice, which is just an impossibility. I am not a singer! It was just my summer of singing, and I think that's passed.'

Julia plays Von in *Everyone Says I Love You*. Woody Allen is Joe who falls in love with Von on sight. She visits a psychotherapist and tells him about her ideal lover. Joe's daughter listens in on the sessions and tells Joe everything that Von says. Joe engineers a meeting and by coincidence they have the same tastes. Again the critics gave Julia a hard time. *Newsweek* said, 'Julia Roberts is charming as an unhappily married woman, but no one is going to be casting her in *Tosca* any time soon.' The *Sunday Times* was no kinder: 'What is Julia Roberts, cinema's sunniest comedienne, doing with a shrink? It's not just her singing that's flat; so is the part.'

Everyone Says I Love You opened on 6 December 1996 but was not a commercial success. It took just $9.7 million in the United States and Canada.

Julia's career was looking to be in terminal decline. She had appeared in three consecutive flops in a town where you are only as good as your last effort. One commentator called her the 'Farrah Fawcett for the new millennium'.

It was a cruel, but at the time looked to be an accurate, description of the star who had shot to fame in *Pretty Woman* and then appeared in a number of turkeys. Could her career be resuscitated or was she doomed to straight-to-video B-movies and to be the subject of trivia quizzes and 'Where are they now?' features?

HOGS AND HEIFERS BAR, NEW YORK, 8 SEPTEMBER 1996
Julia had once complained that the press alleged that she was a hermit and then when she did go out described her as a party girl. 'I can't do anything right. When I stayed out of the limelight they started calling me the new Greta Garbo, someone who just wanted to be alone. I was criticised for being a recluse. But when I do go out and have fun, like I did the other evening when I danced on the bar and took my bra off and had lots of laughs, I'm vilified. Well I just want the world to know that I intend to live my life as I see fit. If that doesn't agree with them that's their problem.'

'The other evening when I danced on the bar and took my bra off and had lots of laughs'? That doesn't sound like Julia Roberts. Here is what happened . . . or possibly didn't happen.

On 7 September Julia and Pat Manocchia went drinking in New York and after midnight ended up in an after-hours establishment called the Hogs and Heifers, a hang-out frequented by Hell's Angels.

With four other women Julia jumped on the bar to dance to the country standard 'The Devil Went Down to Georgia'. Then the stories diverge depending on who is telling them. According to Gary Miller of the *Daily Mirror*, Julia danced with a girl called Margaret Emery who was wearing a skimpy bra top and a hat. According to Miller, the two women did more than just dance together. They French kissed for between 30 and 50 seconds. However, the bar owner Allan Dell claimed that the snog never happened. Emery also denied that anything happened. 'Julia Roberts did not kiss me. That's a long time for a first kiss. I don't know whether I could even do that with a guy.'

No one seriously believed that Julia was or is a lesbian or even bisexual but nevertheless Nancy Seltzer had to spend the next day fielding calls from journalists. 'No, Julia isn't gay, she was just having fun, out dancing with friends. The only person who got a serious kiss that night was Pat Manocchia.'

Julia was told that it was a long-standing tradition at the Hogs and Heifers for ladies[1] to donate their underwear. Without a second thought, Julia whipped off her bra (a 34B Maidenform for those aficionados of ladies' undergarments) and handed it over.[2]

---

[1] Gwyneth Paltrow and Elle Macpherson danced together at the Hogs and Heifers.
[2] On show alongside Julia's bra is a pair of Daryl Hannah's knickers.

17. YOU ARE CORDIALLY INVITED TO THE REBIRTH OF JULIA ROBERTS' CAREER. RSVP. ELAINE GOLDSMITH

'She's a very giving person. There are people who are selfish, and people who are as generous as a dishwasher. She gives out rather than taking in. And she's not out to grab the whole thing for herself. She was very keen for me to do more in the film. And it is up to her in the end, because the film was very much based around her. She's in control of the whole show more or less. And what she wants, she gets.'

Rupert Everett on Julia

CHICAGO, 1997

One of the bizarre aspects of Julia's seeming career decline was why her representatives allowed her to appear in films that were unlikely to be commercial successes. Did Julia insist on appearing in the worthy but ultimately unpopular projects? Was she not advised that her forte was light comedy? Don't cast against type. No one believed in John Wayne in films where he wasn't playing John Wayne. When he portrayed Genghis Khan in Howard Hughes's *The Conqueror* (1956) the critics fell about laughing. The *Los Angeles Times* opined, 'John Wayne as Genghis Khan – history's most improbable piece of casting unless Mickey Rooney were to play Jesus in *King of Kings*.' Cast *with* type. Woody Allen is a neurotic. Tom Cruise is heroic. Arnold Schwarzenegger is violent. Bruce Willis is put upon. Shannon Tweed shows her breasts. Julia Roberts smiles and giggles in romantic comedies. Otherwise it simply does not work.

Thankfully someone realised this before Julia's career was permanently wrecked. The critics were writing off Julia. Her knight in shining armour riding to her rescue was Joel Schumacher. He had recently made *A Time to Kill* starring Sandra Bullock who, despite being three years older than Julia, was being labelled 'the new Julia Roberts'. Schumacher went into bat: 'What's wrong with the old Julia Roberts? She's all of 28. And what do people mean when they talk about Julia trying to make a comeback? A comeback from what? Puberty?'

My Best Friend's Wedding was Julia's kind of film. The kind of film that she did better than anyone else. Julia plays Julianne Potter, a food critic who is devoted to her career. She is also a commitment-phobe who has split from Dermot Mulroney (Michael O'Neal), a sports reporter, but they remain best friends. They decide that if the other has not found love by the age of 28 they will marry each other. But just before O'Neal hits the figure he falls in love with Kimmy Wallace (Cameron Diaz). Far from being happy for her pal, Julianne who is known as 'Jules' – Julia's own nickname – does everything she can to wreck her happiness and to steal O'Neal back for herself. Having played 'worthy' rôles in her previous films, it is a tribute to Julia's skill and talent that she makes Julianne delightful rather than devious despite her bad behaviour. Once again it was her grin that won it. Dermot Mulroney said, 'Julia's smile is like a thousand-watt bulb. Everybody falls for it, but there's nothing like it when she smiles and laughs. You can't help but be drawn into it.'

Chris Lee, the president of TriStar, disagreed. 'If you look at her performance closely, you'll realise it's not just the smile, it's all in her eyes. That was a very tough rôle. The big question mark with the script was, who do we get to play this part? Because, easily, the audience could have hated that character. It's a testament to Julia and how the audience feel about her. They just went with it completely.'

The screenwriter Ron Bass commented, 'It's in her eyes and it's in her heart and it comes right out of her mouth. She is just gifted.'

Julia opined, 'It's really difficult to find a really good, original comedy. They are rather impossible to come across. I was so overjoyed because I like doing comedy and this one was very appealing to me.' The producer Jerry Zucker agreed. He recalls, 'My wife read [the script] and loved it. She said, "Jerry, you've got to stay home from work today and read this. Cancel your appointments and read this script." Not long after I joined [the production], Julia was signed and she had a strong presence in the shaping of the movie.' *My Best Friend's Wedding* was directed by the Australian P.J. Hogan who had a hit with *Muriel's Wedding* and he created a happy set. Hogan remembers, '[What] made me want to [make the film] was the scene on the boat with Julia and

Dermot Mulroney. She has an opportunity to tell him that she loves him and she can't do it. That just really pierced me and I wanted to do the film for that scene.

'Julia is wonderful at comedy, she's a brilliant dramatic actress. There's very little that she can't do and she makes it all look easy. You are never aware of her acting.'

Julia said, 'I went to see *Muriel's Wedding* with my sister. It was so beautifully executed and so well done. P.J. has an amazing capacity for detail. I think that his sense of humour is vast and precise. He really has a clear idea of how he wants things to go. I like the fact that in America he is still considered rather new so he still has that energy that I have for making movies. He'll do some kooky thing off in the corner that's just brilliant while the main scene is going on.'

'Reading the script the first thing I really liked was the story,' said Cameron Diaz. 'I always look to see if the story is something I am interested in. Imagining Julia saying those words, I thought it would be incredibly fun.'

'Julia is very underrated as an actress,' was Rupert Everett's view. 'Because she became such a big star people don't really think of her any more as an actress but she is an incredibly clever actress and comedienne.'

After some unfortunate experiences and bad press coverage Julia enjoyed her time on the set of *My Best Friend's Wedding*. She memorised the names of all one hundred crew members and found out their birthdays. Fourteen crew members had a birthday during filming and for each one Julia arranged a surprise birthday cake. She also relaxed when out in public either shooting or just sightseeing. She shouted an apology to members of the public in Chicago who were inconvenienced by the filming. One day out walking her three-year-old mongrel Diego, Julia came across Jim Meir, a policeman who was selling T-shirts to raise money for the Special Olympics. Julia told the cop that she did not have any money on her but would come back the next day. The policeman was sceptical but at 11 a.m. the next day Julia did indeed return and bought $100 worth of the T-shirts.

Julia felt that she had an unwarranted reputation for not being a very nice person. She complained, 'I can't tell you how many times on a set, whether it be two weeks into it or the day we wrap, I have people come up and say, "I thought you were the biggest bitch and, wow, you're really nice," and I say, "Thanks." I don't overcompensate, because I'm not going to beg someone to like me. Take it or leave it, it's all up to you. But anybody who has had anything particularly nasty to say about me, I'd lay odds they've never met me.'

Julia even allowed an impromptu scene where the gay actor Rupert Everett groped her breasts. Everett played George, her editor, who pretended to be her boyfriend to make Dermot Mulroney's character jealous. However, Julia did draw the line when Everett repeated the trick off camera. He lamented, 'Julia does not like people touching her tits. She did get pissed off at me once – I did it again when we were playing around.' He added that Julia was 'enormous fun to be with and tremendously generous as an actress. She's a very giving person. There are people who are selfish, and people who are as generous as a dishwasher. She gives out rather than taking in. And she's not out to grab the whole thing for herself. She was very keen for me to do more in the film. And it is up to her in the end, because the film was very much based around her. She's in control of the whole show more or less. And what she wants, she gets.'

Julia said, 'Rupert Everett is just one of the funniest people on the planet. It's very difficult to act with him because I am not supposed to be laughing at all the things he's telling me. He is always hilarious. He never loses his spontaneity.'

In the scene in the Crab House where the ensemble sing 'I Say A Little Prayer' after George tells them that he met Julianne in a mental institution, director Hogan bet Julia $100 that she couldn't get through the scene first time without laughing. She won the wager.

My Best Friend's Wedding was due to open in America on 27 June 1997 – what would have been Julia and Lyle Lovett's third wedding anniversary. The weekend before Joel Schumacher's Batman & Robin, which starred Arnold Schwarzenegger as Mr Freeze, George Clooney as the Caped Crusader, Chris O'Donnell as the Boy Wonder and Uma Thurman as Poison Ivy was set to be released and the rationale was to open My Best Friend's Wedding a week later so as not to clash with what was bound to be a box office smash. However, TriStar decided to take the bull by the horns and arranged the release of *My Best Friend's Wedding* to be on the same day as Schumacher's blockbuster. The rationale was that if people did not want to see an action flick, they would gravitate towards a romantic comedy. It seemed to work . . . almost. *Batman & Robin* took $42 million in its first three days on general release. *My Best Friend's Wedding*[1] grossed $21 million at the box office. TriStar was very pleased because *My Best Friend's Wedding* broke the record for a romantic comedy opening weekend set by *Sleepless in Seattle*.[2]

The critics also welcomed the renaissance of Julia's career. *Newsweek* said, 'Julia Roberts is back in glorious comic form.' *Rolling Stone* said, 'Julia Roberts glitters like gold dust.' Writing in the *Daily Telegraph*, Mick Brown said, 'Roberts is delicious in the rôle; feisty, beguiling and funny. And it is her misfortune, perhaps, that, while *My Best Friend's Wedding* has been a huge success in America with both audiences and critics, the main talking point of the film seems to have been the flowering of Roberts's co-star Rupert Everett, playing the rôle of her gay confidant. Indeed, Everett proved so popular with test-audiences that the producers were obliged to shoot another twelve minutes of him on screen.' There was criticism in one unexpected quarter. The First Lady Hillary Clinton complained about Julianne's smoking. Wrote Mrs Clinton, '[Julianne] smokes when she's upset. She smokes when she's tired. She smokes when she's happy. In fact, she seems to smoke throughout the movie. This portrayal of a modern woman so reliant on cigarettes is particularly troubling given that more young women are taking up the deadly habit.' Julia, who smokes Marlboro Lights and votes Democrat in real life, did not comment.

The film played well around the world earning $126 million in America and $165 million worldwide. It led to her next major film

---

[1] A rather embarrassing faux pas befell TriStar in London. Souvenir brochures for preview audiences announced a splendid cast-list including Rupert Everett and Cameron Diaz but Julia was not listed. 'Oh God,' groaned a TriStar spokesman. 'It's all our fault – we produced the programme in London.'

[2] The record would next be broken by the film *Notting Hill*.

with one of Hollywood's biggest stars – in terms of box office if not physical stature – Mel Gibson.

NEW YORK, OCTOBER 1996–FEBRUARY 1997

Conspiracy Theory brought back together the creative brains behind the *Lethal Weapon* series: producer Joel Silver, director Richard Donner and, of course, the star Mel Gibson. The film was franchised by Warner Bros who were so convinced that they would have a smash hit on their hands that the studio bosses, Terry Semel and Bob Daly, agreed to the $80 million budget without first seeing a script. One quarter of the budget went on paying the salary of Mel Gibson. However, despite the fact that Warner Bros were happy to pay for Donner, Silver and Gibson they were not so enthusiastic about hiring Julia.

There were two reasons for this. The first was that they had heard about the disquiet caused on the sets of *Hook* and *I Love Trouble*. The second was perhaps the most important one. Julia wanted $12 million to make the film. Warner Bros believed that Mel Gibson could and would carry the picture so a lesser-known or at least less expensive actress would be more than adequate to play the female lead, Alice Sutton.

The bean counters at Warner Bros would almost certainly have won the day had it not been for Gibson. Having refused to make *Renegades* in 1991 with Julia he now wanted to play opposite her because, as he said, 'She is the queen of subtext. She's very expressive, very smart about the way she acts.'

Gibson's pull swayed the day and Julia was hired to play the Department of Justice lawyer who is spied upon by taxi driver Jerry Fletcher as she exercises at home. Fletcher publishes a newsletter devoted to exposing the conspiracy theories that blight the lives of decent American citizens. When he is not publishing his theories, he is expounding them to his captive audience, i.e. the passengers in his cab. The film was written by Brian Helgeland who would go on to win an Oscar for *LA Confidential*. One day Fletcher accidentally discovers a real-life conspiracy and he has Alice Sutton help him bring the bad guys to justice.

The film was shot in Manhattan and on the first day of filming Gibson sent his co-star an expensive-looking present. When she opened the package it contained a freeze-dried rat. Gibson is apparently well known on film sets for his sense of humour. Rather than being outraged, Julia got her revenge by covering Gibson's Winnebago lavatory in clingfilm causing him to ruin a pair of expensive boots as he attempted to relieve himself.

One aspect of the film that did upset Julia was the lack of romance between Jerry Fletcher and Alice Sutton. 'Put me and Mel in a movie and people are going to be waiting for a little smoochie. I hope people realised the value of the reality we give them rather than waiting to see us smooch.'

Julia is completely wrong in this. When one watches the film, one gets the impression that apart from his voyeuristic tendencies, which anyway are more protective than perverted, Fletcher is asexual and mentally disturbed. For Alice Sutton to kiss or bed him would have been wrong and unbelievable on so many levels.

Richard Donner said, 'There was one little scene where Alice comes into the hospital and, knowing Jerry's fears about being killed in his sick-bed, spots a body on a gurney in the corridor. For a moment she thinks it's Jerry and, as she pulls back the sheet, someone says that the FBI want to see her. As usual I had written a series of notes – guilt; my career down the tubes; why does the FBI want to see me? – so if she was floundering, I'd have something to throw at her. But she came in on the first take, did the whole thing and, as she leaned back against the wall, I saw every one of my ideas roll across her eyes. She's a great little actress.'

Conspiracy Theory opened on 8 August 1997 and took $19 million in its first weekend displacing Harrison Ford's *Air Force One* from the top spot after three weeks. The film grossed a respectable $137 million worldwide.

In October 1997 Julia split up with Ross Partridge, a part-time barman, after a brief fling. He was so upset that he flew home to New York to be comforted by his mother Enid, who told a friend, 'He was so depressed over Julia he couldn't get out of bed for days at a time.'

It was in the next month, November 1997, that Julia met the man who was to become her boyfriend for the next three years. Benjamin Bratt, as with so many of Julia's boyfriends, is an actor.

He appeared in the television series *Law and Order* but his profile was raised considerably by his relationship with Julia. It also opened a world to him that he had previously only read about in glossy magazines.

When Bratt celebrated his 35th birthday, Julia reserved a whole New York restaurant at a cost of $10,000. A three-piece band played while the two lovers danced cheek to cheek. Then Julia handed her boyfriend a gold watch said to be worth at least $20,000, engraved 'Love from JR'.

In an interview Julia spoke of Bratt: 'He's kind and good to his bones. He's very good-looking and his handsomeness pales in comparison to his kindness. That is all a girl could ask for really. I realised immediately that he is someone who will always challenge me in that great way that keeps you moving forward in your life. His presence raises the quality of my life. And I dare say that all my friends echo that sentiment.

'My boyfriend is an actor so we understand what goes through the course of each other's day, that in a relationship you have to meet in the middle. It's not coach and player. It's a team. The beauty of the whole tangled wonder is that I don't have to give up anything. The idea that a woman just serves her man, that you just stand down in the background and be the caretaker, and the man's persona is the head of the household? Well, there was something of that within the framework of how I entered into relationships as a young person. But I'm 31 now and I've become an adult in a lot of ways.'

Benjamin Bratt was born in San Francisco, California, on 16 December 1963, the middle of five children. His Peruvian-born mother is a Native American activist and took part in a demonstration at Alcatraz in 1970. Like Julia, Bratt's parents also divorced when he was young. Also like Julia, Bratt is estranged from a close member of his family. In his case it is his father with whom he has not exchanged a word since Bratt was 25.

Bratt began acting at his father's instigation while he was still at school. He attended the American Conservatory Theatre in San Francisco and then studied for a BA in fine arts at the University of California at Santa Barbara. From 1995 until 1999 he played Detective Reynaldo Curtis on *Law and Order*. In 1999 *People* named Bratt as one of the fifty most beautiful people of the year. Like his mother, Bratt has become a vocal supporter of rights for ethnics. 'The idea of fair and equal representation for coloured people in this business is a joke,' he once moaned. 'How can we as artists remain optimistic about our prospects when the personification of this industry is an overpampered, self-satisfied, middle-aged white male whose only contact with coloured people is the people who clean his house? We can't.'

On 5 May 1999 Julia appeared as a guest star on his show *Law and Order* and was paid just $4,000. The things that Julia does for love . . .

18. MONKEY BUSINESS

'Susan is the ideal woman to me. I think I'm secretly in love with her. You know if anything happens to [her boyfriend] Tim [Robbins] I'm more than willing to step in there. She's loving and generous and infinitely clever and smart.'

Julia's take on her friend and *Stepmom* co-star Susan Sarandon

BORNEO, AUGUST 1997

In the summer of 1997 Julia took a break from the glamour of Hollywood to travel to the depths of a Borneo jungle to make a British television documentary called *In the Wild* for the London-based Tigress Productions.[1] When Julia was approached about taking part, the opportunity appealed to her. 'My reaction was the same as when I'm asked to do anything,' she says. 'It's a knee-jerk kind of instinct to do something. I'd never been to that part of the world before and I love primates. I thought it would be an adventure as well as doing something to raise awareness of the orang-utans' terrible plight.

'Making a documentary is different to making a movie but I felt I was still kind of in my league. It wasn't like I'd gone off to write a novel or something. We were a very small group and we really had to pull together. Our trip, from start to finish, couldn't have been more hilarious, more enjoyable, more entertaining. Those guys, they're all English and they are all very, very funny. Director Nigel [Cole] is one of the funniest men I've ever met. His asides were classics and that was great. But some nights you'd really begin to feel it because just being out there takes its toll, traipsing around day after day. So in those respects it does become kind of gruelling but even saying that sounds kind of ridiculous because I truly loved every minute of it.'

Julia was filming a scene and two yards behind her was a 28-stone male orang-utan called Kusasi. Suddenly the old man of the forest clutched Julia to his mighty chest. Julia recalls the event: 'At that moment I was both full of fear and full of wonder. First

---

[1] Julia would make another documentary with Tigress, *In the Wild* – 'Horsemen of Mongolia with Julia Roberts'.

of all his hands are so enormous, they are like the size of my head and they have the strength of an entire person's body in one finger. Let's face facts, he could have crushed me. And he weighs 400lb. That's like four of me. It was scary on a level of just not knowing where it was going to end. But it wasn't scary like it would be if someone mugs you in Central Park – that's a hostile act, a person who has set out to hurt you, who wants something from you and is going to get it. I firmly believe that he meant no harm to me. He was purely motivated by curiosity, wonderment and just wanted to be close to me for whatever reason, so I wasn't scared thinking, "Oh my God! He wants to kill me . . ." But I was thinking, "He doesn't realise how tiny I am . . ." We cut that scene at a certain point. We didn't go on because it gets a little bit more scary and we don't want to frighten people.'

The crew put down their cameras and attempted to yank Julia away from Kusasi. 'It was a bit like a little girl who has a doll and you tell her that it's time for bed and try to take the doll away but she won't let it go. There's this struggle and it's like, "No, I want to play with it . . ." It was like that for a while, which was a bit intense for me. But if he'd wanted to hurt me he could have done so in a second. I did feel that he didn't have any anger in what he was doing. You see me pat him on the side as if to say "It's OK, don't worry about this . . ." But I guess that's exactly when people were getting worried. But I didn't want to freak him out or to scare him into thinking he had done something wrong.'

Then, fortunately, Kusasi simply released her. 'Our director Nigel, who was there the moment I was released, said to me, "You know what happened there, I have to tell you that there was nothing I could have done. Absolutely nothing. I was pulling and pulling and it was like trying to push a car that has the brake on. He just let you go . . ." '

Julia and the Tigress team – producer Andrew Jackson, director Nigel Cole, cameramen Mike Eley, Luke Hallam and Gil Domb and soundman Adrian Bell – set out on the three-week expedition to Borneo. Their ultimate destination was the orang-utan sanctuary in the Tanjung Putting Park known as Camp Leakey, where German-born anthropologist Dr Birute Galdikas has run a research centre for the past 25 years. There the professor and her colleagues provide a home for the orphaned orang-utans for up to eight years before returning them to the wild. On their journey, Julia and the team visit Balikpapen where a Dutch botanist Dr Willie Smits runs a rescue and rehabilitation centre. There Julia saw a five-year-old female, Holly, on the first stage of her reintroduction to the wild. Holly's first staging post – 'A kind of orang-utan motel,' said the actor – is a wooden hut in the middle of the forest where she will spend the night and where Julia stayed by her side. 'It was a sort of wooden shelter with a piece of foam on the floor and a mosquito net. I was a little scared and a little tired and I didn't really want to go to sleep for fear of spiders.'

Julia said, 'One amazing fact is that orang-utans share 97 per cent of human genes. What I want to know is, what is the three per cent that's different? And I love some of the mythology that you hear out there. There's one myth that says that orang-utans know how to speak and keep it a secret. Now, that wouldn't surprise me.

'They are so very human. The mothers look after their babies for eight years, they have this amazing relationship with their young. Camp Leakey is an incredible place and one of the rules of the trip was that I would never instigate interaction with the orang-utans. But they are so curious, you can be walking around and they'll come up and take you by the hand.'

The meeting with Kusasi did not spoil the expedition. 'At the end of the trip I just felt like the luckiest girl in the world because I had been able to experience this great adventure. I left there and I know more about a place and an animal than I had when I started. In our world we become so accustomed to luxury and technology that we sometimes forget that the most important thing in the world is just to love and respect each other, particularly our families and those closest to us. And do you know, these orang-utans do that on a daily basis, they do it with such effectiveness and with such ease, it's just who they are – they are these big red love thingies – that's who they are.'

NEW YORK, AUTUMN 1997–98

For her next project Julia linked up with Susan Sarandon who had been one of her bridesmaids when she married Lyle Lovett on 27 June 1994. *Stepmom* is a heart-warming film about two women who develop a close friendship, much like Julia and Sarandon off screen after they met on the set of *The Player*.

Julia often spoke of her admiration for Sarandon. 'Susan is the ideal woman to me. I think I'm secretly in love with her. You know if anything happens to [her boyfriend] Tim [Robbins] I'm more than willing to step in there. She's loving and generous and infinitely clever and smart.'

The script of *Stepmom* was discovered by Julia's agent Elaine Goldsmith. Made by Wendy Finerman, the producer of *Forrest Gump*, and Chris Columbus, the director of *Mrs Doubtfire*, *Home Alone* and *Home Alone 2: Lost in New York*, *Stepmom* is about Isabel Kelly, a New York photographer, who is dating a lawyer called Luke Harrison. She tries her best to deal with his two young children three years after their parents' divorce. Their mother Jackie and Isabel are deadly rivals. Julia remarks, 'We've all had those feelings about somebody. Your place is threatened. Your space is threatened. That can bring out the worst in anybody.'

Remembers Sarandon, 'We had a good time fighting. We had some fun fights. It's so much easier to hate somebody than to look at their positive points.' Then Jackie is diagnosed with terminal cancer and the women overcome their differences for the sake of the children.

The original script was written by Gigi Levangie and then four script doctors were brought in to beef up the film including Ron Bass. It was also the first time that Julia received a credit as executive producer. Julia took her responsibilities seriously and sat in on rewrite meetings with director Columbus but she always let him make the final decision. 'If it flows smoothly it's because of Chris. There were times when I said this scene doesn't seem right and he'd say, "Well, what doesn't seem right?" And I'd say, "I just want it to be better, I just want it to be more forceful. I think she should be more aggressive here. Or wherever." It's easy to make this wish list, but you don't always get what you want. But the next day, we'd come into rehearsal and he'd pass out little scenes for everybody. Pretty amazing.'

When filming began Julia stopped wearing her executive producer's hat and stuck firmly to what she knows best. 'Once we got on the set, I never considered myself a producer. Once we started shooting, I was an actor. I mean, that's what I do. And that's enough, particularly with this movie, I had enough on my plate.'

Susan Sarandon did not forgo her duties quite as lightly. She suggested that Columbus include her and the children dancing to the Marvin Gaye and Tammi Terrell[2] standard 'Ain't No Mountain High Enough' when she tells them she is dying of cancer. Janet Maslin of the *New York Times* did not think that this was a good idea. 'Motown music is tacked on as heavily as possible, working overtime to make feeling bad another way of feeling good . . . Miss Sarandon's Jackie is together enough to bop with the children to a Motown song just after they've heard really bad news.'

In interviews to promote the film Sarandon admitted that she had used experiences from her own life as a mother of three to bring life to the movie. As a consequence reporters asked Julia what she had in common with her character. Julia replied, 'We're the same height and weight.'

The actor was getting slightly tired of the media always assuming that she was the character she played. 'I have a certain understanding for particular aspects of [Isabel's] life. I can relate to the fact that we're both into our careers and not yet ready to raise a family. At the same time I want to say to reporters, "Do you really want to know where these things interact?" And I include myself as an avid moviegoer when I find myself wondering how much an an actor and a character are alike. And I say, "What difference does it make?" Just go and listen to the story and believe in the characters and let that be the joy, instead of approaching it as a puzzle where you try figuring out the components of the actor in the character. That's like seeing the strings. And where's the joy in that?'

Julia's remark that she was 'not yet ready to raise a family' elicited a barrage of questions at the Los Angeles première, so many that she eventually snapped at one reporter, 'Why is everybody so obsessed with my uterus?'

Stepmom opened in America on Christmas Day 1998 and took $19 million at the box office on the first weekend. It ended up

---

[2] Tammi Terrell died of cancer aged 24.

grossing $155 million worldwide although once again the reviews were mixed. The *Los Angeles Times* said, 'Roberts does an especially appealing job as the striving step-parent. Though Sarandon is one of those actresses who never gives a bad performance, her work here is not among her best, suffering in subtlety and credibility.' The *Village Voice* commented, 'Loathsome though *Stepmom* is, the eternally coltish Roberts is always a pleasure to watch.'

In 1998 the National Association of Theatre Owners named Julia as their International Star of the Year at ShoWest, their annual filmfest in Las Vegas. It was the first time in their twenty-year history that a woman had received the honour. Julia's career was definitely back on track. Her next picture would see her co-starring with Britain's leading actor.

19. TAKEN FOR GRANTED

'I was struggling with playing a person who really only shares an occupation and a height and a weight and a status with me. Just because you share an occupation with someone doesn't mean you're the same person.'

Julia talking about her character in *Notting Hill*

NOTTING HILL, WEST LONDON AND SHEPPERTON STUDIOS, SPRING 1998

Hugh John Mungo Grant, Latymer Upper School and New College, Oxford, is probably Britain's currently most successful actor who still lives in the UK. His only possible contenders for the title, Sir Anthony Hopkins and Sir Sean Connery, both make their homes abroad. With his beautiful then girlfriend Elizabeth Hurley, Grant was also one half of Britain's most glamorous couple. As an actor Hurley had few good rôles under her belt. It could be said that with the help of a Versace dress Grant launched Hurley's career by taking her to the première of his film *Four Weddings and a Funeral*. The press went into raptures at the revealing outfit and Hurley's stardom was assured although probably not for the reasons she would have liked.

The following year Grant almost blew his stardom when he was arrested for 'lewd conduct' at 7560 Hawthorn Avenue, near Sunset Strip, Los Angeles, California, at 1.15 a.m. on 27 June 1995 after police spotted him receiving a blowjob in his white BMW convertible from $60-a-time black prostitute Divine Brown who has a tattoo of her nickname Pancake (supposedly for the shape of her nipples) just below her left knee. Grant, who used the name Lewis, did not have time to be satisfied before he and Brown were arrested by LAPD vice cops. Grant, who was released on $250 bail, later described what he did as 'an insane act'. On 11 July he pleaded *nolo contendere* (no contest) *in absentia* and was fined $1,000 with two years' unsupervised probation and ordered to undertake an Aids education programme.

Julia had loved *Four Weddings and a Funeral* and described its creator Richard Curtis as a 'genius' on a television chat show. Curtis wanted Julia for his next film – named *Notting Hill* after the area in which it is set – about a Hollywood superstar who falls in love with a shy bookseller called William Thacker. Julia was not at first impressed with the concept. 'How boring. How tedious – what a stupid thing for me to do.' Then she read Curtis's script and changed her mind. 'F*** it, I'm gonna do this movie.' That was not the reaction she gave to Curtis, producer Duncan Kenworthy and director Roger Michell when they met Julia for lunch in New York's Four Seasons Hotel to discuss the picture.

Remembers Curtis, 'It was an extraordinary experience to see the real Julia Roberts waiting at the dining-room table. She was ten years younger than some of us – twenty years younger than one of us – and yet so obviously in charge that it was alarming.' At the end of the meal Julia stood and said, 'Good luck with your film.' It looked as if they would have to find someone else to play the rôle of Anna Scott.[1] A few days later, the Englishmen received the call that Julia was on board.

Filming on *Notting Hill* began in the spring of 1998 and it would be fair to say that everyone was nervous. Julia was apprehensive because she was a movie star working with people whose usual *métier* was Shakespeare and Jane Austen. She had also finished school at eighteen while Hugh Grant was an Oxford graduate.

Julia also thought that playing a movie star might be easy but in the end she said, 'I was struggling with playing a person who really only shares an occupation and a height and a weight and a status with me. Just because you share an occupation with someone doesn't mean you're the same person.

'Anna is still unsure of her own worth whether as an actor or as a person. What is written about her concerns her a lot more than it would concern me. She's a lot more fragile. The screenwriter Richard Curtis wrote a very specific type of actress in a very specific situation who has very precise ideas and values: I had to just reconcile the differences between us and not to judge her choices, because I didn't always agree with them.'

---

[1] In June 1999 Anna Scott, an Irish actress that no one had ever heard of, announced that she was suing Universal Pictures, the film's distributors, after they used her name for Roberts's character. 'People are confusing *Notting Hill*'s Anna with my life. Julia Roberts has robbed me of my good name.' Scott remains in obscurity.

Julia also showed no sympathy over the predicament that Anna found herself in when nude pictures she had posed for earlier in her career came back to haunt her. 'I didn't agree with what she did. Didn't agree with how she got into this mess – I would never have been in that situation.'

Julia was also loath to say one of Curtis's lines in which he misquoted Rita Hayworth's experiences with men, *viz* 'They go to bed with Gilda, they wake up with me.'[2] Julia said, 'I hate to say anything negative about what Richard wrote, because he's a genius, but I hated saying that line. To me, it was like nails on a chalkboard. I don't really believe any of that.'

During a break in filming, Julia and her boyfriend Benjamin Bratt flew on a private jet to Naples, and then sailed to Capri on a private motorboat where they stayed in a £1,250-a-night honeymoon suite at the Europa Palace Hotel.

Thomas Caldwell, a family friend of Julia, reveals, 'When Ben found out how much the honeymoon suite at the Europa cost, he blanched. But Julia said, "Oh, please! I make that much in about five minutes." They checked in as Mr and Mrs Smith, which Julia thought was a riot.'

While they were staying at the Europa, Bratt and Julia had an unofficial ceremony in their suite, during which they ex-changed gold wedding bands – 'From Tiffany's,' Julia told friends – and pledged their love to one another, promising one day to wed.

Julia flew to London for the premiere of *Notting Hill* on 27 April 1999 in Leicester Square and left her fans and the public aghast.

Hugh Grant arrived with Elizabeth Hurley and as usual Hurley looked fabulous. The press therefore could not wait to see what Julia would wear so that they could run comparison pictures in the next day's newspapers. Julia wore a red sequinned knee-length dress designed by Vivienne Tam for the event. The dress was really nothing special and just when the media wondered what angle they could use, Julia spotted someone she knew and gave a wave. As she did, she lifted her arm and revealed about a week's

---

[2] Speaking of her poor romantic track record, Rita Hayworth once commented, 'Every man I've ever known has fallen in love with Gilda and wakened with me.'

growth of armpit hair. The paparazzi clicked and the fashionistas gasped.[3]

'It's something that, on a day-to-day basis, I don't even think about,' Julia later explained to hairy shock-jock Howard Stern of her hirsute appearance. 'You'd think it was like chinchilla I had under there the way the world responded.' However, according to those who know her best, Julia doesn't shave because her fiancé Benjamin Bratt likes her that way. 'To him, it's a turn-on,' revealed an actor who worked with Bratt on the set of the American television show *Law And Order*. 'Ben's mother is Peruvian and his father is English-German, so he has a European sensibility.'[4]

The *Sun* arranged a telephone poll for readers to express their views on whether Julia had just made a fashion faux pas. The blonde surgically-enhanced supermodel Caprice Bourret told the newspaper that she 'shuddered when I saw Julia Roberts's hairy armpits'.

Another columnist wrote, 'A woman's armpit is incredibly sexy to a man. Why ruin it by growing your own carpet under there?' A radio show discovered that 63 per cent of men preferred their women without 'Epping bloody forest' growing out of their axillas. *Time* magazine offered Julia some advice. 'Next time, try cleavage.'

Julia said, 'I thought that I looked pretty. I had on a pretty dress and I felt pretty. Forget that armpit thing, hon. And Elizabeth Hurley has a great figure and she always wears beautiful dresses; not dresses that I would pick, dresses that look really pretty on her. But you know what? We're apples and oranges. You can't say one is better than the next. So for them to put us on the cover of the papers and have it be "Gorgeous Liz, Dowdy Julia", that's not nice. And it was everywhere. Well, you can't read a newspaper through my dresses, anyway – I guess that's a strike against me.'

The film was noticed unusually by a leading British cleric. Dr Rowan Williams, then the Archbishop of Wales and now the Archbishop of Canterbury, addressing the Church in Wales's Governing Body in Lampeter, said, 'Forget the floppy hero and his

---

[3] Few actors choose to display hairy armpits. Helena Bonham-Carter has been seen with them, as has Emma Thompson. Miranda Richardson once caused a fuss when a photographic session which she did for *Harpers & Queen* included shots of hairy underarms.

[4] Julia only shaves her armpits for rôles.

neurotic film star beloved. Look at his married friends, two prosperous young lawyers. She is paralysed and unable to have children, yet every word and gesture they come out with is full of absolute mutual joy – far more erotic, I'd say, than Hugh Grant's clumsy courtship of Julia Roberts. My wife and I both enjoyed *Notting Hill* immensely. When I say "clumsy" courtship I mean that the film seemed to be all about the awkwardness of someone coming to terms with the idea of commitment . . . that their love might be a long-term one. I admired the relationship [of Bella and Max] because it seemed to be one in which there is a great deal of cost involved – where people sacrifice freedom. Not everyone can manage this, of course, but people ought to realise that it is possible. If you cannot see that it is possible then your sense of what human beings can manage has shrunk.'

Notting Hill opened in America on 28 May 1999 and took $22 million in its first three days creating a new box office record for a romantic comedy. Accompanied by Benjamin Bratt, Julia chose to wear a full-length black Calvin Klein dress with demure long sleeves and a high neckline at the premiere at Manhattan's Ziegfeld Theatre. Elizabeth Hurley was unable to attend because of charity commitments in Britain, so Hugh Grant came alone.

20. A RUNAWAY HIT, SORT OF

'They were like magic together. Watching them together was like watching a little dance.'

Masseuse Aimee Moore on the chemistry between
Julia and Richard Gere

BALTIMORE, MARYLAND, OCTOBER 1998

For some time after the release of *Pretty Woman* the public were clamouring for a sequel to the story of the hooker and the billionaire or at least a chance to see Julia and Richard Gere on screen again. If truth be told the Hollywood money men would also like to see a return to one of the screen's most potent – for which read money-making – partnerships.

Director Garry Marshall also felt that a reunion between Julia and Gere, with him at the helm, natch, would be a winner. The one thing holding them all back was the lack of a decent script. '[Richard and I] have incredibly dissimilar tastes,' said Julia, 'as our careers would attest. So it never seemed like anything would come to pass.'

Gere had found a script in which he played a journalist who wrote a mocking feature about a woman who jilted four grooms at the altar. He sent it to Julia but she turned it down as did Sandra Bullock, Geena Davis, Ellen DeGeneres and Demi Moore. Despairing that he would never work with Julia again Gere had another rewrite done on the script and sent it to Julia. This time she hesitated before saying no. She sent it to Benjamin Bratt for his approval and he gave the project the thumbs up.

The cast and crew travelled to Baltimore, Maryland, for the twelve-week shoot. Julia and Gere checked into the Merry Sherwood Bed and Breakfast where they spent their days rehearsing. Hollywood was rife with speculation that this time they might have an affair even though Julia was hot'n'heavy with Benjamin Bratt. One guest at the Merry Sherwood Bed and Breakfast commented, 'You would have thought they were lovers, by observing their hugs and kisses, even if looks can be deceiving because I know for a fact that the two did have separate rooms.'

Local masseuse Aimee Moore was hired by the film's bosses to relax the stars. 'They were like magic together,' she said of Gere and Julia. 'Watching them together was like watching a little dance.'

In spite of whatever feelings Julia still had for Gere, she was determined not to jeopardise her romance with Bratt. While shooting, she chatted on the phone every day to Bratt. Julia celebrated her 31st birthday during shooting and a party was thrown for her. Not all went well. 'Benjamin loves her deeply, and seemed genuinely unhappy when Richard showed up at Julia's birthday party – on a boat chartered by Paramount Pictures off Kent Island in Maryland – and planted a big, lingering kiss on her while the cameras clicked away,' remembered a friend of his. Julia was surprised by Gere's behaviour and Bratt was so furious that he almost took back the purple mountain bike he had given her as a birthday gift.

Some time into the shoot Julia and Gere had to film a scene in a barn. On the fifth take Julia began to cry. According to witnesses, Gere went to his distraught co-star, put his arms around her and kissed her face tenderly, wiping away her tears.

Shawn Hill, a resident of Berlin, Maryland, was hired as an extra for a big wedding scene in the film. 'The scene had Julia climbing out a window in a white wedding gown, hopping on a Federal Express truck with Richard Gere,' said Hill. 'After the scene was over, much to my amazement, Richard swooped Julia in his arms and suddenly started kissing her passionately, really getting into it. The director said, "Hey, that's not in the script. Knock it off." Everyone on the set applauded, as if they were a couple.'

Unlike on previous films Julia did not spend her time chatting with the crew. As soon as Garry Marshall called 'Cut!' Julia went back to her dressing room. This behaviour annoyed Gere who said, 'If Julia doesn't get out here on the set, I'm going in to get her.'

'But she's in the shower,' co-star Joan Cusack protested. 'She's naked!'

Gere replied, with a wide grin, 'Well, good for me, then!'

Later that day, Joan Cusack brought her baby son to the set. According to witnesses, Julia hugged the baby tightly. 'I so want one of these, and I want one now. My biological clock is tick, tick, ticking away.' Julia mischievously looked over to Gere and said, 'Maybe you and I should make one of these?' The actor blushed. 'Sounds like a lot of fun,' he replied with a wink.

Again nothing happened between Julia and Gere and, when the filming of *Runaway Bride* was completed, the flirtation with Gere also seemed to come to a conclusion. Julia went back home to New York and Benjamin Bratt.

Once again the critics got their pens out and dipped them in vitriol. The *Los Angeles Times* headlined their review IT LOOKED GOOD ON PAPER and then spent the review explaining why it looked bad on screen. The *New York Times* bemoaned the lack of expected chemistry between the two leads. 'Gere's and Marshall's reunion with Miss Roberts guarantees a comedy that's easy on the eyes and dependable in the laugh department. But *Runaway Bride* shows signs of strain. Chemistry-wise, it can't bode well for a romantic comedy to feature two stars who apparently posed for the poster art on separate days.'

Daily Variety predicted the film would be a box office smash and so it proved. The film opened on 30 July 1999 and took $34.5 million in its first weekend. It was the best release of Julia's career and eclipsed the previous record for a romantic comedy which was held by *Notting Hill*.

During a round of interviews to promote the film Julia was asked by an Italian journalist if she thought it was ironic that she should be playing a bride who ditches her husband-to-be at the altar when she had just done the very same thing in real life to Kiefer Sutherland. It was probably not the most tactful question, but it did not merit her reply. 'I'm sorry, I don't understand,' she said, looking puzzled. The questioner repeated it. Julia appeared puzzled. 'I'm sorry, I really don't understand what you're talking about.' The hapless Italian repeated it once more and, with evident exasperation, Roberts said, 'Look, I'm trying really hard to work with you, but I can't answer your question if I don't understand it.' It was, according to the journalist John Hiscock, not the first time that Julia was unable or unwilling to answer a question without being nasty. He says, 'Although Julia has never actually lied, she has been evasive – something that those of us who have had dealings in the past with Miss Roberts should have expected. The actress always gives the impression that she would rather be anywhere else in the world than talking to journalists about her latest film. She has developed a fine line in sarcasm and cutting remarks, seeming to enjoy embarrassing her questioners. One of her favourite ploys is to pretend not to understand the question. Or she will snap, "I don't think I know you well enough to answer that." Occasionally she will turn the tables by asking the questioner, "Well, what do you think is the answer to that?" During the four times I have taken part in interviews with Roberts, usually as part of a small group of journalists, I have come to realise that the actress has perfected the technique of saying absolutely nothing, often in an unpleasant manner. Her tactics are in total contrast to those of, say, Catherine Zeta-Jones, who is professional enough to know that it is better to play the game and give interviewers some titbits they can run with: anecdotes about her baby, husband Michael Douglas, or stories of the family back home in Wales. Harmless stuff, and infinitely preferable to "I don't think I know you well enough to answer that." '

By the time *Runaway Bride* was released Julia was deep into filming a movie that would win her her first Oscar.

21. OSCAR GLORY

'It takes a village to raise that cleavage.'

Benjamin Bratt talking about Julia's breasts

VENTURA COUNTY, CALIFORNIA, MAY 1999–2000

Julia had received several awards for her acting (see Appendix 5) but the big one had always eluded her. She had been close on two occasions with *Steel Magnolias* and *Pretty Woman* but her name had never been the one announced on Oscar night. The next film Julia made seemed to critics and moviegoers alike to give her the best shot of nailing the Oscar for Best Actress.

Erin Brockovich, which began filming in several small towns in California's Mojave Desert on 25 May 1999, was the story of a woman who refused to give up. A single parent with three youngsters, she lands a job working for a law firm, Masry & Vititoe, where she discovers documents that suggest a massive utility company has poisoned the water. In 1993, Brockovich and her boss, Ed Masry, put together over 600 plaintiffs and, partnering with a powerhouse law firm, went after Pacific Gas & Electric (PG&E), a $30 billion company. As a result of their efforts, PG&E settled with the plaintiffs for $333 million in 1996, the largest settlement ever paid in a direct-action lawsuit in American history. Brockovich received more than $2 million for her work on the case.

The real Erin Brockovich, a dyslexic who stands 5 ft 10 in and measures 34DD in the bust department, was born in Lawrence, Kansas, in June 1960 as Erin Pattee. She graduated from Lawrence High School in 1978 and joined KMart as a management trainee. In 1981 she was voted Miss Pacific Coast and gave up work to become a professional beauty queen contestant. She soon tired of the frivolity of the beauty pageant lifestyle and joined a law firm where the film begins.

The film came about by serendipity. Executive producer Carla Santos Shamberg was visiting Pam Dumond, her chiropractor, and the medic began chatting. 'I couldn't believe it when my doctor told me about her friend Erin. It seemed incredible that this twice-divorced (from Shawn Brown and Keith Brockovich) woman with three young children, who had no money, no resources and no formal education, had single-handedly put this case together. I thought she seemed like the perfect role model for the new millennium.' Shamberg told her husband, Michael, who along with Carla, Danny DeVito and Stacey Sher are partners in Jersey Films, that she thought this would be a perfect story for their company.

Erin Brockovich was directed by Steven Soderbergh who had won a Best Screenplay Oscar nomination for his film *Sex, Lies and Videotape*, which also won the Palme d'Or at the Cannes Film Festival in 1989. Soderbergh has also directed *Kafka, King of the Hill, The Underneath, Schizopolis, Gray's Anatomy and Out of Sight.* Soderbergh was given a budget of $55 million to make the film, considerably more than he was used to. Julia received $20 million, almost half the budget. 'I don't know how he does it,' recalls Julia, 'but Steven gives me a great sense of security and confidence. I feel like he's really in there with me when he's watching. He takes such care. I think he just loves movies and I think that as a film-maker, he feels a responsibility to make a good film. I love that he runs the camera and is so aware of the precision of our composition and the way things look inside the lens.

'Steven is a constant source of amazement to me. I think that I have learned more about film-making and have seen it at its very best watching him work here. He creates an environment for everybody to participate in that is remarkable.'

Of the real Erin, Soderbergh had this to say: 'This is not really a movie about a lawsuit. It's about a person who cannot seem to reconcile how she views herself with how others view her. Erin is very bright and very quick but she also has a tendency to be very confrontational. She is confrontational in two ways: the way she dresses, which is very provocative and eye-catching, almost audible it's so loud, and in her language. She has a tendency to be very colourful in the way that she expresses herself, very direct. People respond to it in a way that is interesting.'

Soderbergh believes in reality and so he used several of the sites in the true story. Among the sites where filming occurred were Hinkley, where the actual contamination took place; Boron, home to both the Borax mines, where NASA frequently reroutes its shuttle landings; and the Barstow courthouse, where Judge LeRoy A. Simmons (who officiated at the real hearing and discovery for the case) came out of retirement to re-enact for the movie cameras his decision, which sent the case further into the legal system.

'I push for using the actual locations unless there is a compelling reason not to,' explained Soderbergh. 'When I first came to Hinkley, I was struck by how a big company could overpower a small town, how easy it would be for the residents to be forgotten. You know that you're shooting things that you can't buy, that you could only get by going to the exact place.'

Following location shooting in the desert, the cast and crew went back to Los Angeles for a fortnight's filming in and around Los Angeles before continuing to Ventura, California where, after ten days in a residential neighbourhood, the movie wrapped at the Santa Ventura Studios on 5 August 1999.

Soderbergh remembers, 'When we were filming the barbecue scene and the town hall meeting, I was very concerned that the way in which we conducted ourselves was such that the extras, many of whom had been involved in the actual case, would have a good feeling about their film experience. It was important to all of us that they come away thinking that being involved in the production had been a good thing.'

Soderbergh's crew had often worked with him before. 'Putting a crew together is a lifelong process,' he explains. 'You have the idea that the perfect crew is one in which everybody is on your wavelength and likes to work the way you work. It ends up being sort of a jazz ensemble.'

The director of photography Ed Lachman had previously worked with Soderbergh on *The Limey*. He said, 'Stylistically, Steven wanted to film in a point-of-view manner and, because we filmed on location, we were able to shoot it in a very naturalistic way. In several scenes, people from Hinkley who had been involved in the case worked with us as extras and secondary actors. We were able to merge a narrative based on a real story with the reality of the world that was inhabited.'

According to Soderbergh, 'I wanted to come up with a style that wasn't too theatrical. I wanted it not to be glossy, not to feel prepared. I wanted situations to feel like they were caught rather than staged.' As a result, the director had two cameras running which allows for accidents to happen and to be captured on film.

'You don't have to go back and say to the cast, "You know that great thing that happened unexpectedly, could you do that again?" because that can kill a performance,' Soderbergh remembered. 'Also, there is a certain energy in filming in this manner because the actors know they had better be "on" all the time.'

Costume designer Jeffrey Kurland, who was nominated for an Academy Award for his costumes on Woody Allen's *Bullets Over Broadway*, had worked with Julia twice before. The first occasion was on Allen's *Everybody Says I Love You* and then on P.J. Hogan's *My Best Friend's Wedding*. 'Erin is a great character,' says Kurland, 'because she's a total individual. She absolutely kowtows to no one else's opinion and what she wants to do is what she does. She's very true to herself, which makes her strong. She wears what she wants to wear when she wants to wear it and it's always fun to dress women like that.

'My conversations with Steven were mostly about making her true to the real Erin. Erin is an exaggerated personality but we didn't want it to be comical or ridiculous – it had to be acceptable exaggeration. On the other hand, neither did we want to water it down so that she was no longer that woman.

'When I met Erin, I found her to be amazing and intriguing. She showed me photographs taken around the time of the case so that I would have an idea of how she dressed. The truth of the matter is that she did wear eight-inch miniskirts and three-inch heels and plunging necklines. That's what she still wears, and she looked terrific then and she looks terrific now.' To accomplish this look, Kurland selected 52 costumes for Julia, 90 per cent of which he had to have made. 'She also had to get used to running around in very high, spiked heels. And she really does run in them.

'Film-making is a collaboration. I always show the production designer my ideas for the costumes because it helps him choose her furnishings. A woman who wears animal prints is going to have throw pillows that are a reflection of that. She's not going to have needlepoint, she'd probably have big purple mylar pillows. Basically, it all comes out of the script. It's right there for you, you just have to read it and then your ideas will come from that.'

Critics noted a certain difference in the *embonpoint* of Erin Brockovich and that of Julia, normally a much more modest 34B. Steve Daly of *Entertainment Weekly* asked, 'Given her usually modest silhouette, how'd they *do* that?' Kurland said, 'That's all Julia up there.' He added that 'precision engineered' apparel and 'three-inch heels helped to push Julia's bust forward'. Benjamin Bratt disloyally added, 'It takes a village to raise that cleavage.' Sheryl Connelly of the *New York Daily News* decided to experiment with the heels. 'Sorry to report but the only discernible difference that the heels made was suddenly – no surprise – I was taller. The movie magic was definitely in that bra.'

Julia had already signed to make the film when Soderbergh came on board. He said, 'If Julia hadn't already been attached to play Erin, I would have suggested her. The rôle plays to all of her strengths. There is a certain irrepressibility about her that's riveting, and this character allows for all of that. But there's also something more significant, something darker at the core, with this character.'

When Soderbergh first met the real Erin Brockovich, he was amazed to find that she had a very similar energy to Julia. 'There's an inherent charisma and a light in the eye that is very similar and very compelling. Both in person and on the screen Julia has an undeniable energy that is difficult to resist.'

Julia also found the person that she was portraying on screen interesting. 'As a person, Erin really intrigues me. I have great admiration for what she stands for. A lot of women in our culture are facing being a single mother, trying to make ends meet. They are the heroes of our time, aren't they? What's nice about the story is that it's about a person in a very specific situation, which early on is also a dire one. Erin is incredibly self-assured and that is the key that enables her to prevail in all situations. She is who she is and doesn't change for anybody – which is what makes her such a remarkable individual. She can be in a situation where she's completely out of place and have no awareness of that and just focus on what the issue is at hand.'

The only scene that presented Julia with any difficulty was the one in which she appears with the real Erin Brockovich. 'It's a scene where I'm in a diner after I have lost my car accident case.

I have no money, my neck is in a brace and the kids are being really rambunctious and Beth is supposed to be sick. The baby was really tired and screaming at the top of her lungs and Erin comes to the table as our waitress. It was really daunting and bizarre to be playing a person when that person is doing a line with you. The entire time I kept looking at Erin and thinking, "What in the world is she thinking? She's going to think I'm playing a terrible mother." Then, when I looked up, I saw that her name-tag said "Julia". I very nearly lost it.'

Playing Brockovich's boss Ed Masry was four-time Oscar nominee Albert Finney. Of working with Julia, he said, 'I thought it was a great part for her. Now, after working with her, I have to add that the part is very fortunate to have her playing it. She's terrific. She rolls her sleeves up, comes in and gets to work. Julia shoots from the hip. If, as occasionally happens, little adjustments are being made to dialogue, she just takes it on board and comes right up with it. And sometimes Steven has let a scene run on a little after we've finished the scripted dialogue, and she will readily vamp until she cracks Steven or me up and they have to cut. Of course, she is also extremely watchable. Julia is one of those blessed creatures who you like to look at, who you enjoy watching. It's a very sort of magnetic gift.'

The film's producer was Danny DeVito who made his name in front of the camera playing the irascible Louie De Palma in the ABC/NBC sitcom *Taxi*. He recalls, 'From the very beginning there was a company feeling about this film. It would have been very easy to make a caricature version of the players in the story, but the entire cast brought extreme reality to the characters.

'There was this tremendous chemistry between Julia and Aaron [Eckhart who plays Erin Brockovich's boyfriend] and she makes Erin an immensely compassionate and complicated human being. Also, they both have a real ability to retain the whole picture. Actors often play the moment, but Julia and Aaron, while absolutely in the moment, have the uncanny sense of knowing where their character is heading. They give nothing away, but hold some back for later. Every single line is delivered with absolute character conviction. Julia and Aaron are a great combination.'

Most of the critics agreed that here was an excellent film. Jay Carr of the *Boston Globe* stated, 'From start to finish, Roberts's warmth and energy pour off the screen in this film, which is boldly contoured to accommodate her outsize persona. Tapping brilliantly into her high-strung maverick side, Roberts really makes this film stand up and march, or rather totter fearlessly ahead on eight-inch heels. Never has she filled a rôle with so much fire and conviction.' Christopher Tookey of the *Daily Mail* said, 'The open secret behind the film's success can be summed up in two words: Julia Roberts. She makes what could easily have been just another female empowerment fantasy into an exhilarating experience for men and women alike. She can dress like a whore, yet still look wholesome; glare and swear like a football manager, but then charm you with a smile. There are actresses who could have played Erin just as movingly, and much more convincingly – but there is no one who could have played her more charismatically.' Amy Taubin of the *Village Voice* wrote, 'What's pretty original about the picture is that it focuses an investigative drama based on a true story around a comic performance. Without Roberts's combination of exuberance and irony, *Erin Brockovich* would have been a replay of the earnest *A Civil Action*, in which John Travolta brings suit against a big corporation that's been dumping toxic waste in a town's water supply. *Erin Brockovich* has an almost identical plot, but it's closer in tone and even politics to *Thelma & Louise*. Outlaw humour is its survival tool.' A dissenting voice came from Roger Ebert. He moaned, 'Her performance upstages the story. This is always Roberts not Brockovich, and unwise wardrobe decisions position her character somewhere between a caricature and a distraction. I know all about the real Erin Brockovich because I saw her on *Oprah*, where she cried at just the right moment in a filmed recap of her life.' Another came from Eric Roberts who said, 'I saw *Brockovich* and I must say I wasn't that impressed. Everyone's going on about how great she was in it, but what did she do? Wear some push-up bras. It wasn't great acting.'

When the Oscar nominations came out there was no surprise that Julia received a Best Actress nod. *Erin Brockovich* was also nominated for Best Picture, Albert Finney for Best Supporting

Actor, Steven Soderbergh for Best Director (he also received the same nomination for *Traffic*, the first time a double nomination had occurred since Michael Curtiz in 1938[1]) and Best Screenplay Written Directly for the Screen.

THE SHRINE AUDITORIUM, LOS ANGELES, CALIFORNIA, 25 MARCH 2001

The big night finally arrived with one commentator saying that 'if Julia Roberts acts surprised when they call her name, she should get a second Oscar for best performance at an awards ceremony.'

The event began at 5.30 p.m. with Steve Martin doing the honours as emcee. Julia and Benjamin Bratt arrived at the ceremony not in the usual limousine but in an Expedition sports utility vehicle. Julia wore a 1982 vintage black Valentino dress with white piping. She also wore a £1 million diamond bracelet loaned to her by top jeweller Van Cleef & Arpels. The same bauble was later bought for the singer Mariah Carey by her then boyfriend Spanish singer Luis Miguel to celebrate Mariah netting a three-album deal with Virgin worth a reputed £6 million.

Gilbert Cates, the producer of the Oscar show, was so keen to cut down on the waffle from winners that he arranged for the person who made the shortest speech to win a state-of-the-art widescreen television worth $2,500. Perhaps it didn't occur to Cates that the vast majority of the people making speeches could afford a hundred such televisions without noticing a dent in their bank balance. For the record, it was won by Best Animated Short Subject maker Michael Dudok de Wit for his 17.8-second speech. He gave the television to Hollygrove, a home for Los Angeles delinquents.

---

[1] Despite working in Hollywood from 1926, he never quite mastered the English language. Among his lapses were 'Don't talk to me while I'm interrupting' and 'Keep quiet. You are always interrupting me in the middle of my mistakes.' He once told Gary Cooper, 'Now ride off in all directions.' Approached by a man he didn't know, Curtiz was greeted with, 'Hello, stranger.' The director replied, 'What do you mean, stranger? I don't even know you.' According to David Niven while directing the 1936 classic *The Charge of the Light Brigade* Curtiz shouted a request for some riderless chargers to be brought onto the set: 'OK, bring on the empty horses!' Niven and his co-star Errol Flynn fell about laughing. Curtiz was furious. 'You lousy bums. You and your stinking language . . . you think I know fuck nothing . . . well, let me tell you – I know FUCK ALL!' His *Casablanca* (1942) won three Oscars and director Curtiz accepted his with the words, 'So many times I have a speech ready but no dice. Always a bridesmaid, never a mother.'

Julia also had a job to do that evening. She presented the Academy Award for Best Cinematography to Peter Pau for *Crouching Tiger, Hidden Dragon.*

Then at about 8.30 p.m. it was time to present the Academy Award for Best Actress. Kevin Spacey walked out onto the stage to the strains of 'Don't Rain on my Parade' from *Funny Girl.* Spacey went into an anecdote about leaving his tuxedo in Nova Scotia and having Dame Judi Dench deliver it before he announced the news that everyone knew anyway.

'The Academy Award goes to ... Julia Roberts for *Erin Brockovich.*'

Julia had difficulty getting to the stage in her high heels so Benjamin Bratt helped her. Once on stage she hugged Spacey and cried out, 'I'm so happy' and then started laughing.

Then she began her speech mentioning the prize for the shortest acceptance. 'I have a television, so I'm going to spend some time here to tell you some things.' Turning to Bill Conti conducting the orchestra she said, 'And, sir, you're doing a great job. But you're so quick with that stick, so why don't you sit because I may never be here again.' The audience burst into applause.

Julia paid tribute to the other nominees – Joan Allen (*The Contender*), Juliette Binoche (*Chocolat*), Ellen Burstyn (*Requiem*) and Laura Linney (*You Can Count on Me*) – and then, after straightening her frock, thanked Albert Finney. Then she turned her gaze on Steven Soderbergh. 'You made me want to be the best actor that I suppose I never knew I could be, or aspire to and I made every attempt – Stick Man I see you – so I thank you for really making me feel so . . . I love it up here.' Julia then thanked her family, her soon-to-be-ex boyfriend although the world was unaware of that at the time and finished with, 'I love the world! I'm so happy! Thank you.'

Julia later confessed to a faux pas on stage while collecting the Oscar. She had forgotten to thank Erin Brockovich in her 3 minute 37 second speech. At the after-show interviews, she said, 'During my out-of-body experience earlier tonight, I didn't acknowledge her, shamefully, shamefully. And, really, she is the centre of the universe which was our movie. And I've said too many things about her and so many things to her that she knows the esteem in which I hold her, which is quite, quite high. But I was remiss in not acknowledging her tonight. So, with great humility, I acknowledge her profusely.

'I'm thrilled to bits. I don't know how people act cool and calm because this is so huge. I won't have a proper thought for I'd say six to ten days, which is unfortunate because I start a movie[2] in three. But it's with Steven Soderbergh so I think he'll understand. I don't think he'll be making sense for a good four to five days.'

There was an unusual aftermath to Julia's Oscar win. It cost her childhood dentist a fortune. Dr Ted Aspes made a promise 25 years ago when he first opened his practice. The pledge on the surgery wall read then, as today, 'I pledge to give a free tube of toothpaste to every child in Smyrna if any one of my young patients achieves any of the following . . .' The list of achievements reads: winning an Olympic medal, a Pulitzer Prize, a Grammy Award, a Masters golf tournament green jacket, a Rhodes scholarship, a Heisman Trophy (an American football award), and, of course, an Oscar.

Dr Aspes, 50, said, after buying 10,000 tubes of toothpaste, 'I was losing hope after 25 years that any of my patients would ever be great achievers and help me complete my pledge. Of course, I've had my eye on Julia since she first made it big in Hollywood. She was my favourite – even though her brother and sister are both in the business too. I had set some money aside to pay out for the new toothpaste just in case she won on Sunday. I managed to get a pretty good deal. When I made the order, my distributor called and said, "Hey, doc, are you sure there isn't a comma in the wrong place?" On Monday morning there was a queue of parents standing outside the surgery cheering me on as I handed them the free toothpaste. I'd love to say that it was all my own work behind that smile but, really, all I taught her was to keep brushing regularly and have regular check-ups.'

At the ceremony the press made play of the fact that Bratt was wearing an outfit – an Armani tuxedo – that matched Julia's frock. They also wore rings which led people to speculate that they

---

[2] *Ocean's Eleven.*

would be getting married any day. *Access Hollywood* presenter Steven Cojocaru said, 'Remember this folks. The couple that co-ordinates together, stays together, and these two are in it for the long haul.'

If the long haul meant two more months then Cojocaru was correct. In May 2001 Julia and Bratt went their separate ways. There were rumours galore about why they had come to an end – and when. One had it that they had actually split *before* the Oscars but that in order not to wreck Julia's chances at winning they kept quiet until a reasonable time had elapsed. George Clooney, who would co-star with Julia on her next film, was said to be the reason behind the split. He denied it with a merry quip. 'I didn't have time. I was too busy breaking up Tom and Nicole.'

The real reason for the split has remained unclear. Some believe that Bratt could not stand being in Julia's shadow, an allegation levelled at Kiefer Sutherland. Others that she grew tired of waiting for him to propose. A third was a row over Julia's ten-year-old niece, Emma, appearing in *Blow*, the controversial film about America's biggest ever cocaine dealer. It was claimed by the *New York Post* that Bratt told Julia that no child of his would be allowed to be an actor.

Bratt described the attention he got being with Julia as 'like a fly that won't leave you alone. It's that mosquito that buzzes in your ear when you're trying to go to sleep at night. You turn the light on and you can't find it. You turn the light off and it comes back again. It's constant and ever-present and it disrupts any chance of peace . . . When you live your life at that level of fame, it gets beyond your control. By the time you realise it, you're stuck.'

Julia flew to Nashville to see Lyle Lovett after her break-up from Bratt. She spent time with Lovett, still a close friend, and was seen in the city browsing in bookshops and having dinner with the singer.

In July Julia appeared on the *Late Show with David Letterman* ostensibly to publicise her new film *America's Sweethearts* but the subject of her failure to thank Erin Brockovich came up as did the subject of Benjamin Bratt . . . and not in the way Julia would have wanted.

Letterman's Toronto-born, bald band leader Paul Shaffer asked, 'So Julia, you getting laid these days?' 'Bad, bad Paul,' she replied. 'That is so wrong . . . I didn't come out of a cake . . . I'm shocked.' Letterman pretended to scold his stooge and then turned to Julia, 'But what about it?' Julia said that the relationship had 'come to a kind and tender-hearted end and my only regret is that in some odd form, though, the media, not surprising, cannot accept that it's tender-hearted and kind. It has to be messy and ugly. Here's the thing. I love Benjamin. He's a good man, he's a fine man. He is, to the exultation of the female single population, not my man any more. Sad but true. We're just two kids trying to find our way in the world.'

But was she getting laid?

'And to go back to Paul, the answer is no.'

22. HAPPY EVER AFTER?

'I love working with Steven and would do anything for him. I totally believe in him and it's so much fun just being on a set. The movie-star trappings really aren't that important to me – working on this film was a total blast'
Julia on working on *Full Frontal* with Steven Soderbergh

CALIFORNIA, 2001

For most actors any film after an Oscar is an anticlimax unless, of course, you are Tom Hanks and win consecutive Academy Awards. After *Erin Brockovich*, Julia's next released film was *The Mexican* in which she starred opposite pretty boy Brad Pitt who is married to Jennifer Aniston, co-star of Julia's ex-lover Matthew Perry on *Friends*. *The Mexican* was the first of two films that Julia would appear in with Pitt in 2001.

Also appearing in *The Mexican* were Gene Hackman and James Gandolfini who plays a gay hitman, a far cry from his rôle as Tony Soprano on the hit show *The Sopranos*. He was paid nearly £2 million for his work on the film and said, 'Julia wanted me to do it and I didn't want to do anything that was completely different from Tony Soprano as I didn't have a lot of time to do any research. It was a little bit different, but it seemed to fit with me, so I figured, what the hell?'

The film was not a great hit. Writing in the *Daily Mirror*, Jonathan Ross said, '*The Mexican* isn't a bad film, but it's not worth getting that excited about either. Pitt is largely unconvincing as the hapless Jerry, and Roberts exudes all the warmth of a Russian pensioner's bedroom in the middle of an especially cold Siberian winter. There is little chemistry between the two – it's impossible to stop seeing them as a couple of movie stars trying to act quirky.' The *Independent on Sunday*'s Nicholas Barber said, 'Although the poster promises the first ever romantic team-up between two of cinema's most beautiful people, Roberts and Pitt are so rarely on screen together that they have, in effect, cameos in each other's movies. And while it's a shame that the two strands in *The Mexican* have so little in common, a bigger shame is that neither one is all that great in its own right, either. Pitt's is the worse of the two.

Clowning sweetly as if he were auditioning for *Bill & Ted 3*, he's stuck in a stuttering narrative of boy gets gun, boy loses gun, boy gets gun again, boy loses gun again, and boy gets gun yet again. It doesn't do much more than convey the frustration of being stranded in the middle of nowhere with no money, no passport and no friendly faces.'

LAS VEGAS, APRIL 2001

In the late 1950s and 1960s Frank Sinatra led a group of entertainers called the Rat Pack. Comprising Dean Martin, Peter Lawford, Sammy Davis Jr and Joey Bishop among their number, they were a hard-living, riotous crew who made several films – *Sergeants 3* (1962), *4 for Texas* (1963) and *Robin and the 7 Hoods* (1964) – and appeared at Las Vegas casinos in a bid to persuade Americans and tourists to gamble fortunes. In 1959, producer Jerry Weintraub was working in the music business with Frank Sinatra when *Ocean's 11* was being filmed in Las Vegas. 'What people went to see in the original film was Frank Sinatra, Dean Martin, Sammy Davis Jr, Peter Lawford and Joey Bishop on screen together,' Weintraub said. 'They could have been reading the telephone book and it would have been exactly as successful.'

In *Ocean's 11* (1960) Danny Ocean (Frank Sinatra) gathered around him his eleven ex-army paratroop friends to rip off five Las Vegas casinos to the tune of several million dollars on New Year's Eve while the city is watching a boxing match. It is a touch ironic that Sinatra played a character who was ripping off casinos when Sinatra owned shares in several casinos and also had friends who owned them. Throughout his life Sinatra was plagued by accusations of links to organised crime due in no small part to his links to organised crime.

Weintraub asked screenwriter Ted Griffin to adapt and update *Ocean's 11*. 'I had never seen the first movie so I had no reverence for it,' Griffin recalls, 'though I did for that type of movie – films like *The Great Escape* and *The Magnificent Seven*. The basic premise of this new version of *Ocean's Eleven* is the same, but it's set in today's Las Vegas. What might have been considered an incredible heist in 1960 really wouldn't be an incredible heist now. And con-artistry isn't the same today as it was during the Depression.

It's an outdated profession. It's not the same game any more, because all of the money is electronic and even the banks have no cash. The only places left with cold hard cash are the casinos.' According to Griffin, one of the problems he faced was keeping all eleven characters involved, interesting and present in the story. 'In this film, we have eleven guys, plus Julia and Andy,' Griffin explains. 'I had to be quite economical with how much material I could deal to minor characters. In films like *The Dirty Dozen*, you might remember six or seven of the characters, but you don't remember the others. I wanted each of our characters to be memorable. Another problem was defining each member of the gang and not being derivative of other "group of guys" movies, like those "bomber crew" movies where you have one guy from Brooklyn, one from Texas, and so on.'

'When I read Ted's script, I was thrilled and scared at the same time,' Steven Soderbergh reveals. 'I was thrilled because I thought that he had written something that was as close to a perfect piece of entertainment as I'd ever read. It seemed to deliver on all the levels what you want a movie with lots of movie stars and a heist to deliver on. And it was scary because it was physically bigger than anything I'd ever attempted and, in my opinion, required a style of film-making that I hadn't employed before – one that I was going to have to teach myself.

'The issues weren't so much that I was worried I wouldn't be able to handle it as a cinematographer, but whether or not as director I would be up to what I think the technical standards are for this type of film. It's a different way of shooting than what I'd been doing for the last few years, culminating in *Traffic*, which was a very down and dirty, run and gun kind of film. *Ocean's* is exactly the opposite. I thought it should be a very constructed, composed and theatrical kind of film. I did a lot of studying and looking at films made by directors who I thought spoke that visual language very well, trying to figure out what they were doing.'

Soderbergh and Clooney were careful to avoid emulating or comparing their cast with the original film. 'The original *Ocean's 11* is probably more notorious than it is good,' commented Soderbergh. 'It was the first time that the Rat Pack appeared en masse in a film. They were the epitome of cool and none of us felt like we wanted to compare ourselves to them or to what they were up to. You can't beat that. We took a completely different tack.'

'The truth is, most people never saw the original *Ocean's 11*,' said George Clooney. 'They just think they have because those guys were the coolest. Nobody touches Frank and Sammy and Dean, and we won't ever be that cool. But we do have a really great story.'

Clooney starred in the rôle originally played by Sinatra. His co-stars were Julia as his wife, Brad Pitt, Matt Damon, Elliott Gould and Don Cheadle. Other members of the gang were Andy Garcia, Ben Affleck's brother Casey and James Caan's son Scott. Julia played Tess Ocean, Angie Dickinson in the original. After George Clooney and Brad Pitt found out that she was going to be joining them, they sent her a card that read, 'We heard that you get 20 per film'. Enclosed with the card was $20. Julia reputedly was paid $20 million for the film. 'To work with Steven again I would do that for $20. Don't tell [producer] Jerry Weintraub,' joked Julia. 'That was a great lure for me. But I was even more pleased when I sat down and read the script. I thought it was so great and so fun. I liked my little bit in it.'

A twist in the tale in the new film saw the eleven-strong gang as simply various small-time crooks looking for the thrills of one big robbery – $150 million. Apart from Danny Ocean all the other characters' names have been changed. In the 1960 film, Ocean's wife was called Beatrice, but Julia's character was called Tess. Also missing is the sexism inherent in the Rat Pack ethos. Steven Soderbergh explained, 'It has the sensibility of the original, but the story is hipper, sharper and funkier.'

Many of the leading actors took hefty pay cuts for the chance to appear in the movie. Brad Pitt – who plays the Dean Martin-based character Rusty Ryan – can usually demand up to £18 million, but is thought to have settled for around £10 million.

Clooney, who commands £15 million a film, also took less – but took the lead rôle himself because the remake was his idea, and he helped produce it.

Christopher Tookey of the *Daily Mail* said, 'Roberts is likeably spiky and neurotic in her moments with Clooney, which have overtones of the love-hate screen relationship of Tracy and

Hepburn. Their exchanges are the best in the movie, but there aren't many of them.'

The public did not necessarily agree. *Ocean's Eleven* took $100 million at the box office in America.

HOLLYWOOD, CALIFORNIA, JULY 2001

In July 2001 *America's Sweethearts* received its American premiere and Julia arrived with Catherine Zeta-Jones. Gwen Harrison (Jones) and Eddie Thomas (John Cusack) are America's favourite couple – the Douglas Fairbanks and Mary Pickford of their day if you like. They first appeared in *Autumn with Greg and Peg*. The only problem is that they have split up but, for the sake of their careers, they pretend that they are still together. Julia plays Kiki, Gwen's sister and assistant, who falls for Eddie. The film was directed by Julia's old mentor Joe Roth and written by Billy Crystal who plays press agent Lee Phillips.

However, anyone expecting to learn inside secrets of Hollywood was to be sorely disappointed. As Christopher Tookey wrote in the *Daily Mail*, 'Are such people really going to take the lid off the infantilism and nihilistic greed that lie at the heart of Hollywood? The answer is, unsurprisingly, no. What we have instead is an astutely acted but ultimately vapid take on film stars' egotism. There's nothing here that *Singin' In The Rain* didn't do better fifty years ago, or indeed *Once In A Lifetime* 70 years ago; and there's a worrying absence of moral or social perspective . . . But Julia Roberts is miscast as her sister, a browbeaten frump with a weight problem and an unrequited crush on her sister's soon-to-be-ex-husband (John Cusack). Almost any other actress could have played this part more plausibly.'

Matthew Bond of the *Mail on Sunday* was no kinder: 'An early sign of the film's lightweight intentions comes when it takes Lee barely twenty minutes to get the feuding couple (Tom Cruise and Nicole Kidman come fleetingly to mind) to go to the press junket. Lee, you see, has a shortcut. He gets Gwen's sister and PA, Kiki (Roberts), to persuade her to play ball. So much for dramatic tension. And so much for romantic tension, once you've decided to cast Roberts, the world's most popular female film star, as the supposedly less glamorous sister. Sure, she goes gamely through the plain-Jane motions – glasses, scraped-back hair and some nonsense about having just lost 60lb – but she might as well go round with a little arrowed sign over her head saying "He Ends Up With Me". Now, I'm a big fan of Roberts, especially in romantic comedy, but she's not quite at her luminous best in this, although in a film this predictable, I'm not sure that's really her fault.'

Two months later on 11 September 2001 fanatic madmen hijacked four American aeroplanes and flew two of them into the World Trade Center twin towers and one into the Pentagon. The other was brought down by passenger intervention before it could reach its target, thought to be the White House. Ten days later, on 21 September 2001, Julia appeared on the television show *America: A Tribute To Heroes* in honour of those who died on 11 September. Julia gave £1.4 million to the American Red Cross Disaster Relief Fund and The September 11th Telethon Fund. Nancy Seltzer said, 'Like all Americans, Julia was profoundly affected by this horrific tragedy. She sends her deepest sympathies and prayers to everyone who has suffered such an unspeakable loss.'

Fighting back tears, Julia told millions of TV viewers, 'Life is so precious. Let's love one another.' Julia was one of a host of celebrities who appeared on the show, which was broadcast from Los Angeles, New York and London. The stars included Robert De Niro, Tom Hanks, Whoopi Goldberg, Tom Cruise, Jack Nicholson, Sylvester Stallone, Kelsey Grammer, Al Pacino, Bruce Springsteen and his wife Patti Scialfa, Sting and U2. Paul Simon sang a haunting 'Bridge Over Troubled Water', Neil Young performed John Lennon's 'Imagine' and Celine Dion sang 'God Bless America'. A New York City fireman's helmet sat on Billy Joel's piano as he sang 'New York State of Mind'. For the finale all the stars took to the stage as Willie Nelson led a special version of 'America The Beautiful'. The show was seen in 156 countries and raised nearly £130 million.

On 24 March 2002 Julia appeared at the Oscars where she presented the Best Actor award to Denzel Washington for *Training Day*. Going completely over the top Julia had earlier said that she 'could not live in a world' where she had an Oscar and Washington did not. She also said that she was grateful that Tom

Conti was not present. She meant Bill Conti, the orchestra leader, whom she had called 'Stick Man' when she won for *Erin Brockovich*.

WASHINGTON DC, MAY 2002

In May 2002 Julia travelled to the capital and to Capitol Hill where she appeared before a House of Representatives Appropriations sub-committee responsible for public health spending to testify on the effects of the degenerative mental disorder Rett Syndrome. Julia befriended a young victim of the disease. Rett Syndrome is an inherited condition seen only in women, because male embryos affected by it always miscarry. It leads to mental retardation, particularly affecting language and hand movements. There is no known cure.

The sub-committee called an unusual three-hour lunch break so that its members could listen to Julia call for more funding for research into Rett Syndrome. Julia became involved in helping raise public awareness after meeting Abigail Brodsky of Brooklyn, New York and filming a one-hour documentary for the Discovery Health Channel. The child died in June 2001 aged ten. As Julia took her seat, she said, 'This is very impressive and nerve-racking. Abigail was my pal. We spent time together without words. We connected with our eyes.' She added, 'The tragedy of this disorder is that it strikes girls who are too young to comprehend what is happening, and leaves them trapped within their own bodies.'

CALIFORNIA, May 2002

Julia linked up again with Steven Soderbergh to make the low-budget (£1.2 million) drama *Full Frontal*. The film is remarkable because its Soderbergh's first digitally-shot film. It is the story of seven people with little in common who become intertwined.

Julia said, 'I love working with Steven and would do anything for him. I totally believe in him and it's so much fun just being on a set. The movie-star trappings really aren't that important to me – working on this film was a total blast. It is my little nudie flick.' *Full Frontal* has been described as the spiritual sequel to Soderbergh's 1989 acclaimed *Sex, Lies and Videotape*. Julia was rumoured to have been paid $25,000.

Julia spent eighteen days working on the film and drove herself to and from work each day. She went back to her favoured attire of clumpy workman's boots and oversized denim jacket and topped that off with a hairnet that Ena Sharples would have been proud to wear.

Soderbergh called in many favours as Julia, David Duchovny and *Frasier*'s David Hyde Pierce all worked for reduced fees. Brad Pitt made a cameo as himself.

Julia was a tough magazine journalist and said, 'It's very different to anything that I've done before.'

Soderbergh drew up a bizarre set of rules which he sent with the script. His list of guidelines read:

'If you are an actor considering a rôle in this film, please note the following:
  (1) All sets are practical locations
  (2) You will drive yourself to the set. If you are unable to drive yourself to the set, a driver will pick you up but you will probably become the subject of ridicule. Either way, you must arrive alone
  (3) There will be no craft service so you should arrive on set
   • 'having had'. Meals will vary in quality
  (4) You will pick, provide and maintain your own wardrobe
  (5) You will create and maintain your own hair and make-up
  (6) There will be no trailers. The company will attempt to provide holding areas near a given location, but don't count on it. If you need to be alone a lot, you're pretty much screwed
  (7) Improvisation will be encouraged
  (8) You will be interviewed about your character This material may end up in the finished film
  (9) You will be interviewed about the other characters. This material may end up in the finished film
  (10) You will have fun, whether you want to or not.'

Soderbergh's rules quickly became the talk of Hollywood. He said, 'I was trying to send a message that you have to show up ready to work because you could be photographed getting out of your car.

I had cameras going all the time, everywhere, including spy cams that the actors didn't know about. Even Julia drove herself. I didn't want any entourage. The only private area people had was when they had to change clothes for some reason. And that was only because we were required by law to do so. In the one-on-one interviews, it was just me and them and a camera in a room. The questions were about anything: "Do you believe in UFOs? What kind of smell do you hate?" I used the material as narration throughout the film. It was part of the experiment, but a part that really paid off. I had fun. Did they? I think so.' He shot the film mostly on handheld cameras. 'After *Ocean's Eleven*, this was like an antidote. Then, I spent all my time handling logistics. I was anxious to have the opposite experience as soon as possible. This film has raw, emotional urgency.'

As the final words in this book are being written, Julia is working on *Mona Lisa Smile*. The Mona Lisa is famous for her enigmatic smile while Julia is celebrated for her laugh and smile. How appropriate . . .

EPILOGUE: WHERE DO YOU GO TO, MY LOVELY?

'I'm just Julia.'

Talking about herself

BOSTON, MASSACHUSETTS, OCTOBER 2002

Julia has long been painted as a commitment-phobe, someone who cannot find love, but then she married Danny Moder and seemed at last to find contentment. In October 2002 while Julia was filming *Mona Lisa Smile* on location in Boston, Massachusetts, they had a very public argument. Moder was second unit director of photography on the film. But the argument proved to be no more than a tiff as they kissed and made up. Julia then went off with their dog, Louie – a wedding present from Moder – in search of a takeaway for her husband.

The American media ran stories claiming that the couple were desperate to have a baby. Then in April 2003 a story broke that Julia and her second husband were either splitting up, on the verge of splitting up or had indeed split up and called in the lawyers. A few days later they were pictured hand in hand in Pacific Palisades looking very much together. That didn't stop the media bandwagon from again claiming that the couple had gone their separate ways. This time it was due to their inability to have a baby. Julia supposedly believed that the problem lay with Moder rather than with her. Then she was shocked to learn that Moder had impregnated his first wife, Vera Steinberg. She later suffered a miscarriage.

Julia was also said to be angry at Moder's refusal to accompany her to the Oscars on 23 March 2003 where she presented the Academy Award for Best Cinematography. He said that he had not attended the previous year only for Julia to snap that they were not married then.

Julia will be 36 years old at the end of 2003. She is at the peak of her earning power as an actor. She has one Oscar and two nominations to her credit. She has one failed marriage and several engagements that did not lead to the altar behind her. She is said to want to be a mother. Has the pressure of life in the spotlight wrecked her marriage to Danny Moder? If it has – and her family, friends and fans desperately hope that it has not – no one will be too surprised.

APPENDIX 1: FILMOGRAPHY

'I really love [making films] and don't know anything else'

Julia, 1993

BLOOD RED (1986)

(US opening 11 November 1986; 91 minutes; Rated R (USA))

Director: Peter Masterson; Writer: Ron Cutler.

CAST: Eric Roberts (Marco Collogero), Giancarlo Giannini (Sebastian Collogero), Dennis Hopper (William Bradford Berrigan), Burt Young (Andrews), Carlin Glynn (Miss Jeffreys), Lara Harris (Angelica), Al Ruscio (Antonio Segestra), Michael Madsen (Enzio), Elias Koteas (Silvio), Francesca De Sapio (Rosa Collogero), Marc Lawrence (Michael Fazio), Frank Campanella (Dr Scola), Aldo Ray (Father Stassio), Gary Swanson (Senator William Endicott), JULIA ROBERTS (Maria Collogero).

FIREHOUSE (1987)

(US opening 1987; 91 minutes; Rated R (USA))

Director: J. Christian Ingvordsen; Writers: J. Christian Ingvordsen, Steven Kaman, Rick Marx.

CAST: Gianna Rains (Barrett Hopkins), Martha Peterson (Shannon Murphy), Renee Raiford (Violet Brown), Gideon Fountain (John Anderson), Peter Mackenzie (Dickson Willoughby), Joe Viviani (Lieutenant Wally), Jonathan Mandell (Timmy Ryan), Parnes Cartwright (Darnell Fibbs), Peter Onorati (Ron J. Sleek), Andy Ryan (Sid Finegold), Dog Thomas (The Extinguisher), Henry David Keeler (Warren Frump), Dick Biel (Ward Hopkins), Joanne Fox (June Hopkins), Kevin Delaney (Poindexter), Maurice J. DeGennaro (Murray), Ralph Douglas (Pops), Butch Ford (Jerome), Kenny Edwards (Zone), Kristin Roudebush (Estee), Susan Van Deven (Bunny), Elizabeth Richardson (Lizzy), Donna Davidge (Donna), Jamie Lesser (A.D.), Ruth Collins (Bubbles), Jennifer Stahl (Mindy), Charles Tighe Sr (Watchman), Charles Tighe Jr (Pumper driver), Mike Polding (Laddre driver), Ken Lieberman (Hood), Craig Mitchell (Bummy), JULIA ROBERTS (Babs).

SATISFACTION (1988)

(US opening 13 February 1988; 92 minutes; Rated PG-13 (USA))
ALSO KNOWN AS: GIRLS OF SUMMER (1988)
Director: Joan Freeman; Writer: Charles Purpura.
CAST: Justine Bateman (Jennie Lee), Liam Neeson (Martin Falcon), Trini Alvarado (May 'Mooch' Stark), Scott Coffey (Nickie Longo), Britta Phillips (Billy Swan), JULIA ROBERTS (Daryle Shane), Debbie Harry (Tina), Chris Nash (Frankie Malloy), Michael DeLorenzo (Bunny Slotz), Tom O'Brien (Hubba Lee), Kevin Haley (Josh), Peter Craig (Mig Lee), Steve Cropper (Sal), Sheryl Ann Martin (Sylvia), Lia Romaine (Lexie).

MYSTIC PIZZA (1988)

(US opening 21 October 1988; UK opening 5 January 1990; 104 minutes; Rated R (USA), 15 (UK))
Director: Donald Petrie; Writer: Amy Holden-Jones.
CAST: Annabeth Gish (Katherine Arujo), JULIA ROBERTS (Daisy Arujo), Lili Taylor (Josephina Barboza), Vincent D'Onofrio (Bill), William R. Moses (Tim), Adam Storke (Charles Gordon Windsor Jr), Conchata Ferrell (Leona), Joanna Merlin (Mrs Arujo), Porscha Radcliffe (Phoebe), Arthur Walsh (Manny), John Fiore (Jake), Gene Amoroso (Mr Barboza), Sheila Ferrini (Mrs Barboza), Janet Zarish (Nicole), Louis Turenne (Everyday gourmet).
NOTES: Conchata Ferrell would also appear with Julia in *Erin Brockovich*. Lili Taylor also appeared in *Prêt-à-Porter*.

STEEL MAGNOLIAS (1989)

(US opening 17 November 1989; UK opening 9 February 1990; 118 minutes; Rated PG (USA), PG (UK))
Director: Herbert Ross; Writer: Robert Harling based on his own play.
CAST: Sally Field (M'Lynn Eatenton), Dolly Parton (Truvy Jones), Shirley MacLaine (Ouiser Boudreaux), Daryl Hannah (Annelle Dupuy Desoto), Olympia Dukakis (Clairee Belcher), JULIA ROBERTS (Shelby Eatenton Latcherie), Tom Skerritt (Drum Eatenton), Sam Shepard (Spud Jones), Dylan McDermott (Jackson Latcherie), Kevin J. O'Connor (Sammy Desoto), Bill McCutcheon (Owen Jenkins), Ann Wedgeworth (Aunt Fern), Knowl Johnson

(Tommy Eatenton), Jonathan Ward (Jonathan Eatenton), Bibi Besch (Belle Marmillion).

PRETTY WOMAN (1990)
(US opening 23 March 1990; UK opening 11 May 1990; 115 minutes; Rated R (USA), 15 (UK))
Director: Garry Marshall; Writer: J.F. Lawton.
CAST: Richard Gere (Edward Lewis), JULIA ROBERTS (Vivian Ward), Ralph Bellamy (James Morse), Jason Alexander (Philip Stuckey), Laura San Giacomo (Kit De Luca), Hector Elizondo (Bernard 'Barney' Thompson), Alex Hyde-White (David Morse), Amy Yasbeck (Elizabeth Stuckey), Elinor Donahue (Bridget), Judith Baldwin (Susan), Jason Randal (Magician), Bill Applebaum (Howard), Tracy Bjork (Female guest), Gary Greene (Male guest), Billy Gallo (Carlos), Abdul Salaam El Razzac (Happy Man), Hank Azaria (Detective), Larry Hankin (Landlord), Julie Paris (Rachel), Rhonda Hansome (Bermuda), Harvey Keenan (Man in car), Marty Nadler (Tourist), Lynda Goodfriend (Tourist), Reed Anthony (Cruiser), Frank Campanella (Pops), Jacqueline Woolsey (Artist), Cheri Caspari (Angel), Scott Marshall (Child on skateboard), Patrick Richwood (Dennis), Kathi Marshall (Day desk clerk), Laurelle Brooks (Night desk clerk), Don Feldstein (Desk clerk), Marvin Braverman (Room service waiter), Alex Statler (Night doorman), Jeff Michalski (Day doorman), James Patrick Stuart (Day bellboy), Lloyd T. Williams (Bellboy), R. Darrell Hunter (Darryl), James Patrick Dunne (Lounge pianist), Valorie Armstrong (Woman in lobby), Steve Restivo (Italian businessman), Rodney Kageyama (Japanese businessman), Dougl Stitzel (American businessman), Larry Miller (Mr Hollister), Dey Young (Snobby saleswoman), Shane Ross (Marie), Carol Williard (Saleswoman), Minda Burr (Saleswoman), Robyn Peterson (Saleswoman), Mariann Aalda (Saleswoman), R.C. Everbeck (Tie salesman), Michael French (Maitre D'), Allan Kent (Waiter), Stacy Keach Sr (Senator Adams), Lucinda Sue Crosby (Olsen Sister), Nancy Locke (Olsen Sister), Calvin Remsberg (Sod stomping announcer), Lloyd Nelson (Game announcer), Norman Large (Polite husband), Tracy Reiner (Woman at car), Tom Nolan (Vance), John David Carson (Mark), Daniel Bardol (Jake), Karin Calabro (Violetta), Bruce

Eckstut (Alfredo), Amzie Strickland (Matron), Mychael Bates (Usher), Garry Marshall (Bum tour guide), Charles Minsky (Janitor), Blair Richwood (Blair the Secretary), Shelley Michelle (Julia Roberts's body double).

FLATLINERS (1990)

(US opening 10 August 1990; UK opening 9 November 1990; 111 minutes; Rated R (USA), 15 (UK))

Director: Joel Schumacher; Writer: Peter Filardi.

CAST: Kiefer Sutherland (Nelson Wright), JULIA ROBERTS (Rachel Mannus), Kevin Bacon (David Labraccio), William Baldwin (Joseph Hurley), Oliver Platt (Randal Steckle), Kimberly Scott (Winnie Hicks), Joshua Rudoy (Billy Mahoney), Benjamin Mouton (Rachel's father), Aeryk Egan (Young Nelson), Kesha Reed (Young Winnie), Hope Davis (Anne), Jim Ortlieb (Uncle Dave), John Duda (Young Labraccio), Megan Stewart, Tressa Thomas (Playground kids).

SLEEPING WITH THE ENEMY (1991)

(US opening 8 February 1991; UK opening 12 April 1991; 94 minutes; Rated R (USA), 15 (UK))

Director: Joseph Ruben; Writer: Ronald Bass based on the novel by Nancy Price.

CAST: JULIA ROBERTS (Sara Waters/Laura Burney), Patrick Bergin (Martin Burney), Kevin Anderson (Ben Woodward), Elizabeth Lawrence (Chloe Williams), Kyle Secor (Fleishman), Claudette Nevins (Dr Rissner), Tony Abatemarco (Locke), Marita Geraghty (Julie), Harley Venton (Garber), Nancy Fish (Woman on bus), Sandi Shackelford (Edna), Bonnie Johnson (Mrs Nepper), Graham Harrington (Minister), John Ward (Theatre student), Sharon J. Robinson (Sharon), John Lindley (Extra).

DYING YOUNG (1991)

(US opening 21 June 1991; UK opening 30 August 1991; 114 minutes; Rated R (USA), 15 (UK))

Director: Joel Schumacher; Writer: Richard Friedenberg based on the novel by Marti Leimbach.

CAST: JULIA ROBERTS (Hilary O'Neil), Campbell Scott (Victor Geddes), Vincent D'Onofrio (Gordon), Colleen Dewhurst (Estelle

Whittier), David Selby (Richard Geddes), Ellen Burstyn (Mrs O'Neil), Dion Anderson (Cappy), George Martin (Malachi), Adrienne-Joi Johnson (Shauna), Daniel Beer (Danny), Behrooz Afrakhan (Moamar Gadaffi), Michael Halton (Gordon's friend), Larry Nash (Assistant), Alex Trebek (Himself), Richard Friedenberg (*Jeopardy!* contestant).

HOOK (1991)
(US opening 10 December 1991; UK opening 10 April 1992; 142 minutes; Rated PG (USA), U (UK))
Director: Steven Spielberg; Writers: James V. Hart and Nick Castle (screen story), James V. Hart and Malia Scotch Marmo (screenplay) based on Sir J.M. Barrie's book and play.
CAST: Dustin Hoffman (Captain James S. Hook), Robin Williams (Peter Banning/Peter Pan), JULIA ROBERTS (Tinkerbell), Bob Hoskins (Smee/Captain Hook's Servant/Roadsweeper in Kensington Gardens), Maggie Smith (Granny Wendy Moira Angela Darling/Middle-aged Wendy), Caroline Goodall (Moira Banning), Charlie Korsmo (Jack Banning), Amber Scott (Maggie Banning), Laurel Cronin (Liza), Phil Collins (Inspector Good), Arthur Malet (Tootles), Isaiah Robinson (Pockets – Lost Boy), Jasen Fisher (Ace – Lost Boy), Dante Basco (Rufio – King of the Lost Boys), Raushan Hammond (Thud Butt – Lost Boy).

THE PLAYER (1992)
(US opening 10 April 1992; UK opening 26 June 1992; 123 minutes; Rated R (USA))
Director: Robert Altman; Writer: Michael Tolkin.
CAST: Tim Robbins (Griffin Mill), Greta Scacchi (June Gudmundsdottir), Fred Ward (Walter Stuckel), Whoopi Goldberg (Detective Susan Avery), Peter Gallagher (Larry Levy), Brion James (Joel Levison), Cynthia Stevenson (Bonnie Sherow), Vincent D'Onofrio (David Kahane), Dean Stockwell (Andy Civella), Richard E. Grant (Tom Oakley), Sydney Pollack (Dick Mellon), Lyle Lovett (Detective DeLongpre), Dina Merrill (Celia), Angela Hall (Jan), Leah Ayres (Sandy), Paul Hewitt (Jimmy Chase), Randall Batinkoff (Reg Goldman), Jeremy Piven (Steve Reeves), Gina Gershon (Whitney Gersh), Frank Barhydt (Frank Murphy), Mike E. Kaplan (Marty

Grossman), Kevin Scannell (Gar Girard), Margery Bond (Witness), Susan Emshwiller (Detective Broom), Brian Brophy (Phil/Voice of blackmailer), Michael Tolkin (Eric Schecter), Stephen Tolkin (Carl Schecter), Natalie Strong (Natalie), Peter Koch (Walter), Pamela Bowen (Trixie), Jeff Weston (Rocco), Steve Allen (Himself), Richard Anderson (Himself), Rene Auberjonois (Himself), Harry Belafonte (Himself), Shari Belafonte (Herself), Karen Black (Herself), Michael Bowen (Himself), Gary Busey (Himself), Robert Carradine (Himself), Charles Champlin (Himself), Cher (Herself), James Coburn (Himself), Cathy Lee Crosby (Herself), John Cusack (Himself), Brad Davis (Himself), Paul Dooley (Himself), Thereza Ellis (Herself), Peter Falk (Himself), Felicia Farr (Herself), Katarzyna Figura (Herself), Louise Fletcher (Herself), Dennis Franz (Himself), Teri Garr (Herself), Leeza Gibbons (Herself), Scott Glenn (Himself), Jeff Goldblum (Himself), Elliott Gould (Himself), Joel Grey (Himself), David Alan Grier (Himself), Buck Henry (Himself), Anjelica Huston (Herself), Kathy Ireland (Herself), Steve James (Himself), Maxine John-James (Herself), Sally Kellerman (Herself), Sally Kirkland (Herself), Jack Lemmon (Himself), Marlee Matlin (Herself), Andie MacDowell (Herself), Malcolm McDowell (Himself), Jayne Meadows (Herself), Martin Mull (Himself), Jennifer Nash (Herself), Nick Nolte (Himself), Alexandra Powers (Herself), Bert Remsen (Himself), Guy Remsen (Himself), Patricia Resnick (Herself), Burt Reynolds (Himself), Jack Riley (Himself), **JULIA ROBERTS** (Herself/'Marsha Kent'), Mimi Rogers (Herself), Annie Ross (Herself), Alan Rudolph (Himself), Jill St John (Herself), Susan Sarandon (Herself), Adam Simon (Himself), Rod Steiger (Himself), Joan Tewkesbury (Herself), Brian Tochi (Himself), Lily Tomlin (Herself), Robert Wagner (Himself), Ray Walston (Himself), Bruce Willis (Himself), Marvin Young (Himself), Althea Gibson (Herself), Ted Hartley (Party guest), James McLindon (Jim the writer), Derek Raser (Studio post driver), Scott Shaw (Himself), Patrick Swayze (Himself).

THE PELICAN BRIEF (1993)
(US opening 17 December 1993; UK opening 25 February 1994; 141 minutes; Rated PG-13 (USA), 12 (UK))
Director/Writer: Alan J. Pakula based on the book by John Grisham.

CAST: JULIA ROBERTS (Darby Shaw), Denzel Washington (Gray Grantham), Sam Shepard (Professor Thomas Callahan), John Heard (Gavin Verheek), Tony Goldwyn (White House Chief of Staff Fletcher Coal), James Sikking (FBI Director Denton Voyles), William Atherton (Bob Gminski), Robert Culp (President), Stanley Tucci (Khamel), Hume Cronyn (Supreme Court Justice Rosenberg), John Lithgow (Smith Keen), Anthony Heald (Marty Velmano), Nicholas Woodeson (Stump), Stanley Anderson (Edwin Sneller), John Finn (Matthew Barr).

I LOVE TROUBLE (1994)
(US opening 29 June 1994; UK opening 18 November 1994; 123 minutes; Rated PG (USA), PG (UK))
Director: Charles Shyer. Writers: Nancy Meyers, Charles Shyer.
CAST: Nick Nolte (Peter Brackett), JULIA ROBERTS (Sabrina Peterson), Saul Rubinek (Sam Smotherman), James Rebhorn (The Thin Man), Robert Loggia (Matt Greenfield), Kelly Rutherford (Kim), Olympia Dukakis (Jeannie), Marsha Mason (Senator Gayle Robbins), Eugene Levy (Justice of the Peace), Charles Martin Smith (Rick Medwick), Dan Butler (Wilson Chess), Paul Gleason (Kenny Bacon), Jane Adams (Evans), Lisa Lu (Virginia Hervey), Nora Dunn (Lindy).

PRÊT-A-PORTER (1994)
(US opening 23 December 1994; UK opening 3 March 1995; 133 minutes; Rated R (USA), 15 (UK))
Director: Robert Altman; Writers: Robert Altman and Barbara Shulgasser.
CAST: Anouk Aimée (Simone Lowenthal), Sophia Loren (Isabella de la Fontaine), Marcello Mastroianni (Sergei), JULIA ROBERTS (Anne Eisenhower), Tim Robbins (Joe Flynn), Lauren Bacall (Slim Chrysler), Chiara Mastroianni (Sophie Choiset), Kim Basinger (Kitty Potter), Stephen Rea (Milo O'Brannigan), Lili Taylor (Fiona Ulrich), Rupert Everett (Jack Lowenthal), Tracey Ullman (Nina Scant), Jean-Pierre Cassel (Olivier de la Fontaine), Sally Kellerman (Sissy Wanamaker), Richard E. Grant (Cort Romney).
NOTES: The film was retitled *Ready to Wear* in America lest less-educated Americans did not understand the title. A similar

situation occurred with *The Madness of George III* which became *The Madness of King George*, again lest Americans think that they had missed out on parts one and two.

SOMETHING TO TALK ABOUT (1995)
(US opening 4 August 1995; UK opening 5 January 1996; 101 minutes; Rated R (USA), 15 (UK))
Director: Lasse Hallstrom; Writer: Callie Khouri.
CAST: JULIA ROBERTS (Grace), Dennis Quaid (Eddie), Robert Duvall (Wyly King), Gena Rowlands (Georgia King), Kyra Sedgwick (Emma Rae), Brett Cullen (Jamie Johnson), Haley Aull (Caroline), Muse Watson (Hank Corrigan), Anne Shropshire (Aunt Rae), Ginnie Randall (Eula), Terrence Currier (Dr Frank Lewis), Rebecca Koon (Barbaranelle), Rhoda Griffis (Edna), Lisa Roberts (Kitty), Deborah Hobart (Lorene Tuttle).

MARY REILLY (1996)
(US opening 23 February 1996; UK opening 26 April 1996; 108 minutes; Rated R (USA), 15 (UK))
Director: Stephen Frears; Writer: Christopher Hampton based on the novel by Valerie Martin.
CAST: JULIA ROBERTS (Mary Reilly), John Malkovich (Dr Henry Jekyll/Edward Hyde), George Cole (Mr Poole the butler), Michael Gambon (Mary's father), Kathy Staff (Mrs Kent), Glenn Close (Mrs Farraday), Michael Sheen (Bradshaw), Bronagh Gallagher (Annie), Linda Bassett (Mary's mother), Henry Goodman (Haffinger), Ciaran Hinds (Sir Danvers Carew), Sasha Hanau (Young Mary), Moya Brady (Young woman), Emma Griffiths Malin (Young whore), David Ross (Doctor).

MICHAEL COLLINS (1996)
(US opening 11 October 1996; UK opening 8 November 1996; 127 minutes; Rated R (USA), 15 (UK))
Director/Writer: Neil Jordan.
CAST: Liam Neeson (Michael Collins), Aidan Quinn (Harry Boland), Stephen Rea (Ned Broy), Alan Rickman (Eamon De Valéra), JULIA ROBERTS (Kitty Kiernan), Ian Hart (Joe O'Reilly), Richard Ingram (British officer), Brendan Gleeson (Liam Tobin),

APPENDIX 2: BOYFRIENDOGRAPHY

'[I'm] infamous for the people that I f***'

Julia Roberts, 1993

'I just don't see what all the fuss is about. They get this reputation as being a sex god or something then in the flesh they are very normal. I'm not going to name any names but to be honest I could take them or leave them'

Julia Roberts on Hollywood's male sex symbols

KEITH LEEPER (1983)

Julia lost her virginity to him when she was sixteen. She met Keith Leeper, two years her senior, during a junior disco in a club in downtown Atlanta. 'I was standing at the bar and she came over to me and said I looked like Sting. I asked her to dance and we exchanged phone numbers. She was a good kisser.' Julia lost her virginity in his bedroom in Smyrna on 25 December 1983. He recalls, 'We were alone and kissing [during a Christmas party]. It wasn't anything we planned. The timing was right. I took her by the hand and led her upstairs to my bedroom. We stayed there for about an hour before rejoining the party.' During the next four months he and Julia would drive off in his pick-up truck and park on a remote road where they would make love. 'We were always naked,' he says. 'I saw her differently after we had sex. I started to fall in love with her. I was physically attracted to her at first but then we also became best friends. It was puppy love at first.' The last time he saw Julia was just before she left for New York.

DYLAN WALSH (1986–87)

A New York waiter whom Julia dated before she hit the big time.

LIAM NEESON (1987–88)

Julia began dating Liam Neeson, reputedly one of the best-hung men in Hollywood, after meeting him on the set of *Satisfaction*. They split when she met Dylan McDermott while making *Steel Magnolias*. Neeson has never publicly commented on his relationship with Julia except to testily say to one reporter, 'Is this what it's going to say on my tombstone: "He dated Julia Roberts and Barbra Streisand"?'

DYLAN MCDERMOTT (1988–89)

They met while filming *Steel Magnolias*. They became engaged but the affair ended when she was linked to her co-star in *Pretty Woman*, Richard Gere, even though nothing happened. Gossip columnist Liz Smith noted in her column '[Julia Roberts and Dylan McDermott] started having a wild affair and seemed to be very, very much in love. Julia was very sweet to him, very into him. Then all of sudden she dumped him. Her time limit seems to be twelve to eighteen months. As soon as the romance gets serious she can't handle it. She can't seem to handle the reality of commitment.'

KIEFER SUTHERLAND (1990–91)

'Kiefer and I will be together for ever. He is the person I love and admire and respect the most in the world. Kiefer is probably the most wonderful and understanding person I have ever met,' said Julia in February 1991. They split up just three days before they were due to get married when Julia turned to Sutherland's acquaintance Jason Patric.

JASON PATRIC (1991–93)

Julia found solace with Jason Patric after Kiefer Sutherland in June 1991. 'I'm happier now in my life than I've ever been, despite all the chaos,' she commented in November 1991. They split in January 1993 when Patric's neighbours were awakened by shouts and screams from his Stanley Street apartment in West Hollywood. Then his door burst open and the couple spilled out onto the street. They continued shouting at each other. Witnesses later said that the subject of the argument was Daniel Day-Lewis. One bystander said, 'Jason was almost falling down drunk. Jason kept accusing her of having slept with Daniel Day-Lewis, yelling, "You f***ed him. I know you f***ed him." Then Julia yelled back at him, "I can f*** anyone I want to!"'

DANIEL DAY-LEWIS (1993)

Julia had a fling with the son of the former Poet Laureate. In March 1993 Julia 'spent a fortune on flights from Hollywood to Ireland' but no one had a picture of the lovers together. A photo opportunity did arise on 30 May 1993 when Julia and Day-Lewis spent three cosy hours together in the Wren's Nest of the Strawberry Beds pub in the Chapelizod area near Kilmainham. The couple arrived in a red Mercedes with a chauffeur. Both were causally dressed in jeans and while Day-Lewis quaffed Guinness Julia supped lager. Francis Heffernan, the barman at the pub, remembers, 'They were having great craic, she was all over yer man. If you did not know them you would have thought they were boyfriend and girlfriend. There was a lot of laughing and whispering going on.' Four weeks later, she was a married woman.

LYLE LOVETT (1993–94)

They married in Marion, Indiana, on 27 June 1993. The weather was wet, hot and humid when Julia married at 3 p.m. in a twenty-minute ceremony conducted in the St James Lutheran Church by Pastor DeWyth Beltz, Lovett's childhood minister, and the Reverend Mark Carlson in whose church the wedding took place. There was no confetti but the centre pews were decorated with small bouquets of purple, red and yellow flowers. In the second pew sat Julia's mother, Betty, and half-sister, Nancy. The chief bridesmaid was Lisa Roberts and the other bridesmaids were Elaine Goldsmith, the actresses Deborah Goodrich Porter, Susan Sarandon and Paige Sampson, Julia's closest friend from Campbell High School, who had arrived from Chicago, Illinois to see her old pal married. In September 1993 Julia said, 'I couldn't be luckier or happier. We're in love and will spend our lives together.' They separated in 1994 and were divorced after 21 months in March 1995 but remain close.

MATTHEW PERRY (1995–96)

They briefly dated after Julia appeared on *Friends* in the episode entitled 'The One After the Superbowl, Part 2'. She played Susie Moss who went to junior school with Chandler Bing (Perry). When they were both nine years old Chandler had pulled up Susie's dress in front of the whole class. Having not seen each other since school, they bump into each other and Susie flirts outrageously with Chandler, virtually asking him out on a date. One night as they go out she persuades him to wear her knickers.

In the restaurant she seductively tells him to go to the comfort station and take his clothes off. She comes in and then steals his clothes leaving him naked apart from her G-string. Revenge is indeed a dish best served cold for Susie. The relationship was her most serious since the break-up of her marriage. 'I wouldn't classify [it] as a relationship. We were friends. We are friends. Went out on a bunch of dates, had fun, but the "love affair" never existed. For that to happen, I think people being in love with each other probably helps.' However, she did once send him a saucy note that read, 'I love a man who can fax me five times a day.' For his part Perry was less than gentlemanly: 'She leaves her panties on the bathroom floor and toothpaste all over the sink.'

PASQUALE 'PAT' MANOCCHIA (1996–97)
A fitness trainer and former ice hockey player, they split after she reputedly accepted his marriage proposal.

ROSS PARTRIDGE (1997)
A part-time barman with whom Julia had a brief fling. The romance ended in October 1997 and he was so upset that he flew home to New York to be comforted by his mother Enid, who told a friend, 'He was so depressed over Julia he couldn't get out of bed for days at a time.'

BENJAMIN BRATT (1997–2001)
They began dating in November 1997 and she commented, 'I'm happier than I've ever been in my life . . . he's a force. He's strong, he's powerful, he's heavenly.' Bratt accompanied Julia to the Oscars in March 2001 when she won the Best Actress Gong for *Erin Brockovich* but behind the scenes the romance had already hit the rocks. They split in May 2001 with the break-up becoming public the following month. It was later alleged that the couple had stayed together so as not to harm her chances for Oscar glory.

DANNY MODER (2001–)
Husband number two, they met on the set of *The Mexican* and married on 4 July 2002.

APPENDIX 3: TVOGRAPHY

'Making a documentary is different to making a movie but I felt I was still kind of in my league. It wasn't like I'd gone off to write a novel or something. We were a very small group and we really had to pull together. Our trip, from start to finish, couldn't have been more hilarious, more enjoyable, more entertaining'

Julia on *In The Wild* – 'Orang-utans With Julia Roberts'

TELEVISION FILMS

BAJA OKLAHOMA (1988) (HBO)
Director: Bobby Roth.
CAST: Swoosie Kurtz (Doris Steadman), Lesley Ann Warren (Juanita Hutchens), Carmen Argenziano (Roy Simmons), Dennis Redfield (Vern Sandler), Alice Krige (Patsy Cline), Peter Coyote (Slick Henderson), Bruce Abbott (Dove Christian), Cyril O'Reilly (Weldon Taylor), Paul Bartel (Minister), John M. Jackson (Lee Steadman), Jordan Charney (Beecher Perry), **JULIA ROBERTS** (Candy Hutchens), Rob Nilsson (Chuck), Linda Dona (Martha Healy), Rhonda Dotson (Kathy), William Forsythe (Tommy Earl Browner), Karen Laine (Drive-in girl), Michael Leslie (Yob), John Mayall (Himself), Emmylou Harris (Herself), Willie Nelson (Himself), Walter Olkewicz (Private detective), Billy Vera (Lonnie Slocum), Anthony Zerbe (Ole Jeemy Williams).

TELEVISION PROGRAMMES
Crime Story – 'The Survivor' (Broadcast 13 February 1987) as Tracy
Miami Vice – 'Mirror Image' (6 May 1988) as Polly Wheeler
The Howard Stern Show (1994)
Inside the Actors Studio (1994)
Before Your Eyes: Angelie's Secret (1995)
Friends – 'The One After the Superbowl, Part 2' (28 January 1996) as Susie Moss
Murphy Brown – 'Never Can Say Goodbye: Part 1' (18 May 1988) as Herself
Murphy Brown – 'Never Can Say Goodbye: Part 2' (18 May 1988) as Herself

Sesame Street (28 December 1998) as Herself
Law & Order – 'Empire' (5 May 1999) as Katrina Ludlow
AFI's 100 Years . . . 100 Movies (1998)
In The Wild – 'Orang-utans With Julia Roberts' (1998)
AFI's 100 Years . . . 100 Stars (1999)
In the Wild – 'Horsemen of Mongolia with Julia Roberts' (2000)
Nature – 'Wild Horses of Mongolia with Julia Roberts' (22 October 2000)
The 73rd Annual Academy Awards (2001)
Revealed with Jules Asner – 'Julia Roberts Revealed' (2001)
Joan Rivers: The E! True Hollywood Story (2001)
America: A Tribute to Heroes (21 September 2001)
The 74th Annual Academy Awards (24 March 2002)
Comic Relief 2003: The Big Hair Do (2003)
The 75th Annual Academy Awards (March 2003).

APPENDIX 4: UNOFFICIAL FAN CLUBS

This is by no means a comprehensive list of internet fan clubs for J Ro but many have links to other sites. Some are updated more often than others and by the time this book is published there will, no doubt, be even more and perhaps some of those below will no longer be available.

About Julia: http://www.aboutjulia.com/

Charlie's Place – Julia Roberts: http://www2.netdoor.com/~cpl

Julia Roberts Black and White: http://www.connect.to/julia

Index of Julia Roberts: http://bs.addr.com/julia_roberts/

Julia Roberts on the Web: http://juliaroberts.narod.ru/

Julia Roberts Online: http://www.juliarobertsonline.com/

Thank You Julia!!!: http://www.juliaroberts.de/

APPENDIX 5: AWARDS

'I love the world! I'm so happy! Thank you'
> Julia on winning the Oscar for *Erin Brockovich*, March 2001

Scheme: N = Nominee W = Winner

1989 (N) – Academy Award: Best Supporting Actress, *Steel Magnolias*

1990 (W) – Golden Globe: Best Supporting Actress, *Steel Magnolias*

1991 (W) – Golden Globe: Best Actress in a Motion Picture (Comedy or Musical), *Pretty Woman*

1991 (N) – Academy Award: Best Actress, *Pretty Woman*

1991 (W) – ShoWest: Female Star of the Year

1997 (N) – British Academy Awards: Best Performance by an Actress in a Motion Picture, Comedy/Musical for *My Best Friend's Wedding*

1998 (N) – Golden Satellite Award: Best Actress in a Motion Picture, Comedy/Musical, *My Best Friend's Wedding*

1998 (N) – MTV Movie Awards: Best Female Performance, *My Best Friend's Wedding*

1998 (N) – Golden Globe: Best Performance by an Actress in a Motion Picture, Comedy/Musical, *My Best Friend's Wedding*

1998 (W) – People's Choice: Favourite Actress in a Motion Picture

1998 (W) – ShoWest: International Star of the Year

1998 (W) – Blockbuster Entertainment: Favourite Actress (Comedy), *My Best Friend's Wedding*

1999 (N) – Emmy Awards: Outstanding Guest Actress in *Law & Order* – 'Empire'

1998 (W) – Blockbuster Entertainment: Favourite Actress (Suspense), *Conspiracy Theory*

1999 (W) – Blockbuster Entertainment: Favourite Actress (Drama), *Stepmom*

2000 (N) – Moviefone Moviegoer Award: Outstanding Actress in a Motion Picture, *Notting Hill*

2000 (W) – San Diego Film Critics Society Awards: Best Actress, *Erin Brockovich*

2000 (W) – People's Choice: Favourite Motion Picture Actress

2000 (W) – National Board of Review: Best Actress, *Erin Brockovich*

2000 (N) – MTV Movie Awards: Best Female Performance, *Runaway Bride*

2000 (W) – Los Angeles Film Critics Association Awards: Best Actress, *Erin Brockovich*

2000 (N) – Las Vegas Film Critics Society Awards: Best Actress, *Erin Brockovich*

2000 (N) – Golden Satellite Awards: Best Performance by an Actress in Motion Picture, Comedy or Musical, *Erin Brockovich*

2000 (N) – Golden Globes: Best Performance by an Actress, *Notting Hill*

2000 (N) – Csapnivalo Awards: Best Female Performance, *Runaway Bride*

2000 (3rd) – Boston Society of Film Critics Awards: Best Actress, *Erin Brockovich*

2000 (N) – Blockbuster Entertainment Awards: Favourite Actress, Comedy/Romance, *Notting Hill*, *Runaway Bride*

2001 (W) – People's Choice Award: Favourite Motion Picture Actress

2001 (N) – Online Film Critics Society Awards: Best Actress, *Erin Brockovich*

2001 (W) – London Film Critics Circle Awards: Actress of the Year, *Erin Brockovich*

2001 (N) – Golden Satellite Awards: Best Performance by an Actress in Motion Picture, Drama, *Erin Brockovich*

2001 (W) – Golden Globes: Best Performance by an Actress in a Motion Picture, Drama, *Erin Brockovich*

2001 (N) – Chicago Film Critics Association Awards: Best Actress, *Erin Brockovich*

2001 (W) – Broadcast Film Critics Association Awards: Best Actress, *Erin Brockovich*

2001 (W) – British Academy Award: Best Performance by Actress in Leading Role, *Erin Brockovich*

2001 (W) – Blockbuster Entertainment Awards: Favourite Actress, Drama, *Erin Brockovich*

2001 (W) – Academy Awards: Best Actress in a Leading Role, *Erin Brockovich*

2001 (W) – MTV movie awards: Best Female Performance, *Erin Brockovich*

2002 (W) – People's Choice Award: Favourite Motion Picture Actress

The Oscar is a registered trademark of The Academy of Motion Pictures, Arts and Sciences.

APPENDIX 6: BIBLIOGRAPHY

'At home I love cooking and could easily fill my days reading'

Julia

Baxter, J, *Steven Spielberg: The Unauthorised Biography*, HarperCollins, 1996.

Bernard, J, *First Films Illustrious, Obscure and Embarrassing Movie Debuts*, Citadel Press, 1993.

Bernard, J, *Total Exposure: The Movie Buff's Guide to Celebrity Nude Scenes*, Citadel Press, 1995.

Bona, D, *Inside Oscar 2*, Ballantine Books, 2002.

Clarkson, W, *Mel: The Inside Story*, Blake, 1993.

Donnelley, P, *Fade to Black* (2nd Ed.), Omnibus Press, 2003.

Joyce, A, *Julia: The Untold Story of America's Pretty Woman*, Pinnacle Books, 1993.

Martin, M, *Did She or Didn't She?* Citadel Press, 1996.

Martin, M & Porter, M, *Video Movie Guide 2000*, Ballantine Books, 1999.

McBride, J, *Steven Spielberg: A Biography*, Simon & Schuster, 1997.

Millar, I, *Liam Neeson: The First Biography*, Hodder & Stoughton, 1995.

Parker, J, *Richard Gere: The Flesh and the Spirit*, Headline, 1995.

Paton, M, *Alan Rickman: An Unauthorised Biography*, Virgin Books, 1996.

Pendreigh, B, *Mel Gibson and his Movies*, Bloomsbury, 1997.

People Weekly. People Weekly Almanac 2001, Cader Books, 2000.

Sandys, J, *Movie Mistakes*, Virgin Books, 2002.

Sanello, F, *Julia Roberts*, Mainstream, 2000.

Sangster, J & Bailey D, *Friends Like Us: The Unofficial Guide to Friends*, Virgin Books, 1998.

Topping, K, *Inside Bartlet's White House: An Unofficial and Unauthorised Guide to The West Wing*, Virgin Books, 2002.

Tresidder, J, *Hugh Grant: The Unauthorised Biography*, Virgin Books, 1996.

NEWSPAPERS AND MAGAZINES
Celebrity Sleuth, Closer, Daily Mail, Daily Mirror, Empire, Evening Standard, Los Angeles Times, the *Mail on Sunday, Newsweek, New York Post,* the *New York Times, Playboy, Premiere, Star,* the *Sun, Sunday Mirror,* the *Sunday Telegraph,* the *Sunday Times, Today, Vanity Fair, Village Voice.*

APPENDIX 7: HEIGHTOGRAPHY

'People came up: "I thought you were 6 ft tall." I'm average height – 5 ft 9 in, skinny blonde. One guy says to me "So, where's the fox from Mystic Pizza?*" '*

Julia on her height

How do Julia and her family, friends and colleagues measure up?

Liam Neeson 6 ft 4 in
Nick Nolte 6 ft 4 in
Benjamin Bratt 6 ft 2 in
Daniel Day-Lewis 6 ft 1 ½ in
Lyle Lovett 6 ft 1 in
Matthew Perry 6 ft 1 in
Dylan McDermott 6 ft
Eric Roberts 5 ft 11 in
Jason Patric 5 ft 10 in
Julia 5 ft 9 in
Richard Gere 5 ft 8 in
Mel Gibson 5 ft 8 in
Kiefer Sutherland 5 ft 8 in
Lisa Roberts 5 ft 3 in

END CREDITS

After his split from Julia **Benjamin Bratt** married the actress Talisa Soto, his co-star in *Pinero*, on 13 April 2002. They have one daughter, Sophia Rosalinda, who was born on 6 December 2002 in New York City.

The intense **Daniel Day-Lewis** married Rebecca Miller, the daughter of the playwright Arthur Miller on 13 November 1996. They have two sons, Ronan and Cashel. On 23 February 2003 he won the Best Actor Bafta for his performance in *Gangs of New York*.

Richard Gere has never quite managed to recreate his successes of the 1980s. He married the supermodel Cindy Crawford on 12 December 1991 in Las Vegas but their marriage was plagued by rumours about their sexuality. Eventually on 6 May 1994 at a cost of £17,500, they took out a full-page advert in *The Times* proclaiming their heterosexuality and their fidelity. Six months later they separated. On 9 November 2002 he married the actress Carey Lowell. They have one son. In 2002 he starred in the film version of the West End musical *Chicago*.

Lyle Lovett remains a successful country and western star and is still a close friend of Julia Roberts. She once said, 'I can't imagine Lyle not being in my life. If Lyle met a wonderful girl and got married and had six kids I'd be the first at the party.'

Dylan McDermott has continued to act although stardom has eluded him. In 1995 *Empire* named him as the 67th (of 100) Sexiest Stars in Film History. He is married to Shiva Rose and has one daughter by her. His stepmother, Eve Ensler, wrote *The Vagina Monologues*.

Liam Neeson is still married to Natasha Richardson. He was awarded an OBE in the 1999 New Year's Honours List. In May 2002 he was nominated for a Best Actor Tony for his performance in *The Crucible*.

Matthew Perry continues to star as Chandler Bing in the hit sitcom *Friends* for which he reputedly gets paid $1 million per episode. He is the only member of the cast allowed to contribute to the scripts. His personal life has been beset with drug problems. Most recently he was admitted to a rehab clinic on 27 February 2001. He remains unmarried.

Eric Roberts's career is still eclipsed by his youngest sister's. They are still not close.

Kiefer Sutherland married Kelly Winn on 29 June 1996. That marriage, like his first, also ended in divorce. He has never eclipsed his father's fame and currently stars in the television drama *24*.

INDEX